The Formation of a Persecuting Society

The Formation of a Persecuting Society

Authority and Deviance in Western Europe 950–1250

Second Edition

R. I. Moore

BLACKWELL PUBLISHING
350 Main Street, Malden, MA 02148-5020, USA
9600 Garsington Road, Oxford OX4 2DQ, UK
550 Swanston Street, Carlton, Victoria 3053, Australia

First edition published 1987
Paperback edition published 1990
Second edition published 2007 by Blackwell Publishing Ltd

1   2007

Library of Congress Cataloging-in-Publication Data

Moore, R. I. (Robert Ian), 1941-
    The formation of a persecuting society : authority and deviance in
Western Europe, 950-1250 / R. I. Moore.—[2nd ed.].
        p. cm.
    Includes bibliographical references and index.
    Contents: Persecution (heretics, Jews, lepers, the common enemy)—
Classification—Purity and danger—Power and reason.
    ISBN-13: 978-1-4051-2964-0 (pbk. : alk. paper)
    ISBN-10: 1-4051-2964-6 (pbk. : alk. paper)
    1. Power (Social sciences)—History.   2. Social history—Medieval,
500–1500.   3. Europe—Social conditions—To 1492.   4. Persecution—
Europe—History.   5. Deviant behavior—History.   I. Title.

HN375M66 2006
323.1409′021—dc22   2006050241

A catalogue record for this title is available from the British Library.

Set in 10.5 on 13 pt Sabon
by SNP Best-set Typesetter Ltd, Hong Kong
Printed and bound in Singapore
by Markono Print Media Pte Ltd

For further information on
Blackwell Publishing, visit our website:
www.blackwellpublishing.com

CONTENTS

PREFACE TO THE
SECOND EDITION

Most books are written to answer a question. This book was intended rather to ask one. By the middle of the 1980s I had come to think that the persecution in the twelfth and thirteenth centuries of those whom the Church designated 'heretics' could not be satisfactorily explained either by reference to their beliefs and behaviour, or as a necessary response to any real danger that they presented to the Church itself or to society at large. I had also been increasingly impressed by similarities between the ways in which these 'heretics' were treated and the treatment accorded to some other minority groups in Europe at the same time, including Jews, lepers and gay people. This made me wonder whether the explanation was to be sought not among the victims, but among the persecutors, and connected in some way with changes which were taking place in the world in which they lived. So I began to think of western Europe in the twelfth and thirteenth centuries as a persecuting society. It also seemed to me, however, that Europe had not exhibited the habit of persecution to anything like the same degree before the eleventh century, but that it continued to do so thereafter for the rest of its history, at least until the middle of the twentieth century.

This is what I tried to explain in the first edition of this book, published in 1987. It was intended to establish the legitimacy of a question, and to bring the issues which that question raised to the attention of historians working on related topics, rather than to propose an answer, except in the most general terms. Indeed it could not have done so, for I had myself at that time only the haziest inkling of what such an answer might be, and had given very little thought beyond what was expressed in the book to what might be implied by the label 'persecuting society,' applied either to Europe or any other. In short, like most serious historical writing, *The Formation of a Persecuting Society* reported work and thought in progress. What historians write is always incomplete and provisional, but this was less complete, and more provisional, than most.

The response was astonishingly generous. The idea of the 'persecuting society' has been widely – many may think, too widely – accepted. Many scholars working on other aspects of medieval history, and indeed well beyond medieval history, have taken the trouble to consider how it helps, or fails, to make sense of their own concerns; many more have discussed its wider implications. Since 1987 the people whose histories form part of this argument have moved from positions more or less marginal to the interests of most historians to somewhere very near the centre of the stage. Jews and gay men especially, as well as the heretics with whom I started, have been the subjects of a great deal of fine work. To my regret, since I thought and still think them insufficiently studied, lepers have received less attention, though some of it is very important. If the idea of the persecuting society itself has perhaps been examined less closely than would warrant it fit for use, scrutiny of many of its aspects and implications has been acute and learned.

What is offered now is not so much a second edition in the usual sense as a second layer of reflection and discussion. It naturally takes account, as far as it can, of new research on the many subjects touched on, and of critical discussion. I have learned a great deal, though doubtless less than I ought, from both, and have tried to acknowledge it in the pages that follow. But I have found my original intention to revise and correct the work of 1987 in the light of what has been said since impossible to accomplish. The wise saying that 'if you change one thing you change everything' applies almost as much to historical writing as to history itself. What I wrote in 1987 is inextricably the product of what I knew, and how I thought, at that time; trying to rewrite it with hindsight was like stirring up the mud at the bottom of a pond. To start from what I know now and how I now think would be to write another and quite different book, though not necessarily with very different conclusions. In a sense I have already done so, for though *The First European Revolution* (2001) offers a much broader account of the changes that took place between the eleventh and thirteenth centuries, its principal thesis arises from, and develops, the argument of *The Formation of a Persecuting Society*.

It does not, however, do so directly. After twenty years I hope that I have refined the argument, and extended the knowledge on which that argument rests. I have thought more about the implications of labelling Europe a persecuting society, and those who did the persecuting have in their other capacities been increasingly at the centre of my historical interests. The Introduction and Chapters 1–4 are the text of 1987, unchanged except to correct typographical and a few factual errors and to regularise the references. Chapter 5 is new. It is intended to complete the argument by offering an answer to the question raised, though not clearly posed, by the first edition: what do we mean by calling Europe in the twelfth and thirteenth centuries a persecuting society, and what are the implications of doing so? The most important new element comes not from Europe itself but from the comparison hinted at but not developed in 1987, between western, or Latin, Europe and the other advanced societies of the pre-modern world, which seem to me not to be appropriately characterised in the same way. This chapter also takes up some of the issues which have been raised by the work of others since 1987, but by no means all of them, so I have added a Bibliographical Excursus, reviewing some of the ways in which the argument has been affected by the research and discussion of the last twenty years. The subtitle has been changed from *Power and Deviance in Western Europe, 950–1250* not only to distinguish this new version of the book from the old but as a reminder that while power is a fact authority is a construct, and one to whose construction that of deviance is nearly allied.

In the interests of clarity as to what we are arguing about, three common misconceptions about this thesis should be disposed of at once. First, it did not, and does not, maintain that 'the Church' was the sole, or even the principal agent of persecution; second, it does not pretend to offer a complete or balanced account of medieval society and culture; and third, it does not assume, or suggest, that persecution was somehow more characteristic of the middle ages than it has been of subsequent periods of European history. These misapprehensions are dealt with in more detail at the appropriate points below; meanwhile new readers may be interested to notice how far they have arisen from what I actually wrote. The last point, however, may require some immediate explanation. I contended in the 1987 Preface that at some time around 1100 'western Europe *became* a persecuting society,' and that it had remained one, mentioning the scale of persecution described in the records of 'the witch hunts of the sixteenth and seventeenth centuries, the totalitarian regimes of the twentieth century, and numberless others' to illustrate the point – bearing in mind, of course, that for recent centuries the term 'Europe' must be expanded to include societies in other parts of the world which derived their modern history and institutions largely from European colonisation, and latterly from industrialisation. I remarked that in this respect the Enlightenment assumption of 'progress,' that persecution is a feature of barbarous societies which civilization leaves behind, could not have survived far into the twentieth century. Nevertheless, a new reader today may detect a certain complacency underlying those comments of 1987. Although much of the world was still in thrall to persecuting regimes, in the decades since the end of World War II the advanced nations, led and inspired by the wealthiest and mightiest among them, had firmly espoused human rights and the rule of law. Arbitrary arrest, imprisonment without charge or trial, torture, invasion of privacy by the state, might still be widely practised, but they were unhesitatingly and unequivocally rejected, both on moral and on prudential grounds, wherever the future seemed to lie. It was possible to write – I, at any rate, was not wise enough not to write – as though their eventual disappearance was assured, at least in the more developed parts of the world.

The Formation of a Persecuting Society was still in proof when Angeliki Laiou, at Harvard, stimulated what has been the most fruitful and widest ranging of my reconsiderations, the comparison between Latin Europe and other complex civilizations, by pointing out that I was mistaken in asserting that religious persecution was 'familiar in Byzantium throughout its history.' Since then this book has brought me numerous invitations to give lectures and papers, attend seminars and conferences, address meetings and visit campuses. I have been the beneficiary of the most generous hospitality, and the most stimulating and enjoyable company. I have been granted the enormous pleasure and privilege of getting to know many of the brightest and liveliest of a younger generation of scholars. To everybody who has arranged these occasions, and participated in them, my gratitude is beyond measure. Many of them have become friends whose continuing influence is reflected in everything I write. I cannot list them all here, but they know who they are, and I know where they live. In preparing this new version of *Formation* however, I have incurred some specific debts. Scott Ashley's advice greatly influenced the form it has taken. Carole Rawcliffe gave invaluable advice on leprosy, and allowed me to see a substantial part of her major forthcoming book. Mark Greengrass, Ralph Hexter and Mark Pegg responded promptly and generously to pleas for advice and assistance. Tessa Harvey has been a constant support, and she and Angela Cohen have worked heroically to prevent my dilatoriness from delaying publication. A. E. Redgate, as always, has laboured to make me withhold hostages from fortune and say what I mean. All the errors and infelicities are my own.

R. I. Moore
Newcastle upon Tyne, June 2006

PREFACE TO THE
FIRST EDITION

For me this book is a record of new friendships made and old ones
refreshed as successive versions of its argument were read at Gregy-
nog, Swansea, Edinburgh (where the honour of appearing as an
Antiquary lecturer brought an additional and piquant stimulus),
Oxford, Leeds and Birmingham. I owe an enormous debt of pleasure
and gratitude to the gentle efficiency and boundless hospitality of
those who organized these meetings and the acute and generous
criticism of those who came to them.

Since the argument is now presented in a form intended to be
accessible to those who are not already familiar with the period of
European history in which it originates a few words of caution are
in order, not to disarm criticism but to invite it. It will be obvious
that the discussion which follows is not founded on an original
investigation of most of the subjects upon which it touches, or even
on a comprehensive review of scholarship. The variety of the subject
matter would have made either task not only prolonged but repetitive, since the hypothesis presented is so general that most of its parts
are already familiar. Such novelty as it may possess lies not in the
parts but in the connections proposed between them; the interests of
accuracy and efficiency alike, therefore, suggest that the connections
should be exposed to scrutiny in the clearest and briefest form possible. For the same reason this book neither pretends nor attempts
to offer in any sense a complete or even a fair account of the nature
and achievements of European society and institutions in one of the
most vigorous and creative periods of their history. There are many

such accounts, some of the best of them in the works of the historians whose comments on persecution I have singled out for dispute; my aim is to qualify, not to supersede, their characterizations of the period as a whole.

The wider obligations accumulated in the course of devising and exploring a thesis as general as this one are too numerous to record, but at least I can thank Michael Bentley, Richard Hodges, Simone C. Macdougall (Simone C. Mesmin) and Constant Mews for their help and advice, and Robert Bartlett for his generosity in making not only the conclusions but the text of his *Trial by Fire and Water* available to me before its publication. If my debt to the learning and friendship of Bernard Hamilton is but churlishly repaid in the use I have made of his writings here the fault lies in part with the clarity and cogency which make them representative of some of the best traditions of medieval scholarship. None of these, of course, is responsible for my errors and opinions, any more than are the scholars whose work and influence are acknowledged in the text: I am very conscious that among them some of those to whom I owe most will care least for the use to which I have put their work.

R. I. Moore
December 1986

INTRODUCTION

It is very odd that these three crimes, witchcraft, heresy and that against nature, of which the first might easily be proved not to exist; the second to be susceptible of an infinite number of distinctions, interpretations and limitations; the third to be often obscure and uncertain – it is very odd, I say, that these three crimes should amongst us be punished with fire. (Montesquieu, De l'esprit des lois, xxi. 6)

Some years ago I asked in an examination paper for school-leavers, 'Why were heretics persecuted in the thirteenth century?' The question was very popular and the answer, with great confidence and near unanimity, 'because there were so many of them'. The existence of people whose religious convictions differed from those approved by the church was in itself the cause of persecution. The diffusion of their teachings and the appearance of their organization in the Rhineland, the Low Countries, the Languedoc and the cities of Lombardy and Tuscany during the eleventh and twelfth centuries was a sufficient explanation of the formulation of laws to prohibit the expression of their beliefs, and the creation of institutions to identify them and secure their retraction on pain of the loss of liberty, of property and, in the last resort, of life. I have no doubt that if I had asked the reasons for the rapidly increasing severity of action to segregate lepers at this time I should have received precisely the same answer – 'because there were so many of them' – or that the persecution of Jews which was also being greatly intensified would have been accounted for by the increase not of their numbers but of their wealth and economic influence.

As is often the case when their answers in examinations seem unusually absurd or simplistic, the candidates were reflecting, with a frankness which years of scholarly discipline has generally overcome in their betters, an assumption that was, and is, very widely held among those who taught their teachers and wrote their text books. That it was in some way natural or appropriate, or at any rate inevitable, that the medieval church should seek to suppress religious dissent by force, has come to be accepted as a matter of course. Thus, in a work which long held the field as the most authoritative introductory survey of its period in English, Z. N. Brooke wrote of the legislation enacted by the Third Lateran Council in 1179: 'Finally, a strong decree against the Cathari, Patarines and other heretics shows how much the growth of heresy, especially in the South of France, was *at last* beginning to disturb the rulers of the church' (my emphasis).[1]

Those two words – 'at last' – distance their author quite distinctly from the clear assumption which the great liberal historians of the nineteenth and early twentieth centuries – men like Lea, Bury and Coulton – had inherited from the enlightenment, that persecution was one of the leading characteristics of medieval society, perhaps the outstanding symptom of its superstition and barbarousness. Many of their preconceptions, of course, were derived from the hatred of the Roman Catholic Church and its institutions, and the mythology about them, which grew out of the Reformation and its aftermath. In the nineteenth century such emotions were refuelled by the revolution and the long and bitter struggles between legitimacy and liberty, church and state, in which the writing and teaching of history itself, in its apprentice days, were deeply involved. It is, no doubt, very largely the consciousness of the sectarian and ideological passions underlying the clear and vigorous comments of their predecessors on the subject of religious persecution which has led more recent historians to make less of it. Those passions, inevitably, had their counterpart in a Catholic reaction in historical writing, at best mildly apologetic, at worst openly propagandist, which has occasionally achieved academic reputation and more often (through the likes of Chesterton and Belloc) popular notoriety. But what has led most medievalists to express themselves more cautiously on persecution is not any inclination to condone it but the honourable and proper struggle to which serious historians of all religious persuasions and none are condemned, to achieve a sympathetic comprehension of a distant civilization and its institutions. They have sedulously striven, with Spinoza, not to ridicule men's actions, or bewail them, or despise them, but to understand.

[1] *Europe 911–1198*, p. 457.

Yet if sympathy is a necessary condition of understanding, it is not a sufficient one. In recent generations the attempt to come to terms with the persecuting mentality by associating it with the religious convictions which, it is universally acknowledged, characterized and inspired the noblest minds and the highest achievements of medieval civilization, has stifled curiosity and, it will be argued here, prevented us from giving due consideration to some of the profoundest changes in the history of Western society. Sir Richard Southern, for example, probably the finest English medievalist of his generation, comes as near to accounting for persecution in this passage as anywhere in his work. Once more, the emphases are mine:

> those who bore authority in the church were agents with very limited powers of initiative. They were not free agents. *Doubtless* they were responsible for some terrible acts of violence and cruelty, among which the Albigensian crusade holds a particular horror. But on the whole the holders of ecclesiastical authority were less prone to violence, *even* against unbelievers, than the people whom they ruled.[2]

From there it is a short and logical step to the argument of Bernard Hamilton's recent and excellent appraisal of the medieval inquisition, that it 'substituted the rule of law for mob violence in the persecution of heresy'.[3]

These two judgements epitomize the view against which the argument of this book is directed. The reason for taking issue with them is not a moral or political one. We do not follow Lord Acton – the limits of whose liberalism are sharply exposed in this context by his justification of the persecution of the Cathars as 'not against error or non-conformity simply, but against criminal error erected into a system'[4] – in thinking it our business to hold up the sins of our ancestors to the reprobation of their more enlightened descendants. The objection is that the judgements rest on unexpressed and fundamental assumptions about the nature of European society which are historically unfounded, and therefore foster a mistaken understanding of the nature of persecution itself. In particular, Southern's words imply what Hamilton says explicitly, that 'the attitude of the clergy

---

[2] *Western Society and the Church*, p. 19.
[3] *The Medieval Inquisition*, p. 57.
[4] *Lectures on Modern History*, 1969 edn, p. 119.

was shaped by the society in which they lived, which regarded the persecution of heretics as normal'.[5] This is to suppose, first that holders of ecclesiastical – and presumably secular – authority merely reflected sentiment in the society around them, and did not form or direct it, and secondly, that violence and persecution – which are, in any case, by no means the same thing – were simply endemic in the medieval world, a 'norm' which historians must take for granted.

The first of these propositions, relating as it does to the relationship between authority and society, and raising the question whether religious unity was in fact necessary – as is often asserted – to the cohesiveness of medieval society, is an extremely complex one, and will be addressed in the third and fourth chapters. The second is almost self-evidently false. Religious persecution had, of course, been familiar in the Roman Empire, and remained so in the Byzantine world throughout its history. But in the West, far from being 'normal' in medieval society, it faded away with the Roman Empire, and did not reappear until the eleventh century; even then, as the first chapter will remind us in detail, it became regular and established only gradually during the next hundred years or so. Of course it might be argued, and is almost universally assumed, that this is because there were no heretics in the medieval West before that time, and that if there had been they would have been persecuted. As we shall see in chapter 2, neither of those propositions is so obvious, or so simple, as it sounds. But even if they were true it would remain the case that the eleventh and twelfth centuries saw what has turned out to be a permanent change in Western society. Persecution became habitual. That is to say not simply that individuals were subject to violence, but that deliberate and socially sanctioned violence began to be directed, *through established governmental, judicial and social institutions*, against groups of people defined by general characteristics such as race, religion or way of life; and that membership of such groups in itself came to be regarded as justifying these attacks.

The victims of persecution were not only heretics, but lepers, Jews, sodomites, and various other groups whose number was added to from time to time in later centuries. There is no need to list them here. Historians have been assiduous in chronicling and analysing the appalling records of the inquisition of the later middle ages, the

[5] *The Medieval Inquisition*, p. 33.

witch hunters of the sixteenth and seventeenth centuries, the totalitarian regimes of the twentieth, and numberless others. But though
tremendous labour, often of immense distinction, has been devoted
to particular persecutions, relatively little attention has been paid to
persecution as such, as a general phenomenon, and none at all, as
far as I know, to its origin in these centuries. One of the reasons, no
doubt, is that for so many of its greatest historians, who grew up
before the First World War and died before the Second, liberty and
progress went hand in hand. If societies progress away from persecution its approach does not require explanation: persecution is a
feature of barbarous societies which civilization leaves behind. That
confidence could hardly survive far into the twentieth century. But
its replacement by the correspondingly pessimistic conviction that
persecution is a normal component of the human condition is the
result of the same historical error, the familiar one of failing to identify change by taking too short a view. Whether we choose to see
the epoch since 1100 as one of progress or decline, to step back a
little further is to see that around that time Europe *became* a persecuting society. Even if had not remained one, the reasons for such a
change would be worth exploring.

CHAPTER 1

PERSECUTION

The Community of the Faithful

All the faithful of both sexes shall after they have reached the age of discretion faithfully confess all their sins at least once a year to their own priest, and perform to the best of their ability the penance imposed, receiving reverently, at least at Easter, the sacrament of the Eucharist, unless perchance at the advice of their own priest they may for a good reason abstain for a time from its reception; otherwise they shall be cut off from the Church during life, and deprived of Christian burial in death.[1]

In this famous decree the prelates assembled at the Fourth Lateran Council in November 1215 promulgated a working definition (after baptism) of the Christian community, and stated the essential conditions of membership for all Western Europeans for the next three centuries. It took its place, inconspicuously enough, among a comprehensive battery of canons designed to reorganize and reinvigorate the clergy, whose teaching and discipline were traditionally a preoccupation of councils like this, and to lay down a complete pattern of faith and worship in what has been described as 'the first attempt by a council inspired by the papacy to legislate for the Christian life as lived by layfolk'.[2] Although, as with all medieval legislation, there

[1] Peters, *Heresy and Authority*, p. 177. For the full text see Mansi, 22, cols 979–1058.
[2] Knowles, *The Christian Centuries*, p. 219.

was an immeasurable chasm between enactment and implementation, the Lateran decrees provided a programme whose infinitely slow, piecemeal and haphazard influence gradually reshaped the institutional and spiritual framework of European society.

Among the reasons for undertaking this work, one of the most pressing was the defence of the Catholic faith against its perceived enemies. The last three canons required Jews to distinguish themselves from Christians in their dress, and prohibited them from holding public office, and those who converted to Christianity from continuing to observe any of their former rituals, to prevent them from avoiding the penalties of infidelity by means of false conversion.

Even more strikingly – and in this a departure from tradition – the Lateran decrees opened with a declaration of faith. It was clearly and precisely formulated in a manner calculated to repudiate the tenets of the Cathar heresy which in the last two generations had been establishing itself rapidly, particularly in the Languedoc, Provence and Lombardy. This creed was followed by the third and longest canon, which anathematized 'every heresy that raises itself against the holy, orthodox and Catholic faith', and prescribed detailed measures to extirpate them. Heretics were to be excommunicated and handed over to the secular power for punishment, and their property confiscated. Those suspected of heresy were also to be excommunicated, and given a year in which to clear themselves. If they failed, the same punishment would follow. Holders of secular office 'ought publicly to take an oath that they will strive in good faith and to the best of their ability to exterminate in the territories subject to their jurisdiction all heretics pointed out by the Church'; if any should neglect to do so his men would be free to withdraw their allegiance and the Pope to bestow the territory in question on good Catholics 'who on the extermination of the heretics may possess it without hindrance and preserve it in the purity of the faith.' Catholics undertaking military action in this cause would have the same indulgences and privileges as crusaders.

The stigma of heresy was extended to those who sheltered or defended its adherents, and to magistrates who failed to act against them. If they had not cleared themselves after a year they were to be deprived of office and of the power of voting, giving evidence or suing in court, making a will or receiving an inheritance, and would be boycotted in their business or profession. Any who continued to associate with them would expose themselves to excommunication in turn, and clerics were forbidden on pain of deprivation to 'give the sacraments of the church to such pestilential people . . . to give them Christian burial, or to receive their alms and offerings'.

To enforce these regulations

> every archbishop or bishop should . . . twice or at least once a year make the rounds of his diocese in which report has it that heretics dwell, and there compel three or more men of good character or if it should be deemed advisable the entire neighbourhood, to swear that if anyone know of the presence there of heretics or others holding secret assemblies, or differing from the common way of the faithful in law and morals they will make them known to the bishop.

Any lack of zeal on the bishop's part would render him liable to deposition, 'and let another who can and will confound heretical depravity be substituted'.

It is important not to exaggerate the novelty, the effectiveness, or the ecclesiastical character of these measures. The Lateran canon was closely modelled on the bull *ad abolendam* issued at Verona in 1184 by Pope Lucius III jointly with the Emperor Frederick Barbarossa.[3] This was the first truly European-wide measure against heretics, but it was derived from a variety of precedents and procedures of the previous century or so, including the first secular legislation against heresy, chapter 21 of the Assize of Clarendon (1166) in which Henry II had forbidden help or succour of any kind to be given to those whom he had recently condemned as heretics at Oxford. When in 1194 Alphonso II of Aragon ordered convicted heretics to be expelled from his kingdom, and in 1197 his successor Pedro II decreed that they should be burned, they were the latest to display a tradition of ferocity on the part of secular rulers towards those accused of heresy. This tradition went back to the burnings at Orléans in 1022 under the auspices of Robert I of France and at Milan in 1028 on the insistence of the magnates of the city, and to the hangings ordered at Goslar in 1052 by the Emperor Henry III, although it had been frequently and courageously resisted by churchmen. It was reinforced by Innocent III's decree *vergentis in senium* (1199) which declared heretics liable to the same procedures and penalties that Roman law

---

[3] Peters, *Heresy and Authority*, pp. 170–3; Moore, *Origins of European Dissent*, pp. 250–8.

laid down for treason, and opened the way for the launching of the Albigensian crusade against the County of Toulouse in 1208 and the incorporation into secular law of increasingly severe and wide-ranging measures against heretics. In 1226 Louis VIII barred heretics from public office and declared their lands confiscated. During the same decade Frederick II's *Liber Augustalis* laid down draconian measures for the Empire, and in 1233 Jaime I of Aragon gave the provisions of Lateran IV the force of law in his kingdom.

The importance of these provisions lay not only in the formidable array of legal sanctions which they provided against heresy, but in the legitimacy which they gave to action against it. By the beginning of the thirteenth century it had become plain that legislation which relied on the bishops for its implementation would never be effective, however fiercely expressed: where they had the will they often lacked the means and the support to identify, convict and punish members of their communities. The Albigensian crusade itself was the largest and bloodiest illustration both of local reluctance to pursue heresy with the vigour which the Church required and of the opportunity which was provided to outsiders in consequence. At a more ordinary level, Blanche of Castile gave orders in 1229 for an inquisition in the kingdom of France, to be conducted by royal officials, and Raymond VII of Toulouse was compelled to follow suit in 1233. In the same year Gregory IX bypassed episcopal authority by instructing Dominican friars to act as inquisitors in the Languedoc under the direct authority of a papal legate. He had already ordered Conrad of Marburg to hunt German heretics on similar terms, and was about to do the same for the French kingdom through the person of Robert le Bougre.

While both of these officials exercised their licence with legendary ferocity, it was in Toulouse that the papal inquisition took on its regular, formal and enduring institutional form. As its activities spread through Western Europe they also became wider in scope. The first example was the stroke of singular irony by which at the instance of conservative Jews the inquisition ordered the burning of the works of the great speculative philosopher Moses Maimonides at Paris and Montpellier in 1234. The implications of that act became obvious enough at Paris in 1240 when the Talmud itself was solemnly tried in public debate, convicted and burned.[4] By this time the laws against heretics were being held to apply to lapsed converts from

---

4 Poliakov, *History of Anti-Semitism* 1, pp. 68–70.

Judaism, and by 1271 the inquisition had added to its duties that of searching for such people and bringing them to judgement.

We need not enter here into the debates on the brutality or otherwise of the inquisition, and on the extent to which the decline of Catharism in the thirteenth century was the result of repression rather than of the waning of its own spiritual vitality. What is essential to the present argument is that Lateran IV laid down a machinery of persecution for Western Christendom, and especially a range of sanctions against those convicted, which was to prove adaptable to a much wider variety of victims than the heretics for whom it was designed. Jews had been the objects of increasing brutality during the previous two or three decades. They had been expelled from the kingdom of France by Philip II in 1182 after a series of forced loans and confiscations. They were permitted to return in 1198, but only to be the subject of a series of treaties between the king and his princes designed to maximize the exploitation of the Jews and their dependence on the arbitrary and fitful protection of their lords. In England, where the massacre of the entire Jewish community of York in 1190 – perhaps one hundred and fifty souls – was the worst single atrocity committed against them in this period, the crown was equally ruthless in exploiting its rights over Jews, whose position was now deteriorating rapidly everywhere in Europe except where the creation of new communities and enterprises required capital and skills which only they could provide.

Jews had not enjoyed the legal rights to hold land or transmit property by inheritance, or the use or protection of the public courts, in many parts of Western Europe, and to that extent their position was already similar to that which Lateran IV laid down for heretics. But the prescription of identifying clothing (a device which the inquisition later applied to the punishment of heresy, and found to be greatly feared) and the prohibition of Jews from public office served to underline their disabilities, and to confirm their place with heretics in the category of those who were subject to repression. At the same time, precisely the same conditions were being laid down with increasing stridency and stringency for another group of outcasts, not mentioned by Lateran IV largely because the job had been done already by its predecessor, the Third Lateran Council of 1179. Lepers were to be segregated from the rest of the community by expulsion or confinement and deprived of legal rights and protection, and of their property and its disposition – logically enough, since confirmation of the diagnosis of leprosy was announced by a ceremony closely modelled on the rite for the dying. The leper was treated thenceforth as being effectively dead, with all the cruelty and all the ambivalence that implies.

Before examining the implications of these similarities in the fates of heretics, Jews and lepers, it should be considered in more detail how far they extended.

HERETICS

The Legacy of Antiquity

Neither the theory nor the practice of persecution was the invention of the twelfth century. On the contrary the danger, or at least the fear, of schism had attended the church since its infancy. During the last centuries of antiquity the embrace of the imperial power provided the means, and the intelligence of the greatest of the fathers the rationale, of coercion. When the bishops and popes of our period became anxious about the heresy they saw around them there was no difficulty in identifying either a justification or a mechanism of persecution, and no necessity to resort to novelty. 'The factious man (*hereticum hominem*) after the first and second correction avoid,' wrote Paul, 'knowing that he is perverted and sinful and condemned by our judgement' (Titus 3, 10–11). The ambiguity of these words, implying that persistent deviation in belief threatened not only intellectual but social division, is readily understandable in the context of the small and persecuted communities of the early Christians in which the values of fraternity and loyalty must stand supreme.

After his conversion the Emperor Constantine made it clear that the privileges which he conferred on Christians 'must benefit only adherents of the Catholic faith' – that is, adherents of the Nicaean creed and of the bishop of Rome – while 'heretics and schismatics shall not only be alien from these privileges but shall be bound and subjugated to various compulsory public services'.[5] Constantine's successors prohibited the meetings and confiscated the churches and property of sects which attracted opprobrium. Sometimes membership of a heretical sect was held to incur legal infamy, and with it the loss of civil rights: Theodosius I prohibited heretics from holding

---

[5] Peters, *Heresy and Authority*, p. 45; Jones, *Later Roman Empire*, pp. 954–5.

public office, and purges to exclude them were conducted in 395 and
again in 408. In 381, and periodically thereafter, Manichees were
declared incapable of making wills, inheriting, testifying or suing in
the public courts. These measures were invoked from time to time
against other sects, notably in the years after 405 against the
Donatists in North Africa, as part of the great drive to force their
reconversion to Catholicism in defence of which Augustine composed
the first substantial Christian justification of religious coercion and
of the forced conversion which it implied. All this was consolidated
by the Emperor Justinian in what became for the middle ages the
definitive statement of Roman law. Determined to 'close all roads
which lead to error and to place religion on the firm foundation of
a single faith', he debarred heretics from the public service, the practice of law and teaching, the power of inheritance and the right to
testify against Catholics in court. In short, he made right belief a
condition of citizenship and also, on occasion, approval by local
priests or attendance at communion the test of right belief.[6]

In the eastern empire the death penalty for heresy was prescribed
only for a few very remote sects, and applied on a handful of
occasions. In the West in 383, Priscillian of Avila, suspected of
Manichaeism, was handed to the local prefect for punishment in
spite of the protests of Bishop Martin of Tours, and executed on a
charge of witchcraft.[7] Priscillian's accusers were excommunicated by
Ambrose of Milan and Pope Siricius, and he remained not only the
first Western European to be burned as a heretic (though not, it is
emphasized, accused as such) but the only one before 'fourteen of
the higher clergy and more respectable laity of the city' of Orléans
were burned at the order of King Robert I of France in 1022. Heresy
itself largely died in the West with the Arian faith of the Germanic
settlers of the fifth century. For a time their Arianism epitomized the
exclusion of the immigrants from Roman society and served to
justify it, but it disappeared from Francia with the conquests of
Clovis and his sons in the early years of the sixty century, from Italy
with the destruction of the Ostrogothic kingdom in Justinian's wars,[8]

[6]   Bury, *Later Roman Empire* ii, 361, 364.
[7]   Chadwick, *Early Church*, pp. 169–70.
[8]   Against the tradition that the Lombards were Arian at the time of or
shortly after their invasion of Italy see Fanning, 'Lombard Arianism
Reconsidered'.

and from Spain shortly after the conversion of King Reccared in 587 and the formal union of the Arian and Catholic churches at the Council of Toledo two years later. Thereafter, while doctrinal disagreements among the clergy gave rise to occasional accusations of heresy there is no record of departure from Catholic orthodoxy being urged upon the laity of the Latin West, let alone of any of their number being seduced by it, until the last years of the tenth century. That is to say – since we are talking of continuity – for a period as long as that which separates the reign of Elizabeth I from the present day.

The Eleventh Century

That this long silence is broken by the Cluniac chronicler Rodulfus Glaber (the Bald) is embarrassing in itself. His *Five Books of History*, written in the second quarter of the eleventh century, are largely designed to illustrate the apocalyptic prophecy that 'Satan will be released when a thousand years have passed.' Accordingly Rodulfus grouped ominous happenings around the years 1000 and 1033, and demonstrated their allegorical significance by whatever additions or elaborations he thought appropriate. Rodulfus was even less concerned than most of his contemporaries with what a modern mind conceives as 'the facts', and is therefore not a reliable recorder of them. However, granted that each may contain a large element of myth, his stories of Vilgard the schoolmaster of Ravenna and Leutard the shepherd of Champagne may be accepted as typifying in their ways the two threads of heresy which become visible in the first few decades of the eleventh century.[9]

Vilgard, according to Rodulfus, was condemned by Bishop Peter of Ravenna (d. 971) for maintaining that Ovid, Virgil and Horace were divinely inspired, but his teachings subsequently gained a wide circulation. The story obviously reflects monastic suspicion of the revival of interest in classical literature, but apart from that relates to nothing that is recorded in any other source.

Shortly before the time that Rodulfus was writing an equally strange but somewhat more fully recorded incident led to the burning of a number of people from the castle at Monforte near Asti, apparently including the countess. The group was uncovered by Aribert,

[9] Wakefield and Evans, *Heresies of the High Middle Ages*, pp. 72–3; Stock, *Implications of Literacy*, pp. 101–6.

archbishop of Milan, in 1028. Cross-examination of its leader, Gerard, revealed that he and his followers were vowed to chastity, 'loving their wives as they would mothers and sisters', would not eat meat, held their goods in common and dedicated their lives to prayer. Aribert carried them off to Milan, whose leading citizens (*majores*) insisted that those who would not renounce their heresy must die.

It used to be thought that Gerard and his companions were influenced by the Bogomil heresy from Bulgaria, but it is now considered that the formative influence on them, as revealed by Landulf Senior's account of Gerard's interrogation by Aribert, was the neoplatonist approach to the understanding of the scriptures which had been developed in the late Carolingian schools and was much in vogue both north and south of the Alps at this time.[10] This view laid heavy emphasis on the liberation of the individual from the bonds of fleshly preoccupation through personal abstinence, and on the allegorical interpretation of the scriptures, especially the New Testament, to achieve a higher degree of understanding than was attainable through a merely literal reading of the text.

Another group dedicated to that goal had provided the fourteen, or in one text sixteen, victims of the purge at Orléans in 1022 which has already been mentioned. Its members, led by two canons of the cathedral name Etienne and Lisois, have long occupied a legendary place in the history of medieval heresy not only because they were the first to be burned in the West, but because of the sensational nature of what was accepted as the primary account of them, that of Paul of St Père of Chartres, according to whom they not only offered in intensely mystical language to initiate newcomers into their sect, but conducted diabolic orgies of the most dramatically promiscuous character, burning the consequent babies to make a magical ointment from the ashes.[11]

Paul has been exposed by R. H. Bautier not only as late, poorly informed, and a pedlar of literary stereotypes, but as the apologist of the winning side in what was a highly political affair.[12] The truth has turned out to be less strange than his fiction, though considerably

---

[10] Moore, *Birth of Popular Heresy*, pp. 19–21; *Origins of European Dissent*, pp. 31–5; Taviani, 'Naissance d'une hérésie, pp. 1224–52.

[11] Moore, *Birth of Popular Heresy*, pp. 10–15.

[12] Bautier, 'L'hérésie d'Orléans; see also Stock, *Implications of Literacy*, pp. 106–20, and Moore, *Origins of European Dissent*, pp. 285–9.

more interesting. The trial at Orléans was a central episode in a long running rivalry between King Robert the Pious and Count Eudo of Blois. It was designed to discredit Queen Constance, whose marriage to Robert had been a major setback for the Blois connection, and to bring to a head the protracted dispute over the bishopric of Orléans, in which the king had succeeded in placing his own candidate, Thierry, against Eudo's, Odalric. Etienne, the leader of the 'heretics', had been chaplain to the queen, and Lisois was also a recipient of royal patronage. On the other side, the 'sect' was uncovered by the evidence of Aréfast, who claimed to have infiltrated it. He was an uncle of the Count of Normandy, who was closely allied with Eudo of Blois, and he acted on the advice of the sacristan of Chartres, whose bishop Fulbert, though away at the time of this affair, had conducted a bitter campaign against Thierry's appointment as bishop of Orléans. To complete the picture, Etienne and Lisois were associated with other pupils and followers of Gerbert of Aurillac, who as archbishop of Reims had been subjected to similar attacks and forced to abjure a number of heresies in which there is not the slightest reason to suspect him of having indulged.

The Orléans affair, whose results included the deposition of Thierry in favour of Odalric, must be understood as a successful attack on an influential court circle united by ties of spiritual tendency and patronage, planned and carried out by a similarly coherent and similarly motivated rival faction. If the intellectual background of the accused is similar to that of the Monforte group, as the language of spiritual cleansing and renewal that they used clearly implies, the origin of the affair nevertheless lies in the world of the court and political power, and not in that even of learned, let alone popular heresy. In this respect the affair at Orléans should be seen as the precursor of sensational intrigues such as those which broke out at the English, French and papal courts around the beginning of the fourteenth century, rather than of the popular movements of the eleventh and twelfth.

It may be worth noticing that another episode, when Henry III ordered some men hanged at Goslar in 1052 for refusing to kill a chicken, might, for all we know to the contrary, have reflected something similar. The test that was used suggests a charge of Manicheeism, which could, as we have seen, plausibly be levelled at those whose neoplatonist theology exposed them to suspicion of esoterically ascetic beliefs and practices.

Leutard of Vertus, near Châlons-sur-Marne, is the prototype of a very different sort of heretic. He is described by Rodulfus Glaber as a peasant who was impelled by a vision to renounce his wife, break the crucifix in his local church, and preach against the payment of tithe and in favour of literal adherence to the New Testament. He gained some following for a time, but Bishop Gebuin succeeded in convincing the people that he was a heretic, and he drowned himself in a well. Gebuin was the first of three successive bishops of Châlons to be confronted by reports of popular heresy. In 1015 his successor Roger (1008–42) convened a synod apparently to combat Leutard's influence. Roger was probably the recipient in 1024 of a letter from his neighbour Bishop Gerard of Cambrai which accused him of having dealt ineffectually with heretics whom he had detected, examined and released. Twenty years later Bishop Roger II, perhaps to avoid similar rebuke, sought the advice of Bishop Wazo of Liège on how he should deal with some peasants whom he had caught holding secret meetings in the diocese, and in particular whether they should be handed to the secular power for punishment, which Wazo was firmly against.[13]

There is no reason to believe that these groups formed a single sect or tradition, but they did share certain leading characteristics. All, it seems plain, were peasants, or at any rate not privileged, and their religious doctrine appears to have amounted to a simple and literal adherence to the precepts of the New Testament, especially the Gospels and Apostles, which made them sceptical of some of the teachings and claims of the church. Much of the fullest account of any of them comes from Gerard of Cambrai's description of his interrogation of the people whom he examined at Arras in the new year of 1024, and whom he believed to have entered his diocese from that of Châlons.[14]

The men whom Bishop Gerard confronted at the splendid council which he convened for the purpose were illiterate, since they were unable to understand the Latin confession of faith to which they were eventually required to subscribe, and probably unfree, since it seems that they were tortured during their preliminary interrogation. They

[13] Moore, *Origins of European Dissent*, pp. 35–41.
[14] Ibid., pp. 9–18, 288–9; this text, partly translated by Moore, *Birth of Popular Heresy*, pp. 15–19, is crucial to the argument of Duby, *The Three Orders*, pp. 21–44.

were rather humble objects, therefore, for the extensive and wide-ranging sermon which Gerard preached in refutation of a range of heterodox propositions that ran from denial of the virgin birth and the real presence in the mass through objections to the use of bells and psalmody in church services, the veneration of the cross and payment for burial in holy ground.

If those to whom the bishop ostensibly addressed his words had promulgated half of these doctrines in his diocese, or deployed a quarter of the arguments which he set himself to rebut, they would have been formidable heresiarchs indeed. But it is easily shown that they did not. In reality Gerard's discourse was directed against the same theological tendency which had already provided the basis of the condemnation at Oriléans, and would soon do so again at Monforte. Gerard had his own reasons for seizing the opportunity presented by the discovery of these unschooled enthusiasts to attack what he regarded as the forces of change and disorder in the late Carolingian world, and especially the movement for ecclesiastical reform which was associated with the new direction of theology. He was not really much interested in the men before him, whose beliefs, though certainly radical enough in their implications, were very simply stated. They lived, they said, according to the tenor of the Gospels and the Apostles, which they summed up as being 'to abandon the world, to restrain the appetites of the flesh, to do injury to nobody, to extend charity to everybody of our own faith'. 'If these rule are followed,' they continued, 'baptism is unnecessary; if they are not it will not lead to salvation.' They concluded by denying that baptism was a sacrament, on the grounds of the evil lives of the priests by whom it was administered, the probability that the vices renounced at the font would be resumed in later life, and the inability of the infant to understand the confession of faith made on his behalf.

These are the best documented of the episodes which constitute the much-discussed revival of heresy in the eleventh-century West. Sharply though the two currents which it comprised contrasted in their intellectual sources and their geographical and social settings, they converged on one proposition, that the church needed to be reformed, and the corruption of its government and the laxity of its priests expunged, so that it could respond to the spiritual needs of those who sought salvation through illumination of the soul, the rejection of worldly wealth and power, and the imitation of the apostles. The currents of heresy were therefore swept up in the far

broader and faster streams of reform which from the middle of the
century turned the church and half of Europe upside down. In Milan
the Patarenes could drive priests from their churches, denouncing
them as ministers of Satan and their orders as invalid. They could
defy the archbishop for a generation (1056–75) in the name of apostolic purity as they defined it, with the full support of the papacy,
and therefore without entering the list of those whom posterity
usually discusses as heretics. In Flanders, Ramihrdus of Cambrai
could preach in 1076 that the priests had forfeited spiritual authority
through their worldly corruption, refuse to confirm the good faith
of his statement of orthodox doctrine by accepting the sacrament
from any of the bishops, abbots and clerks who interrogated him on
the ground that all of them were simoniacal or unchaste, and be
hailed as a martyr by the pope when the bishop's servants burned
him for his refusal. Heresy did not disappear in those years, as is
sometimes said: the goals of the 'heretics' became those of the
church.

The Growth of Popular Heresy

As the Gregorian revolution lost its zeal and began to come to terms
with the world again, heresy reappeared with greater vigour and
again in two guises, though very different ones from before. On the
one hand, as after every revolution, were those who thought that the
reform had been betrayed, had failed to keep faith with the uncom-
promising ideal of apostolic poverty and dissociation from the corruption of secular power which Leo IX, Cardinal Humbert and
Gregory VII and their emissaries had carried to so many corners of
Europe. On the other, less commonly at first but increasingly important as the twelfth century wore on, were those who rejected not
only the achievement, but the objective of the Gregorian reform, the
ideal of a hierarchically organized church which claimed the right to
intervene in every area of life and thought. There were many throughout the twelfth century whose views might be described in one of
those two ways, especially the first, but who because of their station
or conduct were never arraigned as heretics.

The message of betrayal was borne by wandering preachers, men
of wild aspect, conspicuous poverty and ferocious language, who
railed against the avarice and lechery of the priests and drew followers to themselves in alarming numbers. At first their reception was

ambivalent. Bishop Marbod of Rennes might have no doubt of the impropriety of Robert of Arbissel's wandering Brittany and Anjou in the 1090s clad in skins, barefoot, with staring eyes and unkempt hair, 'wanting only a club to complete the outfit of a lunatic', his tattered retinue of thieves and whores swarming over the country-side, and his indictment of the morals of the clergy calculated 'not to preach but to undermine'.[15] But Robert, like his friend Bernard of Tiron who denounced the archdeacon of Coutances as unfit for office in the market square outside his own cathedral, had been commissioned by the pope to preach the crusade. He died in 1115 a hero of the church and founder of one of its admired religious orders, even if some sharp footwork was needed to preserve the respectability of his memory. The ambivalence was clearly demonstrated in the following year when another of Robert's friends, Bishop Hildebert of Le Mans, welcomed another ragged and fervent preacher to his city at the beginning of Lent, as he was setting out for Rome. He returned to find his clergy overthrown, some of them beaten up, their authority destroyed, and the city presided over by Henry of Lausanne, whose adoring disciples included not only the lay people but some of the younger clergy, who had helped to provide Henry with a platform from which to decry the vices of their seniors. This was the beginning of the longest and most successful recorded heretical career of the century. For another thirty years Henry was active throughout the south-west of France, enjoying much influence in Toulouse and the villages around it in the early 1140s. It took a full-scale preaching mission, complete with a battery of miracles from St Bernard of Clairvaux, in 1145, to shake Henry's command over popular affection enough to let him be captured by the bishop of Toulouse, in whose prison, we are bound to surmise, he died.

A little farther to the south, along the coastal plain between Provence and Narbonne, was the stamping ground of another famous heresiarch of the 1120s and 1130s, Peter of Bruys, whose ferocious and allegedly violent attacks on the teachings, personnel and buildings of the church were repaid in kind when the citizens of St Gilles tossed him onto the bonfire which he and his followers had made of a crucifix.

[15] Marbod of Rennes, Ep. vi, in 171, cols 1483, 1484. For what follows see in addition to Moore, *Origins of European Dissent*, pp. 46–114, Leyser, *Hermits* especially pp. 52–77.

It is impossible to say categorically whether Peter and Henry were exceptional in their talents and their capacity to exploit popular indignation in a part of Europe where ecclesiastical authority was particularly weak, or only in having attracted the attention of two of the most famous churchmen of their day in Bernard of Clairvaux and Peter the Venerable sufficiently to prompt them to leave descriptions of their activities, but probability points to the former. We should not be quite ignorant of either of them even without the works of Bernard and Peter, and churchmen of this generation were nervous enough of effective anti-clerical preachers to create a fair likelihood that something would reach a source which happened to survive. From the first two decades of the twelfth century, for example, there are fragmentary accounts of such preachers near Trier (a priest) and Soissons (Clement of Bucy), of whose precise doctrines and popular influence we know nothing. And it is difficult to evaluate the lurid account of the activities of Tanchelm in which the canons of Utrecht begged the archbishop of Cologne to come to their help. According to them, he terrorized the coastal regions of Flanders for some three years before he was killed in 1115 by an indignant priest, drawing such crowds to him that it was impossible to oppose him. Tanchelm's theme too was the avarice of the clergy and the tyranny of the church, which he illustrated by presenting a wooden statue of the Virgin to his crowds, pronouncing his own marriage to it, and demanding gifts of silver and jewels in the buckets which he hung from its arms. Like the Milanese Patarenes his followers, on at least one occasion, expelled a priest from his church and took it over for their own use, and like Henry's they included both the poor and artisans, though they cannot be characterized precisely.

Together with the part which Arnold of Brescia played in the rising of the people of Rome against the Pope in 1146 and their subsequent defiance of both papal and imperial authority, these are the most spectacular manifestations of popular anti-clericalism in the twelfth century. No less significant are the growing indications that groups of lay people took to gathering together for spiritual comfort and social support by means of private worship and gospel study. Except when for one reason or another they incurred the suspicion of authority we know little about them. It is impossible to suggest how far we should generalize Bernold of Constance's picture (from the 1090s) of whole villages forming themselves into religious communities under clerical guidance and obedience, though he says that they did so all over southern Germany, or Lambert le Bègue's account of the manner in which the ladies of his parish in Liège met in their homes after service on Sundays to read the Bible and sing psalms in the 1160s.[16] But such a background of widespread, discreet but often determined lay piety, whose very existence constituted in some sense a criticism of the Church and its performance, is an essential context for the growing appeal of the heretical movements. There are signs of it in Champagne, the Rhineland and the Low Countries in the 1120s and 1130s, and sporadically thereafter.

In 1143 the first clear signs that this native tradition of dissent was being joined by emissaries of the heretical communities of the Byzantine world – probably refugees – arose from a clash between two groups of heretics in Cologne which led to their arrest. The subsequent interrogation revealed that the leaders of one group preached the doctrines and claimed the history and orders of the Bulgarian Bogomils. It would be wrong to exaggerate the contemporary impact of this discovery. Western churchmen had always been strongly inclined to attribute heresy to alien (though not yet Manichaean) infection, whether there was evidence of it or not. Nevertheless, this was a momentous episode in the history of heresy in the West. By the 1150s at the latest the Cathars, as they came to be known, had an organized ecclesiastical structure in the Rhineland, with its own churches, rituals and bishops. By the 1160s they were spreading rapidly into the Languedoc, which became their most notorious stronghold, and thence into Italy, where in the 1170s they made contact – by no means friendly contact – first with other sectaries of Bulgarian origin who had spread into Veneto and the Marche from Dalmatia during the same two decades, and then directly with missionaries of their counterparts in Constantinople.

In all these regions the Cathars struck deep social roots very rapidly, perhaps because they were areas where authority was already fragmented and rapid social change was creating tension and

[16] Moore, *Birth of Popular Heresy*, pp. 101–11; 'New Sects and Secret Meetings', pp. 49–51. The account of twelfth-century heresy in the remainder of this section is defended by Moore, *Origins of European Dissent*, *passim*; for other views see Lambert, *Medieval Heresy*, pp. 39–66; Wakefield and Evans, *Heresies of the High Middle Ages*, *passim*; Peters, *Heresy and Authority*, *passim*; Wakefield, *Heresy, Crusade and Inquisition*, pp. 15–49.

conflict. By 1165 leaders of the Cathars could openly debate with the bishops of Toulouse and Albi, setting them at defiance before a great meeting of churchmen and nobles at Lombers, near Castres. Thirteen years later a papal mission was greeted with jeers and obscene gestures in Toulouse, though it did succeed in securing the conviction and punishment as Cathar heretics of some prominent citizens. By that time there were Cathar churches – in many cases more than one, because of their sectarian rivalry – in all the major cities of northern and central Italy, and civic unrest and faction often enabled them to preach and practice their faith quite openly. It would be fruitless to attempt any numerical estimate of their strength, but there is no doubt that during the next three decades the Cathars entrenched themselves firmly in the Languedoc, Provence, Lombardy and Tuscany, and secured a degree of toleration and protection from influential laymen which in many places gave them substantial immunity from the disciplines of the Church. Indeed, it was an attempt to counter their influence which led to the formation of the other great and enduring heresy of this period, when Valdès of Lyons and his followers were excommunicated in 1181 for refusing to acknowledge the bishop's right to licence them to preach, as they had vowed to do against Catharism.

The Waldensians spread perhaps as rapidly as the Cathars, and (not surprisingly in view of their origins) were even more bitter against the claims and authority of the Roman clergy. It is therefore probable that the period between the Third Lateran Council of 1179 (which in response to the previous year's mission to Toulouse promulgated strong condemnations of a number of heresies) and the Fourth in 1215, saw the most rapid diffusion of popular heresy that Western Europe had yet experienced.

The Response of the Church

The dissemination of heretical teaching to the laity was for all practical purposes a new problem for the bishops of the eleventh and twelfth centuries. Analysis and prescription could be found in the pages of St Paul and the fathers of the church, to whom they naturally turned for guidance. The powers and penalties laid down in Roman law eventually provided the basis of their response, but the fact that when, around 1002, Burchard of Worms made the most comprehensive collection of ecclesiastical law to date he did not include such provisions, or otherwise consider the question of popular heresy, is striking confirmation that our ignorance of heretical sentiment in the centuries immediately before is not attributable simply to deficiencies in the surviving evidence. As we have seen, in some of the earliest cases the initiative was taken by the secular powers, for reasons of their own. In the absence of pressure from them the bishops tended to act on the principle laid down by Wazo of Liège that reports of heresy should be investigated, heretics examined and excommunicated, and their teachings publicly rebutted. The Councils of Montpellier in 1062 and Toulouse in 1119 demanded that heretics and their supporters should be handed over to the secular power for punishment, but it seems that most bishops (unlike Aribert of Milan) shared Wazo's view that to do so would amount to participation in the shedding of blood, for after that episode in 1028 there is no further case until 1148. In that year a notorious and violent heretic, Eon de l'Etoile, who had been responsible for looting and burning monasteries in Brittany, was handed over to a council at Reims presided over by Pope Eugenius III. Eon himself was spared as being obviously mad, but a number of his followers were delivered to the lay power and burned.

This case together with the execution of Arnold of Brescia a few years later (even though he was charged with rebellion, not heresy) marks a very clear watershed in the history of the Church. In earlier years even notorious heretics had been treated comparatively leniently. Tanchelm, for instance, was imprisoned for a time by the Archbishop of Utrecht, but released. As late as 1135 Henry of Lausanne was captured by the Archbishop of Arles and brought before a council at Pisa which simply ordered him confined to a monastery. These judgements may have been influenced by particular considerations of which we know nothing. Even so, we cannot ignore the contrast between the years up to 1140 or thereabouts, when the episcopal response to heretical preaching was piecemeal, *ad hoc* and often mild, and the increasing determination to deal severely with it which becomes evident after that time.

The change was certainly associated with movement towards a more centralized approach to the problem. The responsibility for dealing with heresy lay with the bishops. But far from being adequate to check the dissemination of heretical teachings their main remedy, the expulsion of the heretic from the diocese, actually assisted it. As the Le Mans chronicler observed, when Hildebert of Lavardin expelled Henry from the city which he had temporarily ruled 'he fled to disturb other regions and infect them with his poisonous breath'.[17] The letter which Peter the Venerable, abbot of Cluny, wrote in about 1139/40 to the bishops of four dioceses in which Peter of Bruys had been active marks a change not only in calling for the invocation of the secular power (a call the more striking in coming from the head of an order which, until about that time, had been particularly notable for its abhorrence of violence), but in explicitly intervening in what was usually regarded as a diocesan matter.

The novelty of Peter the Venerable's letter is softened by the fact that the abbots of Cluny had long felt and exercised a degree of supervisory responsibility in this region of small and poor dioceses, where episcopal authority was especially fragmented and weak. The next step, however, marked a decisive advance both in the assumption of central responsibility in dealing with heresy and, fatefully, in external intervention in the affairs of the Languedoc. In 1145 Bernard of Clairvaux wrote to the Count of Toulouse to announce his intention of entering the Count's dominions in the company of a papal legate, Bishop Alberic of Ostia, and Bishop Geoffrey of Chartres, to undo the work of Henry of Lausanne. His mission set an important precedent both in itself and in its tactics of attacking not only the heretic but his sympathizers. In the city of Toulouse Bernard secured a judgement from the citizens that 'the heretics, their supporters and all who gave them any help would not be eligible to give evidence or seek redress in the courts, and nobody would have any dealings with them, either socially or in business'.[18] There is perhaps some irony in the last point, which recalls so clearly the boycott that Henry had organized against the canons of Le Mans thirty years earlier.

The Council of Reims of 1148 confirmed the end of inhibition against invoking the secular power by handing the Eonites over for burning, and the papacy's increasing concern with heresy wherever it might arise, by demanding that no succour should be given to the followers of heretics in Gascony and Provence (i.e. the disciples of Henry and Peter) on pain of interdict on the lands of any who sheltered them. Nine years later another council at Reims, presided over by the archbishop, showed a new savagery in proscribing the follow-

---

[17]   *Gesta Pontificum Cenomannensium*, Bouquet XII, p. 551.
[18]   *PL* 195, col. 412.

ers of the '*Piphiles*', the Balkan missionaries whose activity at this time has already been noticed. Those who persisted in the heresy were to be excommunicated and their goods forfeited. The missionaries themselves were to be imprisoned for life, and those suspected of being their disciples to be put to the ordeal of the hot iron, and if found guilty branded on forehead or cheek. It was also ordained that suspected heretics could be arrested by whoever chanced to discover them. Formerly bishops had reacted to what were generally, in the recorded instances, dramatic and aggressive acts on the part of notorious – in effect, self-proclaimed – heretics; now it was their business to go looking for heretics on the premise that they were there to be found, and that any failure on the part of the heretics to proclaim their infamy would only prove their duplicity. A papal council at Tours in 1163 confirmed this transition. Heresy was now alleged to be spreading secretly but with great rapidity in the region of Toulouse. Reports of meetings or houses that sheltered heretics were to be speedily investigated; those suspected of adherence to heresy were to be socially and commercially boycotted, the secular power invoked against them, and their property confiscated.

In these years, in short, the Church went on the offensive. In 1178 another papal mission to Toulouse, headed by another abbot of Clairvaux, Henry de Marcy, put the last major element of inquisitorial procedure in place when, exasperated by the slowness of the Count and citizens of Toulouse to denounce the heretics whose presence in the city was beyond question, it instructed

> the bishop and certain of the clergy, the consuls of the city and some other faithful men who had not been touched by any rumour of heresy to give us in writing the names of everyone they knew who had been or might in future become members or accomplices of heresy, and to leave out nobody at all for love or money.[19]

In the following year, Henry de Marcy inspired the Third Lateran Council to order that there should be no social or commercial dealings with heretics or their supporters, on pain of excommunication, and of the dissolution of the ties of homage and liability to confiscation of land and goods. The ground for *ad abolendam* and for Lateran IV and the inquisition beyond it had been prepared.

[19]   *PL* 204, col. 237.

JEWS

The Legacy of Antiquity

Roman law placed Jews under the same disabilities as Christian heretics. They were excluded by Justinian's *Codex* from the imperial service and the legal profession, from making wills and receiving inheritances and from testifying or suing in the public courts. These prohibitions originated as the counterpart of the privileges accorded to the Jews in the wake of the bloody wars of the first century AD, which culminated in the great dispersion.[20] Alone among the citizens of the empire, Jews were excused from making obeisance to the divine emperor, which would have offended their religious principles. Scattered through the empire and beyond it though they were, they lived by their own law, which regulated civil and commercial as well as religious affairs, under the authority of a hereditary patriarch who resided at Tiberias in Palestine, until the line failed in 429. The patriarchs were usually accorded high civil rank in the imperial hierarchy, and maintained a staff of *apostoli* through whom they collected taxes from their people all over the empire and exercised discipline over their clergy. This was the ambiguity which continued to govern the relations of the Jews with the other peoples of Europe. By setting them apart it accorded a measure of protection to their religious and cultural identity at the price of exposing them, when the current ran that way, to special obloquy as well as special privilege, and of a dependence on their protectors which made them both peculiarly vulnerable to tyranny and often identifiable as its instruments.

The rise of Christianity in the fourth and fifth centuries brought home the problem. Jews were forbidden to marry Christians, acquire Christian slaves, or convert those slaves they had to their own religion. Early in the fifth century the Emperor Honorius I forbade the construction of new synagogues, though the repair of old ones continued to be permitted, and worship in them remained a protected liberty. The famous protest of Ambrose of Milan against the fines imposed on the bishop of Callinicium and his flock for burning down the synagogue there in 415 – 'should not the rigour of the law yield to piety?' – seems to have been exceptional both in its cynical bigotry

---

[20]   Jones, *Later Roman Empire*, pp. 946–9.

and in its success. In this as in so many things Pope Gregory the Great was more Roman, insisting that damage to synagogues must be compensated.

Prohibitions designed to prevent Jews from exercising political and domestic power over Christians and from proselytizing their religion were contained in some fifty provisions of the Theodosian code and repeated in law codes of the Germanic successor kingdoms of the fifth and sixth centuries. The extent to which they were enforced is another matter.[21] There is no doubt that at the courts of Charlemagne and his successor Jews enjoyed imperial protection. A famous letter of Bishop Agobard of Lyons in which he called upon Louis the Pious to enforce the prohibitions on the ownership of land and the keeping of Christian servants by Jews was categorically rejected. The emperor was even prepared, no doubt for venal reasons, to ignore blatant violations of the ban on trading in Christian slaves. Whether such protection benefited the Jews in the long run is an open question. It certainly contributed, after the partition of the empire in 843, to a vigorous campaign of the west Frankish clergy headed by Archbishop Hincmar of Reims for the restoration of the prohibitions, notably on the building of new synagogues and the holding of public office and dignities by Jews. Other projects to undermine Jewish communities, such as removing Christian children from Jewish homes, and legally separating Jewish children from their parents were also mooted. Charles the Bald took no notice, but in the long run the bishops had the stronger cards.[22]

The Emergence of Anti-Semitism

The change which took place in the next century and a half is vividly expressed by the scene in the *Song of Roland* (lines 3658–71) which shows Charlemagne revenging the death of his friend by the destruction of the synagogues of Saragossa along with the mosques, and the forced conversion of the worshippers in them. It is quite out of

---

[21]   The view of Bachrach, *Early Medieval Jewish Policy*, vigorously opposing accounts in the 'lachrymose tradition' (as S. W. Baron dubbed it) such as that of Katz, *Jews in the Visigothic and Frankish Kingdoms of Spain and Gaul.*

[22]   Bachrach, *Early Medieval Jewish Policy*, pp. 84–123; Wallace-Hadrill, *The Frankish Church*, p. 393.

keeping with the historical Charlemagne, but not with the northern French world of the eleventh century in which the *Song* was written. The first general indication of the changing atmosphere came in 1010–12, with a series of attacks at Limoges, Orléans, Rouen, Mainz and elsewhere, after a rumour that the Holy Sepulchre in Jerusalem had been sacked on the orders of the Prince of Babylon. In 1063 several Jewish communities in south-western France were attacked by knights on the way to fight the infidel in Spain; the archbishop of Narbonne earned a papal rebuke for leaving his Jewish quarter open to them, whereas the *vicomte* protected his on the other side of the city.[23] These episodes foreshadowed the massacres of 1096 in the Rhine cities and at other points on the route of the first crusade.

The magnitude of the atrocities associated with the first crusade cannot be estimated precisely. Rouen is the only French city which is known to have been the scene of a massacre, but both Christian and Jewish sources say that there were others. At Rouen, according to Guibert of Nogent, the crusaders 'herded the Jews into a certain place of worship, rounding them up either by force or by guile, and without distinction of age or sex put them to the sword. Those who accepted Christianity, however, escaped the slaughter.'[24] More than a dozen chroniclers add to the tale which followed the crusading armies, and especially that led by Emicho of Leiningen. At Speyer the bishop was able to intervene when eleven Jews had been killed, but at Worms eight hundred died, some by their own hands, to avoid forced conversion. 'This one killed his brother, that one his parents, his wife and his children; the betrothed killed each other even as wives killed their children.' Others were killed by the crusaders, 'granting quarter to none save those few who accepted baptism'. Two days later the same thing happened at Mainz, and then at Cologne, Trier, Metz, Bamberg, Regensburg, Prague and many other places.[25] It is difficult to assess the scale of these massacres numerically. As always, the estimates of the chroniclers differ widely and are inherently unreliable. It seems unlikely that cities whose populations did not exceed two or three thousand contained as many hundred Jews, and they do not appear to have lost the whole of their Jewish populations. As recently as 1982

[23] Little, *Religious Poverty*, pp. 46–7, citing *PL* 146, cols 1386–7.
[24] Guibert of Nogent, II. 5, trans. Benton, pp. 134–5.
[25] Riley-Smith, 'The First Crusade and the Persecution of the Jews'; Poliakov, *History of Anti-Semitism*, I, 41–6.

the site of a substantial and well-constructed house which can be securely dated to the very beginning of the twelfth century, within a few years of these events, has been excavated at Rouen.[26] But that is hardly to the point. Though it has been questioned whether the events associated with the first crusade left a lasting impact on French Jewry[27] there is no doubt that the savagery and ruthlessness of the killings, which disturbed many Christian commentators, left the Jews of Germany and the Rhineland not only shocked and despairing but exposed as the objects of cruelty, insults and exploitation – and therefore also, of course, of the secret fear that they might, by one means or another, seek their revenge.

The preaching and preparation of crusades, the religious fervour and social unrest associated with them, continued to represent danger for Jews. In 1146 the intervention of Bernard of Claivaux seems to have prevented a catastrophe on the scale of that half a century earlier, though not before many more killings in the Rhenish cities, including Mainz, Worms, Speyer, Strasbourg and Wurzburg, had been incited by the apocalyptic preaching of a monk called Ralph. Bernard, arguing that the scriptures enjoined the dispersal, not the killing of Jews, confronted Ralph at Mainz and persuaded him to give up preaching and return to his monastery. 'The people', says Otto of Friesing, 'were very angry, and wanted to start an insurrection, but they were restrained by regard for Bernard's saintliness.'[28] The prominence of King Richard I in the organization of the third crusade helped to spread the fever to England, where his coronation, on 3 September 1189, was attended by the burning of the London

---

[26] Varoqueaux, 'Découvertes médiévaux à Rouen'; on Jewish populations in the cities Little, *Religious Poverty*, pp. 44–5 and Fossier, *L'enfance de l'Europe*, pp. 593–4, though Fossier's observation that 'if it is true as Ralf Glaber says [in itself an improbability] that 900 Jews were massacred at Mainz (in 1015) the numbers would be comparable with those in the Mediterranean south' is difficult to reconcile with the rest of the data which he gives.

[27] Chazan, *Medieval Jewry in Northern France*, pp. 26–8. But cf. the comments of Langmuir, 'From Ambrose of Milan to Emicho of Leiningen', on the casualness of Christian chroniclers towards these events, in contrast to the agreement of Jewish ones that they constituted a traumatic turning point.

[28] Otto of Freising, *Deeds of Frederick Barbarossa*, pp. 37–40; Scott James, *The Letters of St. Bernard*, pp. 462–3, 465–6.

Jewry, with the loss of at least thirty lives. In the next few months there were attacks on Jews in several places, especially in East Anglia, where Kings Lynn, Norwich, Stamford, Bury St Edmunds and Lincoln prepared the way for the death by fire and mass suicide of the Jewish community of York in March 1190.[29]

From the beginning, then, the crusades undoubtedly stimulated hostility to the Jews and provided the most appalling occasions of its expression. But they did not cause it, and may too easily serve as a portmanteau explanation of events whose real causes and connections with each other are obscure. It is a useful caution, for instance, that we know enough about the background of the largest single atrocity against the French Jews in our period – the killing of eighty people or more by Philip Augustus at Bray-sur-Seine at the end of 1191 – to say firmly that it had no connection whatsoever with the crusade, or with any other attack on the Jews, even though it took place less than two years after the massacre at York. It is difficult, and may be misleading, to fashion the very fragmentary incidents of which we have knowledge into a coherent story, and still more to know how far the increasingly coarse and violent anti-semitism which is not so much betrayed as flaunted by the monastic chroniclers should be taken as representative of other sections of the Christian population. However, it does seem certain that the Jews of Europe were being subjected to a growing weight and variety of daily vexations throughout the eleventh and twelfth centuries, and there may be something more than coincidence in the tendency of such indications of it as survive to shift from mediterranean to northern Europe as the period unfolds.

The success of Ratherius, bishop of Verona from 931–8, in securing the expulsion of the Jews from that city probably represents a thread of continuity between Carolingian and later traditions of ecclesiastical reform, in strict adherence to canon law. In 1020 or 1021 a number of Jews were accused of mocking a crucifix in Rome, and savagely punished, and there is a reference to some unspecified hostility against the well-established community at Lucca around the same time. In 1062 Jews were accused of blaspheming a holy image at Artemo, near Pescaro, and in the next year the Jewish community was expelled from Benevento.[30] It seems to be from the early years

[29] Dobson, *The Jews of Medieval York*, pp. 18–28.
[30] Roth, *Jews of Italy*, pp. 72–3.

of the eleventh century that we should date the 'tradition' which appeared in some towns of south-western France, including Toulouse, Béziers and Arles – and also in Chalon-sur-Saône in Burgundy – of striking a Jew on the face outside the church on Easter Sunday.[31] That the ceremony was commuted to a tax on the Jewish community in Toulouse at least as early as 1077[32] prompts the suspicion that like other 'customs' of this period it was developed specifically for the purpose of raising revenue, in this case levied by the Church in a region where its resources were under particularly severe pressure. Even so the custom was real enough on at least one occasion, for Adémar of Chabannes reports that in Toulouse about 1020 the appointed striker performed his task with such vigour that he knocked out the eye of his victim, who died in consequence.[33]

It is impossible to strike a true balance of the general situation of European Jews in the twelfth century. In many ways they shared in the general prosperity and expansion of the period. Jewish communities spread to many parts of Europe, especially in the north and west, where they had not been before. Their members often occupied positions of influence, and many of them accumulated great wealth, not only through local money-lending (which was not invariably lucrative) but as part of a banking and trading network which extended through Europe and the middle east. Jewish thought and culture experienced, like their Christian counterpart, a twelfth-century renaissance. 'In numbers and cultural wealth,' as John Mundy has put it, 'western European Jewry reached its peak in the late twelfth and early thirteenth centuries... both in the north and in Mediterranean Europe Jews flourished as never before.'[34] Yet, while that is as true as any statement so general could be, it is hard not to be conscious of the precariousness of such well-being, and to suspect that apart from the occasional, sudden and devastating riot, apart from the growing depiction of the Jew as the dedicated enemy of the Christian community which carried such sinister portent for the future, there was an increasing vulnerability in everyday life to the casual obloquy and abuse of the faithful. That, at any rate, is what is suggested by the question put to Gilbert Crispin by a Jew from

---

[31]   Little, *Religious Poverty*, p. 47.
[32]   Mundy, *Liberty and Political Power*, p. 8.
[33]   Ibid., p. 225, n. 21.
[34]   Mundy, *Europe in the High Middle Ages*, p. 81.

Mainz which Gilbert records in his *Dialogue between a Christian and a Jew* in the early 1090s: 'If the mosaic law is one that ought to be observed why should you treat those who observe it as though they were dogs, driving them forth and pursuing them everywhere with sticks?'[35]

In 1179 an appendix to the decrees of the Third Lateran Council provides a sufficient commentary on these words, in the pope's instruction that Jews were not to be deprived of land, money or goods without judgement, nor to be assaulted with sticks and stones during the celebration of their religious festivals, and their cemeteries were not to be invaded or violated.[36] By this time casual, almost instinctive anti-semitism had become commonplace in the chronicles. Rigord, the biographer of Philip Augustus, for example, reflects the king's hostility to Jews in depicting them as immensely wealthy, grasping and cruel, killers of Christian children and desecrators of sacred vessels deposited for loans; in England, says R. B. Dobson, the rich crop of northern chroniclers of the last part of the twelfth century 'wrote of the Jews in a manner which reveals their complete commitment to the classical medieval Christian stereotype of the blaspheming and sacrilegious enemy of Christ'.[37]

It seems certain that the formation of that stereotype together with the specialization of the Jews in the business of money-lending and the activities associated with it, and with the establishment in most areas of their peculiar juridical status as the posessions – the serfs – of the king, was in practice though not in principle the work of the twelfth century. These three developments were intimately inter-linked, and together constituted the essential elements of the vulner-ability of the Jews to persecution.

The Jews as Enemies of Christ

The identification of the Jews as the particular enemies of Christ, and therefore of Christians, has been the central and cruellest thread of European anti-semitism. Norman Cohn puts it like this:

[35] Quoted by Richardson, *The English Jewry Under the Angevin Kings*, p. 34; on the date, Southern, *St. Anselm and his Biographer*, p. 91 n.
[36] Mansi, 22, col. 356.
[37] Luchaire, *Social France at the Time of Philip Augustus*, p. 195; Dobson, *Jews of Medieval York*, p. 20.

As I see it the deadliest kind of anti-semitism, the kind that results in massacre and attempted genocide, has little to do with real conflicts of interest between living people or even with racial prejudice as such. At its heart lies the belief that Jews – all Jews everywhere – form a conspiratorial body set on ruining and then dominating the rest of mankind. And this belief is simply a modernized, secularized version of the popular medieval view of Jews as a league of sorcerers employed by Satan for the spiritual and physical ruination of Christendom.[38]

The idea of a special association between the Devil and the Jews had a basis in scripture. John (8, 42–44) has Christ say to the Jews: 'If God were your father ye would love me . . . Ye are of your father the devil, and the lusts of your father ye will do. He was a murderer from the beginning. . . .' The phrase 'synagogue of Satan', which was often used of the Jews in our period, came from Revelations 2.9 ('I know the blasphemy of them that say they are Jews and are not but are a synagogue of Satan') and 3.9. The Christian fathers did not invent the belief that Jews were especially skilled in sorcery, but they did give it wide currency. By the seventh century these two ideas were connected in the Byzantine legend of the apostate priest Theophilus on whom a Jewish magician conferred supernatural powers.[39] This was an important source of the notion of the diabolic pact which became so important in the witch craze of the later medieval West. In 992 a convert accused the Jews of trying to murder the Count of Maine by sticking pins into a wax image they had made of him.[40] Guibert of Nogent, one of the early historians of the first crusade, was particularly fond of anecdotes which associated Jews with sex, sorcery and the devil. The many which crowd the pages of his auto-biographical *Monodiae*, written in 1115, include a tale in which through the mediation of a Jew skilled in medicine a renegade monk acquires mastery of the black arts by selling his soul to the Devil; his apostasy from Christianity was sealed by a libation of sperm.[41] This is the first example of a theme which at the end of the middle ages became a standard component of the stereotype of the witch.

[38]   Cohn, *Warrant for Genocide*, p. 12.
[39]   Peters, *The Magician, the Witch and the Law*, pp. 13–4; more generally, Trachtenberg, *The Devil and the Jews*, pp. 23–31.
[40]   Chazan, *Medieval Jewry*, p. 12.
[41]   Guibert, *Autobiographie*, i, xxvi, 115; Trachtenberg, *The Devil and the Jews*, p. 213.

By this time a link was already familiar in monastic literature between diabolic associations, sexual libertinism and the murder of children. Enemies of the early Christians had claimed that their secret meetings were attended by orgiastic behaviour which culminated in the slaughter of a child, and the Christians in their turn said the same of heretics. In the eleventh century the tradition was revived by Paul of St Père of Chartres, who claimed that the 'heretics' burned at Orléans in 1022 had used the ashes of children born of their orgies to make a powder which bound those who took it irreversibly to their sect. Guibert of Nogent, never backward in peddling superstition, was happy to attribute the same behaviour to the followers of the 'Manichees' whom he believed he interrogated in 1114 in the persons of Clement and Everard of Bucy.[42]

The death a of skinner's apprentice named William in a wood near Norwich early in 1144 did not at first create much stir.[43] The claim of his mother and uncle that the Jews were responsible for it was quickly squashed by the sheriff. It was only six years later, under a new sheriff and a new bishop, that the accusation that William had been tortured to death by the Jews of Norwich was elaborated, and began to be vindicated by a series of miracles at his tomb. The cult built up a considerable if local following over the next century or so, and continued to provide gruesome material for East Anglian church artists until the reformation. Similar accusations, of which detailed accounts do not survive, were aimed at the Jews of Gloucester in 1168, Bury St Edmund in 1181, Winchester in 1192 and Norwich again in 1235. The discovery of a boy's body in a well at Lincoln in 1255 brought the fever to its peak. The dean had the body of little St Hugh interred beside that of Robert Grosseteste, despite the protest of the boy's parish priest. A royal justice was prepared to give credence to the accusation that he had been tortured to death by the Jews, who were dragged off to London for trial. Nineteen were hanged, and only the intervention of the king's brother, Richard of

[42] Cohn, *Europe's Inner Demons*, pp. 1–22; Moore, *Birth of Popular Heresy*, pp. 10–15 and *Origins of European Dissent* (1985), pp. 285–6; Guibert, *Self and Society*, iii, 18, trans. (here inaccurately) Benton, pp. 212–14.
[43] Thomas of Monmouth, *William of Norwich*; Langmuir, 'Thomas of Monmouth'; on the cult Ward, *Miracles and the Medieval Mind*, pp. 68–72 and Finucane, *Miracles and Pilgrims*, pp. 118–21, 161–2.

Cornwall (as a paid agent, not a principled defender of justice) prevented some ninety more from sharing their fate.[44]

In telling the story of how a Jew of Winchester was accused of doing away with a Christian boy at the time of the Passover in 1190, Richard of Devizes adds the element of international conspiracy to the stereotype.[45] It was alleged that the boy in question was French, and had been directed to Winchester by a Jew of Rouen who provided him – what could be clearer proof of foul intent? – with a letter in Hebrew to show to the Winchester Jews. On this occasion the story was dismissed by the royal justices, whom Richard said had been bribed, and the matter was dropped. But it brings into the arena of religion another ancient calumny against the Jews which had begun to reappear in the eleventh century. The stories of their having betrayed Visigothic Spain to the Arabs in the eighth century and Bordeaux and Barcelona to the Vikings in the ninth seem to have started then.[46] The first attacks of the eleventh century, as we have seen, seem to have been sparked by the assertion which Rodolfus Glaber records, that it was at the instigation of the Jews of Orléans that Caliph al Hakim destroyed the Holy Sepulchre.

It has been estimated that the allegation of child murder was the basis of some one hundred and fifty known trials during the high middle ages.[47] It appears on the continent at almost the same time as in England. In 1147 the Jews of Wurzburg were blamed for the death of a boy found drowned in the River Main. By 1171 the Count of Blois accepted an accusation, even though no body had been found or boy reported missing, as a sufficient reason to hang thirty-one Jews, though King Louis VII subsequently disagreed with him. In 1191 Louis' successor Philip Augustus seized the opportunity of an unsubstantiated allegation that Jews had killed one of his vassals

---

[44] Hill, *Medieval Lincoln*, pp. 224–32, and the excellent article on Little St Hugh by William Hunt in the *Dictionary of National Biography*.

[45] *Richard of Devizes*, ed. Appleby (London, 1963), pp. 64–9. I doubt Appleby's view (p. xv) that Richard himself did not believe the story he told, but in any case he did not invent it: Thomas of Monmouth, *William of Norwich*, p. 94, claimed that William's murder was ordered by the Spanish Jews.

[46] Bachrach, *Early Medieval Jewish Policy*, pp. 114; Blumenkranz, *Juifs et Chrétiens*, p. 381.

[47] Trachtenberg, *The Devil and the Jews*, p. 125.

to assert his presence at the important frontier stronghold of Bray-sur-Seine by surrounding it and executing more than eighty Jews.[48] In those two cases no elaboration of the accusation was necessary: the purposes of count and king respectively were sufficiently served by the simple assumption that Jews killed Christians. By the middle of the thirteenth century belief that Jews slaughtered Christian children for their own ritual purposes had become widespread, in spite of repeated disavowals by the papacy, notably in 1242 and 1253, and the conclusion of a commission established by the ever-curious Frederick II to investigate the question, that there was nothing in it.[49]

Closely associated with the ritual murder myth, and responsible for perhaps another hundred trials, was the suggestion that Jews served their diabolic master by profaning the host. At Cologne in 1150 the two were neatly combined in a story that the son of a converted Jew took home the wafer which he received at mass on Easter Sunday and buried it in his garden; when the hole was opened by a priest the wafer had assumed the shape of a child which miraculously ascended to heaven.[50] This theme too had made its appearance around the time of the first crusade, when those who charged a French Jew with boiling a communion wafer in oil and water said that they saw it turn into a child in the cauldron. At Belitz near Berlin in 1263, and again at Brussels in 1320, large numbers of Jews were burned on accusations like these, whose potency was no doubt increased by the establishment from 1264 of the feast of Corpus Christi as a means of arousing popular enthusiasm for the doctrine of transubstantiation, and against heretics who doubted it. Another blasphemy which was attributed to the Jews more and more often, obviously reflecting their activity as money-lenders, also helped to associate the idea of the Jew with that of dirt and especially of defecation. In the middle of the twelfth century Peter the Venerable, abbot of Cluny, warned King Louis VII that Jews would subject sacred vessels which came into their hands to disgusting and unmentionable indignities, and a hundred years later Matthew Paris produced his tale that Abraham of Berkhamsted used his privy as a place of storage for a picture of the Virgin and Child lodged with him as security.[51]

[48] Chazan, *Medieval Jewry*, pp. 37–8, 56–9, 69–70.
[49] Poliakov, *History of Anti-Semitism*, I, 60–1.
[50] Ibid., pp. 59, 62–3; Little, *Religious Poverty*, p. 52.
[51] Chazan, *Medieval Jewry*, p. 44; Denholm-Young, *Richard of Cornwall*, p. 69.

The Jews as Royal Serfs

'The Jew can have nothing of his own, for whatever he acquires he acquires not for himself but for the king; for the Jews live not for themselves but for others and so they acquire not for themselves but for others'[52] Thus Bracton epitomized the legal position of the Jew, which is often described as servitude to the crown, and indeed the serf 'acquired not for himself but for his master'. In principle the Jew's property was the king's, to seize at will, and in hard practice debts owed to the Jew were owed to the king and reverted to the exchequer at the death of the creditor.

The servitude of the Jews was essentially an innovation of the eleventh and twelfth centuries. It had been foreshadowed in 694 when the Council of Toledo reduced the entire Jewish population of Spain (but not of the provinces of the Visigothic kingdom to the north of the Pyrenees) to slavery. The motive may have been directly fiscal, to bring the resources of the Jews into the hands of the crown, or political, to prevent them from providing a base for opposition.[53] But there is no evidence of any direct link between this legislation and the principle which began to be enunciated in charters of Aragonese and Castilian towns towards the end of the twelfth century that 'Jews are the serfs of the crown and belong exclusively to the royal treasury.'[54] If that idea has a single origin it is Frankish, in the act of Louis the Pious which reserved the hearing of cases involving Jews to himself, through an official called the *magister judaeorum*. This must be regarded as part of the favour which the Carolingian kings in general and Louis in particular accorded the Jews, and may even have been intended to protect them against the enforcement of the traditional prohibitions for which some of his subjects were calling.

As so often in Jewish history special treatment was dangerous in itself, and what began as a privilege later became the means of oppression. Protection of the Jews and jurisdiction over them became one of the rights which the counts usurped from the crown in the tenth century, and the feudatories from the counts in the eleventh.

[52]   Pollock and Maitland, *History of English Law*, 1, 468.
[53]   The views respectively of Collins, *Early Medieval Spain*, pp. 135–6, and Bachrach, *Early Medieval Jewish Policy*, p. 21.
[54]   Baer, *Jews in Christian Spain*, 1, 85.

At Macon the count acted as lord of the Jewish community, and intermediary between Jews and Christians, regarding them in turn as part of his patrimony, exercising justice over them and inheriting their lands when they died.[55] In 985 the Count of Barcelona considered himself heir to the Jews killed in Almanzor's seige of the city, and in 1022 confiscated the goods of a Jew convicted of committing adultery with a Christian woman. According to the *Usatges* of Barcelona (*c*.1060) the *wergild* of the Jew was fixed not by custom like that of the free man but by the arbitrary decision of the Count. Elsewhere in Christian Spain the rights and security of the Jews were retained by the crown, which might therefore release them from obligations to other lords, as when in 1062 the king of Navarre exempted the Jews of Jaca from having their flour ground in the seignurial mill.[56] The position was essentially the same in England, where Jews were introduced by (or at least in the reign of) William the Conqueror, and were treated by his successors as part of their prerogative. As the *Leges Edwardi Confessoris* put it in Henry I's reign, 'All Jews wherever they are in the kingdom must be under the guardianship of the king; nor may any of them be subject to any baron without the licence of the king, because Jews and all their property are the king's.'[57]

In the Holy Roman Empire the same relationship between protection and possession is visible in the twelfth century. At Worms in 1090 Henry IV exempted Jews from episcopal and comital jurisdiction, reserving them to his own. In confirming privileges granted by the bishop of Speyer in the same year he specifically added that the bishop's grant to the Jews of the right to do their own justice was in reality an imperial concession. Having tried, ineffectually, to punish the perpetrators of the massacres of 1096 Henry placed all Jews under imperial protection by the Peace of Mainz in 1103. In 1179 Frederick I described them as 'pertaining to the imperial fisc', a principle reiterated by Frederick II in 1236. For all these monarchs Jews represented a valuable asset, neither to be dissipated nor to be annexed by their subjects.[58]

---

[55]   Duby, *La société aux XIe et XIIè siècles dans la région maconnaise*, p. 120.
[56]   Baer, *Jews in Christian Spain*, pp. 40–3.
[57]   Richardson, *English Jewry*, p. 109.
[58]   Langmuir, '*Judei nostri*', p. 106.

In Spain, England and the Empire the establishment of the position of the Jews as royal serfs therefore represented in effect a reassertion of royal prerogative by reclamation of alienated powers, assisted in the first two cases by the circumstances of conquest. In the French kingdom the disintegration of central power which continued throughout the eleventh century included power over the Jews. So they fell under the sway of the lords, to whom their superior culture made them particularly valuable. The Count of Macon used the Jews of the town as his financial agents, and Guibert of Nogent's classical portrait of seignurial tyranny, brutality and exaction in the person of Thomas of Marle includes several tales arising out of his domination over a number of Jews who ministered skilfully to his most vicious whims. We shall consider later whether it was the closeness of the Jews to the lords that made them need protection by the end of the eleventh century, or their need for protection which brought them close to the lords. In either case it was only as the Capetians began to reassert royal power outside their demesne, in the reign of Philip Augustus, that they started to claim with it a special dominion over Jews. When Louis VII created a *prepositus judaeorum* to enforce debts to Jews, near the end of his reign, he was doing no more than any lord might have thought prudent in his own lands. There was a sign of growing readiness to exert royal power, which would later be less benevolently exercised, after the affair at Blois in 1171, when the survivors of the Count's assault appealed to the king, who dismissed the charge of ritual murder on the grounds that similar accusations against the Jews of Pontoise and Joinville had been proved groundless, and directed officials throughout his demesne to protect Jews and their property more effectively.

From Exploitation to Expulsion

The dramatic deterioration in the situation of French Jews after the accession of Philip Augustus in 1179 owed a good deal to personal antipathy as well as to royal avarice.[59] Within three months of his coronation Jews were arrested at worship by royal agents, their houses searched, and their goods seized and held to ransom. Two years later

[59] Bautier, 'La personnalité de Philippe Auguste', p. 44; cf. Poly and Bourmazel, 'Couronne et mouvance', p. 228.

the expulsion of Jews from the royal demesne was announced, and while they were allowed to sell off their movable goods, their 'houses, fields, vineyards, barns, winepresses, etc. [the king] reserved for himself and his successors the kings of the French', and the synagogues were handed over to the bishops for conversion into churches. The communities affected by the expulsion, which was enthusiastically applauded by the monastic chroniclers of the reign, included those of Paris, Bourges, Corbeil, Etampes, Melun and Orléans.[60]

The king's biographer, Rigord, offers as justification for this action the usury of the Jews and the allegations which had been made against them of murdering Christians – dismissed by the royal court only a few years ago – and desecrating sacred ornaments and vessels. The claim that the king was entitled to appropriate the Jews' property because they themselves were his emerges only at the end of Philip Augustus' reign, in the chronicle of Guillaume le Breton.[61] It seems, therefore, that the doctrine that Jews were royal serfs was embraced in the French kingdom as a *post factum* rationalization of persecution, and did not supply the original basis for it. Indeed, although it was implicit in all Philip's dealing with the Jews after he readmitted them to the royal demesne in 1198, the explicit formulation of the doctrine in French royal documents took place relatively slowly during the thirteenth century. Its legal foundation no doubt owed something to the facts that Philip found it fully established over the substantial Jewries of Anjou and Normandy when he annexed those territories in 1204, and that Innocent III reiterated that the Jews were condemned to perpetual servitude as punishment for the crucifixion in a bull issued in 1205.

Most of those expelled in 1182 took refuge in the lands of the Count of Champagne. The terms of an agreement which Philip concluded with him when they were readmitted to the royal demesne in 1198 show very clearly what were the motives of the two men in their dealings with Jews, whose chattel status is taken for granted:

> Let all whom the present letters reach know that we have conceded that we shall retain in our land none of the Jews of our most beloved and faithful neighbour Theobald, Count of Troyes, unless with the verbal consent of that count; and that none of our Jews will be per-

---

[60]   Chazan, *Medieval Jewry*, pp. 63 ff.
[61]   Ibid., pp. 66–7.

mitted to lend money to anyone nor to seize anyone or anything in his lands unless with [his] verbal consent. The same Count Theobald conceded to us that he will retain none of our Jews in his lands... and that none of his Jews will be permitted to lend money to anyone nor to seize anyone or anything in our lands unless with our verbal consent.[62]

This agreement inaugurates a new and far more systematic exploitation of Jews as a source of profit to the French kings and their baronage. It was sustained with increasing ferocity throughout the thirteenth century. When the direct profits of their financial activities were insufficient for the needs of the moment they could be charged for protection, or to have their goods returned after seizure, or they could be expelled from the kingdom and made to pay to return on still harsher terms than before. The process continued until the final expulsion in 1394.

That the agony was briefer and probably less brutal in England was not due to the superior benevolence of its kings, but to the greater financial sophistication of their government. Under Henry II and Richard I, English Jews were relatively moderately taxed. The formation of the exchequer of the Jews in 1194 to administer the debts which reverted to the crown on the death of Aaron of Lincoln, and thereafter of others, provided the king with a regular and powerful control over that source of income (and through it also an enhanced capacity for the political manipulation of the debtors), but did not in itself produce a deterioration in the situation of the Jews. In John's reign, and especially after the fall of Normandy to Philip Augustus in 1204, things took a turn for the worse. Taxation and arbitary impositions increased sharply, and the Jews incurred growing hostility as the source of the debts whose increasingly ruthless enforcement by the king became a major grievance against them. Nevertheless, after John's death the regents declined to implement the anti-Jewish provisions of the Lateran Council in England, or to provide secular support to bishops who wished to do so. Such restraint would not have been exercised if it had incurred a political cost sufficient to outweigh the relatively modest income from the sale of licences to dispense with the badge of shame, of which almost all English Jews took advantage.[63] Their situation deteriorated in respect

[62] Ibid., p. 75.
[63] Richardson, *English Jewry*, pp. 178–9.

of both financial exaction and discriminatory legislation as Henry III's reign progressed, but the expulsion of Jews from Gascony in 1288–9 and from England in 1291 was the result not of any growing pressure of hostility from the community at large, but of financial exigency which Edward I chose to meet by this single and arbitrary action of spoliation.[64] The expulsion from England was final, but the Gascon Jews returned within a few years to what remained, despite renewed royal directives for expulsion, one of the most tolerant refuges available to them in Western Europe.

The story of the English Jews provides ample caution against assuming that anti-Jewish legislation was always and everywhere enforced, or that royal persecution was inspired or endorsed by popular hostility.[65] Nevertheless, the apparatus for the persecution of Jews in Europe was fully worked out during the thirteenth century and the image of the Jew so firmly associated with it was established. It was not until this time that drawings which depict Jews as physically distinctive – particularly with long, hooked noses – began to appear:[66] like the badge of shame they were necessary because, as the framers of the Lateran decrees had complained, 'in the countries where Christians do not distinguish themselves from Jews and Saracens by their garments relations are maintained between Christians and Jews and Saracens . . . In order that such wickedness in future be not excused by error it is decreed that Jews of both sexes will henceforth be distinguished from other people by their garments.'

LEPERS

And the leper in whom the plague is, his clothes shall be rent, and his head bare, and he shall put a covering upon his upper lip, and shall cry, Unclean, unclean.

All the days wherein the plague shall be in him he shall be defiled; he is unclean: he shall dwell alone, without the camp shall his habitation be. (Leviticus 13, 45–6)

[64] Ibid., p. 213.
[65] Ibid., pp. 192–7, 231–3.
[66] Blumenkranz, *Le juif médiévale au miroir de l'art Chrétien*, pp. 15–32.

'Leprosy'

The history of lepers and leprosy is complicated both by the medical uncertainties which still surround the disease and by the difficulty of knowing what medical conditions are described as leprosy when it appears in historical sources from different periods and cultures.

Leprosy is caused by a bacillus called *microbacterium leprae* which was identified by G. W. A. Hansen in 1874. It is therefore sometimes called Hansen's disease, as it will be from time to time in this section to distinguish it from other conditions which may have been called leprosy at different times. But it was almost another century before clinical proof of Hansen's discovery was established by the successful infection of a healthy organism in laboratory conditions.[67] Until very recently, therefore, there has been great freedom to ascribe the cause of leprosy to an extraordinary variety of circumstances, from an exceptionally lascivious temperament to an excess of bad fish in the diet. To add to the confusion, *microbacterium leprae* manifests itself clinically in several different ways, some of which are relatively mild, and is closely connected with various tubercular conditions. The disease is therefore both difficult to diagnose correctly and easy to confuse with others: even today a standard medical textbook warns that a doctor who is not looking for leprosy may easily miss it, while one who is is liable to see it everywhere.[68]

The next chapter will argue that these difficulties are central to assessment of the problem which leprosy posed for twelfth-century Europe. Nevertheless, it is possible to exaggerate them. The most virulent form of Hansen's disease, lepromatous leprosy, is characterized by loss of sensation at the nerve ends, particularly in the extremities of the body, because they have been invaded and destroyed by the bacteria. They also destroy blood vessels, ligaments and skin tissues with hideous and bizarre effects – the throaty voice of the leper, for instance, is the result of damage done in this way to the larynx – and also produce an erosion of the bones of head, limbs, hands, and feet which can be clearly distinguished by the archaeologist. In this form therefore – though not in the more benign forms which seem to become commoner as resistance to the bacillus is

[67] Cochrane and Davey, *Leprosy*, p. 13; Brody, *Disease of the Soul*, p. 22.
[68] Cochrane and Davey, *Leprosy*, p. 280.

developed in the society in question – there is the possibility, which
has to some extent been achieved, of comparing the assertions of
literary sources about the dissemination of leprosy with scientifically
objective data about its most damaging and most frightening form.
Nor should we be too smug about the scientific advantage which we
enjoy over our forerunners. Twelfth-century doctors (like the priests
of Leviticus) knew that leprosy could easily be confused with several
less dangerous conditions, and some of the tests which they employed,
such as the dropping of cold water on the suspected spot of skin to
watch how it ran, were capable of contributing to an authentic diagnosis of Hansen's disease. However, for the moment these considerations need not delay us. In tracing the responses of eleventh- and
twelfth-century society to the diffusion of leprosy, which was universally believed to be rampant at the time, it is with those who were
called lepers and treated as such that we are concerned, whether a
modern specialist would have confirmed the diagnosis or not.

The Legacy of Antiquity

It is quite clear that the leprosy of Leviticus was not Hansen's disease,
which seems to have originated in China and found its way only
slowly to the Middle East and Europe. As recently as 1980 the characteristic bone deformations have been found in skulls from Egypt of
the second century BC, and in 1974 in the legs and feet of a Romano-
British skeleton of the fourth century AD. Before that the examination
of many thousands of skeletons had yielded no evidence of leprosy
from the ancient world earlier than the traces from the sixth century
AD turned up in Britain, France and Egypt.[69] It may therefore be said
with some confidence that if Hansen's disease was not unknown in
the ancient world it was extremely rare. It was not to sufferers from
it, for example, that the Emperor Constantine referred when he
ordered the expulsion of lepers from the city of Constantinople and
executed an official named Zoticos for giving them shelter instead.[70]
In fact, it looks as though this had more to do with a drive to rid the
city of the swarms of indigents and vagabonds who crowded into it
than with any concern for public health.

---

[69]   Manchester, *Archaeology of Disease*, p. 43, supplementing Andersen,
Studies in the Medieval Diagnosis of Leprosy, pp. 10–14.
[70]   Mollat, *Les pauvres au moyen âge*, p. 26.

In repenting of his action and founding a hospital for lepers dedicated to the memory of Zoticos, Constantine displayed an ambivalence which would remain at the heart of Western attitudes to lepers. The more charitable response remained uppermost, at any rate in the literature, for the next couple of centuries, for the succouring and healing of lepers are fairly common occurrences in the saints' lives of that period. The charitable impulse still prevailed at the Council of Orléans which in 549 ordered that lepers were to be given food and clothing by bishops, to relieve those who 'through severe infirmity are constrained to unbearable destitution'. We have no means of knowing whether the segregation of 'lepers' was practised at this time. It is first prescribed neither in Roman nor in ecclesiastical law, but in the code of Rothari, king of the Lombards, in 635. His decree lays down the future position so clearly that it is worth quoting in full:

> If anyone is afflicted with leprosy and the truth of the matter is recognised by the judge or by the people and the leper is expelled from the *civitas* or from the house so that he lives alone, he shall not have the right to alienate his property or to give it to anyone because on the day that he is expelled from the home it is as if he had died. Nevertheless while he lives he should be nourished on the income from that which remains.

In a later chapter Rothari provides that a betrothed girl who contracts leprosy (or goes mad, or blind in both eyes) may be cast off without penalty. The man will bear no guilt because 'it did not occur on account of his neglect, but on account of her weighty sins and resulting illness'.[71]

Rothari's diagnosis confirms what the circumstances of his reign and legislation would lead us to expect, that we see here the continuation of the tradition of late antiquity, and not a response to any actual change in disease patterns. Similarly, the actions of the abbot of Remiremont a little later in assigning separate cells to leprous nuns and instructing them not to communicate with the healthy, and of St Othmar in the next century in constructing a leper house near his monastery, whose inmates he cared for himself,[72] are more likely to

---

[71] Drew, *Lombard Laws*, pp. 83–5.
[72] Mesmin, 'The Leper Hospital of St. Gilles de Pont-Audemer', p. 11.

represent respect for the Biblical teaching than the appearance of Hansen's disease in these relatively central regions of Western Europe. They also confirm, however, that when the disease did become widely current a framework for dealing with it was already familiar.

Apart from those two incidents the legislation of Rothari inaugurated a silence in the western sources which lasted almost unbroken until the eleventh century. Indeed the recrudescence of leprosy which then becomes visible is often attributed (like heresy, syphilis and gothic arches) to the increased contact with the middle east that came with the crusades. That will not quite do. William of Malmesbury, writing early in the twelfth century, tells the story of a dispute which arose between the monks of St Martin who carried his body from Tours to Auxerre to keep it safe from the Vikings and their hosts.[73] Martin's body was placed in the crypt beside that of the native patron, St Germanus. The question then arose how credit for miracles performed there, and hence the offerings made in gratitude for them, should be divided between the two saints. It was resolved by placing a leper 'nearly at the last gasp, wasted almost to a skeleton' between them. In the morning the side next to Martin was clean and healthy, while that which had been exposed to Germanus' attention remained as it had been. Next night, 'so that they might not attribute this miracle to chance they turned the yet diseased side to Martin. As soon as the day began to dawn the man was found by the hastening attendants with his skin smooth, perfectly cured', a result which William tactfully attributes not to the impotence but to the hospitality of Germanus, 'yielding to the honour of such a welcome stranger'. There is, alas, no certainty that such a story dates from the ninth century to which it is attributed. The tenth century has a little more to offer, in King Athelstan's donation for the care of the poor and leprous of Bath and the fate of Abbot Reginald of St Omer, who in 959 found himself leprous and ruled the abbey from his cell for almost a year before he was betrayed by his efforts to avoid meeting an important visitor and compelled to resign and leave the abbey for a place of seclusion.[74] At a time when the absence of archaeological evidence for Hansen's disease in Western Europe in these centuries is beginning to assume a negative weight it would be rash to take either of these references at face value, but Reginald's story in par-

---

[73] William of Malmesbury, ii. 4, trans. Giles, pp. 115–16.
[74] Bourgeois, *Lépreux et Maladreries*, pp. 158, 301.

ticular suggests at least that the idea of the leper was something more than a biblical metaphor.

The Onset of Medieval Leprosy

Once more it is in the early years of the eleventh century that we pick up the trail again, and towards the end of it that scattered and unrelated episodes begin to form what can be seen as the beginning of a continuous story thenceforth. In 1014, lepers were among those who were cured by the relics which Bishop Gerard translated to his church at Arras.[75] In 1023 at Orléans, 'a district which had many infirm, especially lepers', they were given money and kissed in demonstration of his humility by King Robert I. In 1044 Aelfward was compelled by leprosy to give up the bishopric of London. The monks of his abbey of Evesham refused to receive him, so he took back the books and relics which he had given them and went to Ramsey instead. The same fate overtook Gervase, abbot of St Riquier, who was compelled to resign in 1075, and a little latter there is a similar case from the secular world in a Picard lord who sought the help of St Anselm because he was 'afflicted with leprosy [and] despised and deserted by his own men, despite the dignity of his birth, on account of the foulness of so great an affliction'.[76]

There is every possibility that there was more to incidents like these, which involved the deposition of holders of authority in turbulent times, than simply nervousness of leprosy. They do occur, however, on the eve of a most dramatic alteration in the treatment of lepers, and one which represents a remarkable effort of organization and expenditure – the foundation of hospitals and homes for lepers which took place on a large scale all over Western Europe. Table 1 shows that the chronology of these foundations is very similar in three areas of north-western Europe for which systematic data can be compiled, and this is probably typical of Western Europe as a whole.

The institutions represented by these figures include not only large and permanent foundations but houses which may only have lodged one or two lepers for a few years, or conversely might have existed

---

[75] Ibid., p. 218, n. 161.
[76] *Helgaud, Vie de Robert le Pieux*, pp. 126–8; Barlow, *The English Church*, pp. 74–5, 219; Mesmin, 'The Leper Hospital of St. Gilles', p. 18; *Eadmer's Life of St. Anselm*, pp. 57–8.

Table 1 Leper hospitals first referred to in the years indicated

	1075–1100	1100–25	1125–50	1150–75	1175–1200	1200–25	1225–50	1250–75	1275–1300
England and Wales	4 (4)[a]	10 (4)	19 (5)	29 (16)	42 (4)	19 (3)	37 (3)	24 (3)	18
Pas de Calais	2	1	1	6	9	6	5	1	15
Paris region		2	3	7	21	23	29	17	13

Notes: Paris region = the four departments comprising modern Paris.

[a] The figure in brackets represents the number of houses known to have been founded during the quarter century in question, as distinct from first reaching a surviving record during it. Notice that the proportion which this figure represents declines sharply during the period as a whole. This may suggest (i) that the rate of foundation probably reached its peak somewhat earlier than the figures for first references would suggest; but (ii) that the appearance of leper houses in England after the Norman Conquest is not simply an illusion produced by superior recording, since all of those known to have existed by 1100 and two-thirds of those by 1125 were founded between 1075 and 1125. The more fragmentary records of the Pas de Calais, carefully collected by M. Bourgeois, convey a similar impression.

Source: Paris region: Goglin, *Les misérables de l'Occident Médiévale*, p. 185; other figures compiled from Knowles and Hadcock, *Medieval Religious Houses: England and Wales* and Bourgeois, *Pas-de-Calais*.

for many years before their presence happened to be noted, for one reason or another, in a surviving record. The probability of the latter obviously increased with time. The table is therefore likely to exaggerate the number of leper houses which existed at any one time, at any rate in the later part of the period, and to suggest (as the comment on the figures for England and Wales illustrates) that they came into existence somewhat later than was really the case, Nevertheless, it shows pretty unequivocally that the movement began around the end of the eleventh and beginning of the twelfth centuries, surged to a peak about a hundred years later, and fell away quite quickly in the later part of the thirteenth century. The institutions mentioned for the first time after 1250 in England and Wales are almost all very small and in remote regions (several of them in Cornwall), and from this time there is a growing number of indications both from England and from the continent that there were more vacant places in leper hospitals than lepers to fill them; the decline became rapid in the years after the Black Death.

Lastly, it should be noticed that there is a clear and general explanation for the marked increase in these foundations in the last quarter of the twelfth century. In 1179 the Third Lateran Council reiterated that lepers should be segregated, and were forbidden to go to church or to share churches and cemeteries with the healthy.[77] It laid down that those who were living in communities should be provided with chapels, priests and cemeteries, though this was not to be done in a way which was detrimental to the parochial rights of existing churches. Many of the donations recorded in the following decades, often by bishops and chapters, were plainly designed to implement this decree. In 1186, for example, the bishop and chapter of Arras made a church available for the use of the inhabitants of the leprosarium of Grand-Val, which had probably come into existence about twenty years earlier, and the existence of the leper hospital at Béthune is first signalled by the gift of a chapel to it by Robert d'Hinges and his wife Sarah in 1194.[78]

Towards Segregation

The foundation of shelters and hospitals for lepers on this scale was obviously a great charitable endeavour. Some historians have been

[77]   Mansi, 22, col. 230.
[78]   Bourgeois, *Pas-de-Calais*, pp. 192, 231.

content to view it in that light alone. The foundations of the Anglo-Norman period in England, for instance, have recently been described as a 'momentous break-through to institutional care', part of a movement in which 'the country's rulers enthusiastically embraced challenges in governmental administration, labor-saving technology and public welfare', 'a significant triumph of ingenuity over need... reveal[ing] a whole new era in social welfare'.[79] It is no part of my argument to deny the reality of compassionate motives in these foundations and in many of the other changes which overtook the treatment of lepers in our period. The stylized preambles of charters of donation, at most reflecting such current moral platitudes as that lepers needed charity all the more because segregation intensified their poverty, will not be taken too seriously as evidence of individual sentiment and motive. But Eadmer's account of Lanfranc's foundation of St Nicholas, at Harbledown near Canterbury, reflects a perfectly straightforward humanity of sentiment:

> Outside the western gate of the city, but further away from the northern gate, on the shelving side of the hill, he constructed wooden houses and assigned them to the use of lepers. Here also, as elsewhere, the men were kept separate and not allowed to associate with the women. To these lepers he had all that they needed according to the nature of their disease supplied from his own resources and for this service he appointed men of such character that, at any rate in his opinion, nobody would question their skill, their kindliness, or their patience.[80]

However, although such instances might be multiplied easily enough, it remains the case that these foundations took place in a context of rising hostility to lepers, and a growing conviction that they should be segregated from the community at large. How far the foundations should in themselves be regarded as evidence of these sentiments is a more difficult question. The establishment of a hospital did not necessarily mean that segregation was being introduced for the first time. The hospital at St Omer, for instance, was established in 1106 on land which had been reserved for the use of lepers since the time of Count Robert I of Flanders (1071–93). That example, however,

---

[79] Kealey, *Medieval Medicus*, pp. 82, 105.
[80] *Historia Novorum*, trans. Bosanquet, pp. 16–17.

equally shows that this qualification will not justify the projection of segregation into the distant past in the absence of explicit evidence for it, for a charter of 1056 describes the same land simply as pasture and marsh.[81]

It has been observed with justice that since the strongest sanction which the statutes of most thirteenth-century leper houses provided against persistent infringement of the rules was expulsion, segregation can hardly have been the principal object of the foundations. Conversely, one of the main sources of benefaction was the lepers themselves, who gained admission (or the promise of admission) to the hospitals in that way. This, however, only means that life in a leper hospital was better than the alternative, which is scarcely a contentious point. The image of the wandering leper with his bell or clapper to warn of his approach and the begging bowl which none but he would touch is one of the most familiar and painful that the medieval world has to offer, and life in the leper villages whose existence is abundantly testified by twelfth-century place-names can hardly have been much better.[82] Nor were the lepers alone in their misery. Around 1200 the rules of the general hospital of St Jean at Angers prohibited the admission of lepers, sufferers from ergotism (St Antony's fire, brought on by eating grain infected by fungus), paralytics, those who had been mutilated in punishment for theft, the violent, and children too young to attend to their own needs. As M. Bienvenu observes, we know that the lepers had somewhere else to go, but we know nothing about the rest.[83] In other words, the anxiety of the leper to be admitted to the lazar house, or not to be expelled from it, and the degree of charitable achievement which its foundation and maintenance represented, must be very largely a measure both of the rigour with which segregation was being insisted on and the horrors which attended it.

It is extremely difficult to estimate how generally or how strictly segregation was enforced in the high middle ages. We have already

[81]   Bourgeois, *Pas-de-Calais*, pp. 158, 301.
[82]   Sournia and Trevien, 'Essaie d'inventaire des léproseries en Bretagne', estimate that there were 287 leper colonies in the five departments of Brittany, of which about half are attested by documentary evidence and half by place names alone.
[83]   Bienvenu, 'Pauvreté, misères et charité en Anjou', 73 (1967), pp. 208–12.

met a small group of people who as lepers were excluded from office in the tenth and eleventh centuries. To it might be added famous examples of royal and noble lepers who were not, like Baldwin, the leper king of Jerusalem (1174–85) or Constance of Brittany (d. 1201), but probably not Robert the Bruce or King Henry IV. The powerful were both more vulnerable to political hostility and more able to secure exemption from the laws that governed others, according to circumstance, than ordinary people, whose situation is hard to discern.

The principle of segregation had remained alive since the time of Rothari, and provided the inhabitant of Speyer who wrote to Archbishop Heribert of Cologne a little after 999 with a sharp image of penance in the leper who must be led from the village by the priest before he could be cured.[84] But it is impossible to say whether he drew it from experience or Leviticus. Segregation may be implied but is scarcely proved by Helgaud's account of Robert the Pious' visit to lepers at Orléans, 'ad hos avida menti properans et intrans' ('eagerly hastening towards them and entering'): did he enter a building, an enclosure, or only a crowd? The leper whom Hugh of Cluny found living in a hut in Gascony, and cured, had been a wealthy man, but the circumstances of his isolation are not explained.[85] The nobleman who approached Anselm for help was shunned by his men, but nothing in the story suggests that he had been placed in isolation.

These few incidents will show how difficult it is to guess from the context of these occasional anecdotes about lepers in the eleventh-century sources, which are in any case by no means numerous, what their circumstances were. But it is clear that segregation was not then universal, and did not become so for some time. The charter by which Bonhomme the leper gave land to St Aubin at Angers in 1123 shows that he was living in freedom; in the same area towards the end of the century Pierre Manceau seems to have been under more pressure when he obtained his lord's permission to give himself and his goods to an almonry as an alternative to entering a leper hospital. The Life of St Steven of Obazine tells of a leper who shared a house with a cripple at Pléaux in the Limousin and begged for both, appar-

---

[84]   PL 151, cols 693–8, quoted by Stock, Implications of Literacy, pp. 77–8.
[85]   PL 159, col. 875, 897.

ently in the 1140s.[86] Nor does it seem that segregation was strictly
enforced in England at that time; in 1163 the city of Exeter regarded
as 'ancient' the custom of allowing lepers to walk freely in its streets,
which the bishop revoked in 1244.[87]

On the other hand, there are undoubted signs of increasing nervousness of the contagion of leprosy, and the rapidity with which it
could spread, from the beginning of the twelfth century. Some of the
clearest came from the kingdom of France where in 1118 the inhabitants of Péronne asked Bishop Lambert of Tournai to secure lepers in
a place away from the town because they feared infection. Before
1124, Abbot Arnold of St Pierre le Vif told Louis VI that he had
changed the location of his leper house to remove it from fields and
vineyards because of the growth in the number of lepers and the fear
of contagion. And Louis VI himself gave as his reason for founding
a leper house at Compiègne that the lepers had been wandering in
the streets like beggars until on the advice of the doctors that they
were contagious 'the clergy and inhabitants took it upon themselves
to gather them up and make them leave the town and the ancient
fortress'.[88] The same distinction between lepers and beggars is made
in a letter addressed to Eugenius III by Waleran of Meulan about the
leper house which he had founded *c*.1135 at Pont-Audemer in
Normandy. Here the implication is that the lepers had already been
segregated, and their plight aggravated by their resultant inability
to beg.

Waleran's foundation exhibits another characteristic which may
suggest that the establishment of leper houses responded in some
degree to a perceived collective need, in the provision that a stated
number of lepers would be supported by regular collections of money
and food from the inhabitants of Pont Audemer. If they failed to
maintain their contributions the count would retaliate by reserving
to himself the right to nominate inmates.[89] The construction of a

---

[86] Bienvenu, 72 (1966), p. 401, and 73 (1967), pp. 202–3. Aubrun, *La vie
de St. Etienne d'Obazine*, pp. 164–6. The context suggests a date *c*.1140,
but an earlier one is possible.

[87] Clay, *Mediaeval Hospitals*, p. 57; Kealey, *Medieval Medicus*, pp. 103–
4, holds that segregation was not widely practised or believed in Norman
England; more generally, Brody, *Disease of the Soul*, pp. 93–4.

[88] Mesmin, 'The Leper Hospital of St. Gilles', p. 36.

[89] Mesmin, 'Waleran, count of Meulan', p. 15.

chapel dedicated to St Lazarus for the use of lepers at Angers by a confraternity of citizens, some time before 1120, provided an early example of collective action which also suggests some advance in the strictness of segregation.[90] Examples of the separation of leprous monks from their communities begin to appear a little later. In the 1140s the abbot of Whitby sent Geoffrey Martel to the hospital at Spitalbridge when he was suspected of having contracted leprosy, to avoid the risk of infection to the brethren; the same thing happened at Taunton priory between 1174 and 1185, and at Savigny, in Normandy, before 1173.[91]

Some time between 1146 and 1169 Arnulf of Markene, lord of Ardres near Calais, founded a leper house at Lostebarne, and his neighbour Arnulf of Guines (d. 1169), touched by his example and by 'pity for the poor of Christ, deprived of the use of their limbs and tainted by leprosy', founded another nearby, at Spelleke. The latter was given a chapel and surrounded by a wall in the time of its founder's son, Baldwin (d. 1205), and between 1194 and 1203 it was decided that 'throughout the lands of Guines women tainted by leprosy would be taken to Lostebarne, where they would be fed for the remainder of their lives, and men to Spelleke, where calling daily on death in their hoarse voices they would eat their bread in wretchedness until their final breath'.[92] It does not seem unduly fanciful to see over the half-century or so in which those events transpired a transition from a relatively compassionate to a relatively stern attitude to the lepers and a greater degree of coercion in their confinement. If so it is consistent with such indications as are evident from elsewhere in north-western Europe, though it must be emphasized that these are far too fragmentary for such a conclusion to be anything but tentative and provisional.

The Living Dead

The reinforcement of the law of segregation which was provided by Lateran III was most cruelly expressed in the ritual of separation

[90] Bienvenu, 73 (1967), pp. 202–3.
[91] Kealey, *Medieval Medicus*, p. 93; Clay, *Mediaeval Hospitals*, p. 52; *Vita B. Hamonis*, p. 33.
[92] Bourgeois, *Pas-de-Calais*, pp. 89, 189–90.

from the community, modelled on the rite for the dead, which it ordained, and of which it provided a number of models. At Amiens and elsewhere, the leper was required to stand in an open grave while the ritual was read by the priest; in other places it sufficed to throw a few spadefuls of earth over his head by way of conclusion. Then the priest would transfer to the vernacular to spell out in circumstantial detail the implication of what had occurred:

> I forbid you ever to enter the church or monastery, fair, mill, marketplace or company of persons . . . ever to leave your house without your leper's costume . . . to wash your hands or anything about you in the stream or fountain. I forbid you to enter a tavern . . . I forbid you, if you go on the road and you meet some person who speaks to you, to fail to put yourself downwind before you answer . . . I forbid you to go in a narrow lane so that if you should meet anyone he might catch the affliction from you . . . I forbid you ever to touch children or give them anything. I forbid you to eat or drink from any dishes but your own. I forbid you to eat or drink in company, unless with lepers.[93]

During the thirteenth century these injunctions were translated into a variety of local and municipal regulations for the control and isolation of lepers, such as those which forbade them to walk the streets of London in 1200, Paris and Sens in 1202, Exeter in 1244, whose ruthless though spasmodic enforcement is regularly attested by tales of the expulsion of lepers from towns and cities, individually and *en masse*, which occur regularly in the following centuries. They were paralleled by detailed regulations for the conduct of the privileged among them, the inhabitants of leper houses, which separated the sexes, laid down minute instructions for their daily behaviour, forbade them the amusements of drink, gambling, chess and so forth.[94]

The most fearful dimension of the leper's death to the world, however, was the loss which it carried of worldly protection and property. There was a good deal of variation in its extent.[95] In

[93] Brody, *Disease of the Soul*, pp. 66–7.
[94] Ibid., p. 78.
[95] Ibid., pp. 81–3. Lepers at St. Omer were allowed to leave their possessions to other inmates, but this looks no more than a custom of the house: Bourgeois, *Pas-de-Calais*, p. 166.

Normandy, the leper was allowed to keep the income from his lands, and in Hainault could even dispose of them by will – and therefore retain some hold if not on the affections at least on the assistance of those who might hope to inherit. In England, leprosy had been deemed a bar to inheritance since Norman times, and the right was denied absolutely, together with that of making a will and pleading in court, by the Council of Westminster in 1200. As Bracton put it, 'a leprous person who is placed out of the communion of mankind cannot give and he cannot ask . . . if the claimant be a leper and so deformed that the sight of him is insupportable and such that he has been separated . . . he cannot plead or claim an inheritance'. By the early years of the fourteenth century the inquisitors of Philip V (1316–22) were torturing lepers to obtain confessions that they had hatched a conspiracy to poison wells all over France. The results provided Philip with his justification for burning hundreds of them, and appropriating the revenue of the lazar houses for his ever-hungry treasury. There is little to suggest that the event aroused even as much horror as the similar though larger operation which his predecessor Philip the Fair had carried out against the Templars a few years earlier.

Leprosy was now in retreat. In 1342 the property of the leper house at Ripon was assigned to the poor after a royal inquisition ascertained that there were no longer lepers to use it. All over Europe a similar process, culminating in the sixteenth and early seventeenth centuries, reversed the tide of donation which we have traced in the twelfth and thirteenth.[96] But the image of the leper as the most repellent, the most dangerous and most desolate of creatures, representing the last degree of human degradation, which though certainly not devised in those centuries was then given precise social and legal form, remained so firmly established that the terror of being found to suffer from the disease has remained one of the most powerful obstacles to its control and treatment up to the present day.

---

[96] Knowles and Hadcock, *Medieval Religious Houses*, p. 302; Foucault, *Madness and Civilization*, pp. 3–7. In view of the extent to which the remainder of my argument is indebted to approaches pioneered by Foucault it is ironic that these pages betray no suspicion that the exclusion of the leper from medieval society was anything more than a general response to an objective medical threat.

THE COMMON ENEMY

For Christians the living death of leprosy was an object of admiration and even envy, as well as terror. The leper had been granted the special grace of entering upon payment for his sins in this life, and could therefore look forward to earlier redemption in the next. Orderic Vitalis tells of a monk who was so overcome by the extent of his sins that he prayed, successfully, to be afflicted by leprosy, and the biographer of Yvette of Huy says that she yearned for the disease. Conversely, the ninth-century rule of St Grimlaicus laid down that when a hermit was immured in his cell, never to leave it again, the office for the dead was to be read over him, as Lateran III would prescribe for the leper.[97] Like hermits and monks lepers were often called *pauperes Christi*, and the strict rules governing the conduct of leper houses were in part a reflection of the idea that lepers constituted a quasi-religious order. It was this ambivalance about their condition, as well as its physically revolting character, that lent extra merit to the practice of washing the sores and kissing the lesions of lepers which during this period became a general, almost a fashionable, religious exercise. One of its early enthusiasts was Henry I's wife Matilda, whose devotion on one occasion prompted a courtier to ask what the king's feelings would be if he knew where last her lips had been.[98]

The idea of leprosy as a punishment for sin is by no means exclusively Christian. Among Hindus in the Himalaya region today it is held to be the result of offences in a past incarnation so vile that punishment for them will be visited not only on the leper but on any who approach him, and the Zande of the Upper Nile regard leprosy as the consequence of incest. Some in the medieval Islamic world believed that leprosy was God's punishment for immorality, and that the leper should be shunned accordingly, though Islamic society

[97] Orderic, bk iii, ed. Chibnall, ii, 29, 79; Mesmin, 'The Leper Hospital of St. Gilles', p. 29; Leyser, *Hermits*, p. 14. Bossy, 'The Mass as a Social Institution', pp. 45–6, sees the celebration of such rites over the living as implying the hope that death itself would be hastened thereby.
[98] William of Malmesbury, ii, 494; cf. Hugh of Avalon's ecstatic account of the religious symbolism of leprous wounds, *Magna Vita of St. Hugh of Lincoln* ii, 13–15.

never segregated lepers with the ferocity of its Christian neighbour.[99] No doubt such sentiments arise from the grotesque appearance and revolting stench of putrescent wounds which afflict the sufferer, and perhaps also from the fact that horrible though it is, leprosy is in itself neither life-shortening (although it does leave its victim exposed to injuries and infections which are) nor directly painful, because of its anaesthetizing effect on the nerve-ends. However that may be, leprosy offered itself readily as a spectacle of punishment, for wrong-doing in general or for specific offences that seemed particularly heinous.

The association with sexual misconduct was especially strong. Odo of Beaumont was segregated as a leper after contracting gonor-rhea in the brothels he enjoyed, as was another Norman knight who sought the help of St Edmund at Bury.[100] During the papal revolution in the eleventh-century simoniacs, representing the great threat of lay control against which the church was struggling, were often described as lepers.

One sin above all was identified with leprosy, and had been since patristic times:

> You too are a leper, scarred by heresy, excluded from communion by the judgment of the priest, according to the law, bare-headed, with ragged clothing, your body covered by an infected and filthy garment. It befits you to shout unceasingly that you are a leper, a heretic and unclean, and must live alone outside the camp, that is outside the church.[101]

These words were addressed to the great heretical preacher, Henry of Lausanne, by a monk named William, who engaged him in debate somewhere in the Languedoc around 1130. Leprosy had long been identified with enmity to the church. A miraculous cure was one of the legendary antecedents of Constantine's conversion. The instruc-tions of Leviticus on the treatment of leprosy were held to apply to sin in general (probably a correct interpretation of that text, which

---

[99]   Dols, 'The Leper in Medieval Islamic Society', pp. 895–7, 912–16.
[100]   Sumption, *Pilgrimage*, p. 81.
[101]   Moore, *Birth of Popular Heresy*, p. 57, and for the discussion which follows Moore, 'Heresy as Disease'; *Origins of European Dissent*, pp. 246–50.

is nowadays generally thought to be concerned with religious defilement, and not with disease at all). As William said to Henry in this same debate, when Christ commanded the cured leper, 'Go shew thyself to the priest and offer for thy cleansing as Moses commanded', 'by leprosy we understand nothing other than the stain of sin'. Nor was this thought of simply in an allegorical or metaphorical sense. The treatise *On medicine* of Rhabanaus Maurus (d. 856), for example, explains that illness was caused by an imbalance of the humours which was the result of sin. Diseases could therefore be classified according to the sins of which they were the bodily manifestation: 'Leprosy is the false doctrine of heretics . . . lepers are heretics blaspheming against Jesus Christ'.

The analogy between heresy and leprosy is used with great regularity and in great detail by twelfth-century writers. Heresy spreads like leprosy, running far and wide, infecting the limbs of Christ as it goes. When the Count of Toulouse asked the pope for help against the Cathars who were establishing themselves in the city in 1177 he said that 'the putrid *tabes* of heresy' prevailed there. The *tabes* was the sore of the leper and, according to Isidore of Seville, when it became putrid death was inevitable. Heresy, like leprosy, was spread by the poisoned breath of its carrier, which infested the air and was thus enabled to attack the vitals of those who breathed it, but was also and more efficiently transmitted as a *virus* – that is, in seminal fluid. Against so insidious an infection nothing less than fire was effective; when the leper died the hut in which he had lived and all his belongings were burned. When heretics were discovered in England in 1163 they were driven from the camp – expelled from Oxford, where they were tried – and by royal command refused food and shelter so that they soon perished in the winter's cold. The hut in which they had lived was dragged outside the town and burned. William of Newburgh, whose account is suffused by a sustained use of the metaphor, says that the result of this treatment was that the disease did not appear in England again.

If leprosy and heresy were the same disease it was to be expected that their carriers should have the same characteristics. The leper's tattered and filthy clothing, staring eyes and hoarse voice are also part of the standard depiction of the wandering preacher and the wandering heretic – all, as it were, *pauperes Christi*, or claiming to be. So was lasciviousness and the means to gratify it. Leprosy was believed to be sexually transmitted and inherited, to increase the sexual appetite and to cause swelling in the genitals. Hence the separation of the sexes in the leper hospitals and the strong emphasis in thirteenth-century municipal legislation on banning lepers from brothels; and hence the horror of Isolde's fate in the versions of *Tristan* by Béroul (*c*.1160–70) and Eilhart von Oberge (*c*.1170–80), where she is punished for her adultery by being handed over to a band of lepers. 'I have here a hundred companions,' says their leader in Béroul, 'Give Isolde to us and she will be held in common. Never will a woman have worse end.'[102] The metaphor of seduction was freely used in association with heresy, and sexual libertinism ascribed as a matter of course to heretics and their followers. 'Women and young boys – for he used both sexes in his lechery – became so excited by the lasciviousness of the man that they testified publicly to his extraordinary virility', according to the Le Mans chronicler's account of how Henry of Lausanne established his sway over the people of that city.[103]

By the time those words were written the suggestion that heretics met by night for secret orgies in which they were visited by the Devil and had intercourse with him had already been revived from the writings of the fathers (where it had been particularly associated with the Manichees) to assist in denouncing the clerks of Orléans in 1022 and the followers of Clementius of Bucy, interrogated by Guibert of Nogent in 1114. This became the coven upon which the great witch craze of the later middle ages was founded. We have already seen how anti-semitism contributed to its formation in the elaboration of the idea – also pioneered by Guibert – that there was a special link between the Devil and the Jews, sexually bonded and characterized by the seduction of Christians into the Devil's service by means of Jewish wiles. Jews were also held to resemble heretics and lepers in being associated with filth, stench and putrefaction, in exceptional sexual voracity and endowment, and in the menace which they presented in consequence to the wives and children of honest Christians. A conspiracy between Jews and lepers was alleged to have poisoned the wells of France in 1321.[104] And so it might go on, well beyond nausea and towards infinity. The

---

[102] Brody, *Disease of the Soul*, p. 180.
[103] Moore, *Birth of Popular Heresy*, p. 34.
[104] Trachtenberg, *The Devil and the Jews*, pp. 100–8, and on the identification of Jews with heretics and sorcerers, ibid., pp. 207–16.

images and nightmares are not always consistent, but they always feed the same fear. For all imaginative purposes heretics, Jews and lepers were interchangeable. They had the same qualities, from the same source, and they presented the same threat: through them the Devil was at work to subvert the Christian order and bring the world to chaos.

CHAPTER 2

CLASSIFICATION

Coincidence and Continuity

The parallels in the development of the persecution of heretics, Jews and lepers are very striking. There were differences, but in each case although persecution was rigorous in theory it did not occur in practice until the beginning of the eleventh century and remained intermittent until its end; in each, rising hostility became sharply apparent in the middle decades of the twelfth; and in each a comprehensive apparatus of persecution was worked out towards the end of the twelfth century, codified by the Fourth Lateran Council of 1215 (for lepers the Third of 1179), and perfected by the middle of the thirteenth century or soon after. The forms of persecution were equally similar. If it was not necessary in the case of Jews, as it was for heretics and lepers, to devise any elaborate means of hunting them down and identifying them, they too were required to advertise in their dress the segregation from society at large which was institutionalized by imprisoning heretics and confining lepers to lazar houses or villages and Jews to their increasingly strictly defined residential quarters in the cities. In all three cases exclusion from the community extended to civil rights, denying access to public courts and office, security of property during life and disposal of it after death. Finally, these parallels in treatment were clearly reflected in the language that was used and the fears that were expressed about the three groups, making them in all essentials identical and interchangeable.

This requires us to reconsider the accepted, if not always very closely examined, explanations of the growth of persecution, and in particular to consider whether it can be right to attempt to account for the persecution of each set of victims independently of the others. The explanations most commonly advanced are derived from the assumption that the presence of each group became more evident during the twelfth century, thus making the threat which it is supposed to have presented more ominous. Lepers, like heretics, it is widely assumed, became very much more numerous at this time, and Jews very much more important, because of the special role which they played as money-lenders and bankers in the spectacular growth of commerce and urban communities in this period. The parallels not only in the chronological evolution of persecution but between the forms which it took and the beliefs which engendered it must undermine that approach. The coincidence is too great to be credible. That three entirely distinct groups of people, characterized respectively by religious conviction, physical condition, and race and culture, should all have begun at the same time and by the same stages to pose the same threats, which must be dealt with in the same ways, is a proposition too absurd to be taken seriously. The alternative must be that the explanation lies not with the victims but with the persecutors. What heretics, lepers and Jews had in common is that they were all victims of a zeal for persecution which seized European society at this time. This suspicion is strengthened by the further question which it raises, namely whether the groups from which the persecuted came were in fact as large and as distinctive as they were believed to be – by considering, in other words, the possibilities that heresy, leprosy and Jewishness lay with beauty in the eyes of the beholders, and that their distinctiveness was not the cause but the result of persecution.

These two questions in turn involve a third, which cannot be clearly distinguished from them: that of the continuity both of the existence of those who were persecuted, and of the attitudes of society towards them. Behind the supposition that the growth of persecution represented a response to real change, whether in the numbers or the importance of the persecuted, lies another that – to put it very crudely – if heretics were not persecuted between the seventh and tenth centuries it was because there were none, and that if we do not hear of the enforcement of the canonical prohibitions against Jews and the segregation of lepers it is because the scattered and fragmentary sources for those centuries happen to find no place for what was so commonplace as to be taken entirely for granted. On that view the emergence of persecution, which we have traced so

painstakingly through the eleventh and twelfth centuries, reflects in
the main a change in the record rather than in reality, a gradual
lifting of the curtain of darkness which the decline of the ancient
world laid across our knowledge of European society and its doings.
By its nature a stance taken upon the impossibility of adequate
knowledge is difficult to rebut, and knowledge is indeed less attainable of these centuries, and of these subjects, than most. Nevertheless, we must make what shift we can to marshal a balance of
probabilities, however tentatively.

Heresy: The Problem of Recognition

The proposition that heresy would have been persecuted before the
eleventh century if there had been any is meaningless. A heretic, by
canonical definition, was one whose views were 'chosen by human
perception, contrary to holy scripture, publicly avowed and obsti-
nately defended'.[1] That meant in practice that a person became a
heretic only by refusing to accept a bishop's pronouncement that his
expressed views were heretical, and by refusing to undertake not to
preach without the bishop's permission – and of these, the latter
became far more important during the twelfth century. From the
point of view of the faithful, therefore, the heretic is self-defined, and
indeed self-proclaimed, as the person who by his own deliberate
choice denies the authority of the Church. But by the same token to
put it in that way is to be reminded that heresy exists only in so far
as authority chooses to declare its existence. Heretics are those who
refuse to subscribe to the doctrines and acknowledge the disciplines
which the Church requires: no requirement, no heresy. Heresy (unlike
Judaism or leprosy) can arise only in the context of the assertion of
authority, which the heretic resists, and is therefore by definition a
political matter. Heterodox belief, however, is not. Variety of religious opinion exists at many times and places, and becomes heresy
when authority declares it intolerable. In the early middle ages this
seldom happened. Once Arianism had faded away there is no evidence of the preaching to the laity of doctrines which the Church
found it necessary to prohibit. Certainly nobody now believes, as
some twelfth-century writers did, that the teachings of ancient heretics like Mani and Arius had remained dormant among the peasantry

---

[1] Gratian, *Decretum* II Cxxiv Qiii cc. 27–31, ed. Friedberg, I, 997–8.

to break out again with renewed vigour in the age of the crusades. We are more inclined to agree with Adelman of Liège, writing in 1051, that 'even their memory had rotted away'.[2] Among churchmen themselves, especially during the 'renaissance' of the ninth century, there were disagreements over questions of liturgy and occasionally theology which sometimes spilled over into accusations of heresy. But these remained individual conflicts which did not reverbate beyond the arguments that gave rise to them or stimulate the creation of any mechanisms to deal with them, just as the similar disputes among the intelligentsia of the later period, such as the charges of heresy against Abelard or Gilbert de la Porée, did not impinge upon the growth and development of the persecution of popular heresy which was described in the last chapter.

The structure of the Western Church itself in the early middle ages was one which permitted, and was bound to permit, a much greater variety than would later be thought consistent with the maintenance of Catholic unity. It had not yet developed the means, or, some would say, the inclination, to demand uniformity of worship and practice throughout Western Christendom. Each bishop ruled his diocese as the heir and successor of the patron saint who was usually said to be its founder. Rome enjoyed a general though far from unchallenged pre-eminence, but no universally acknowledged authority to intervene in diocesan or provincial affairs. Its precepts were by no means generally supposed to enjoy greater standing or authority than was accorded by custom. Indeed the papal reform of the eleventh century was precisely, in one of its most central aspects, a struggle to impose Roman authority over local tradition. The most familiar but not untypical example is that of Milan, whose clergy claimed the traditional authority of St Ambrose for their 'customs' of paying for their benefices, marrying, and maintaining a distinctive liturgy – customs which the impassioned reformers denounced as the vilest of heresies.[3]

[2] *Epistola ad Berengariam*, ed. R. B. C. Huygens, 'Textes latins du xiè au xiiiè siècle', *Studi Medievali*, 3rd ser. 8 (1967), quoted by Stock, *Implications of Literacy*, p. 285.
[3] This aspect of the reform is well illustrated, for example, by Cowdrey, 'Archbishop Aribert of Milan', 'The Papacy, the Patarenes and the Church of Milan', and Robinson, 'The Friendship Network of Gregory VII'. For the view of the relationship between heresy and reform which follows see Moore, *Origins of European Dissent*, especially pp. 38–136, 261–83.

These circumstances did not make it impossible that 'heresy' might have been identified and pursued, as indeed it began to be before the papal reform was under way. Churchmen did not forget the threat which had been posed by the great heresies of antiquity, and continued to agree on the necessity of denouncing them and guarding against their revival. It would be carrying scepticism too far to imagine that a substantial movement among the eighth-century laity in opposition, let us say, to baptism or the unity of the trinity would have passed unnoticed or unrebuked. Nevertheless, any comparison of the prevalence of heresy in the high middle ages with the lack of it in the earlier period must make a substantial allowance for the greater sensitivity of the more centralized structure to the manifestation of dissent.

It is unnecessary to dwell at length on the part which the Church itself played in turning dissent into heresy. Three aspects of it, however, need to be noted as diminishing the extent to which the ecclesiastical perception of heresy as a monster ravaging outside the gate can be taken at face value.

In the first place, the amount of latitude that would be allowed to critics or would-be reformers varied considerably with circumstance and with the attitudes of different holders of authority. We have already noticed how thin was the line which separated a Robert of Arbrissel from a Henry of Lausanne. They preached the same message, that the church must be stripped of corruption, to the same people, the poor and the destitute; their dress and demeanour were the same, and there is no reason to suppose that their language was very different. It is difficult, if not impossible, to know what made the difference between them when our knowledge of the one depends largely on sources designed to demonstrate his sanctity, and of the other entirely on those determined to prove his depravity. Robert was educated and in orders but Henry was, at the least, not illiterate or unversed in the Church's teaching. Henry defied secular and spiritual authority, but authority tolerated a great deal of rebuke and even attack from Robert, who was fortunate in his friends. Robert's enemies, like Henry's, accused him of sleeping with his female followers; posterity has chosen not to believe them. And so we might go on. In these two figures the worlds of heresy and reform appear to overlap beyond any discrimination which the sources can sustain at all objectively. A couple of generations later the Waldensians were driven into heresy by an episcopal and then a papal demand for obedience, and the Humiliati rescued from it by the wisdom of a more flexible pope. Obedience was always the test, but it was not always demanded with equal firmness or measured with equal nicety.

Secondly, while the heretic was always accused of innovation, the greatest source of religious novelty in this period was the Church itself, or to be precise the reforming Church. Those who denied the necessity of infant baptism, of the sanctification of matrimony, or intercession for souls in purgatory, of regular attendance at mass and confession to priests, were not rebelling against ancestral patterns of faith and practice. Whatever the theology of the matter, these were innovations in the daily life of the faithful that throughout the period under discussion and beyond were gradually being pressed upon the priesthood and its flocks by the episcopate, which was itself dragged slowly and painfully into line by a papacy captured for reform in the revolution of the eleventh century. Some of these innovations indeed responded to popular demand,[4] but innovations they remained. To a considerable extent, therefore, charges of heresy in the twelfth century must be seen as serving to reflect back upon the recalcitrant the accusations of novelty which they had levelled at their accusers.

Finally, the very process of identifying and rebutting heresy gave it a greater coherence, and therefore a more menacing aspect, than it actually possessed. Those who defied the Church were extremely diverse in their backgrounds, their motives and their convictions. If their teachings resembled each other it was because they rebelled against the same things – at first against the corruption of the priesthood and its entanglement in the structures of secular power and later also against the Church's expanding claims over their lives and purses. Not until the 1140s, when the first missionaries or refugees from the Bogomil church in the Balkans appeared in the Rhineland, was the Western church confronted by any authentic representative of a potentially universal rival, and only over the next thirty years did the Cathars slowly establish an alternative church with its own priesthood, its own bishops and ecclesiastical organization. But from the very beginning, from the arraignment of the men of Arras before Gerard of Cambrai in 1025, those accused of heresy were regarded

---

[4] For example, the demand for a professional priesthood: Moore, 'Family, Community and Cult on the Eve of the Gregorian Reform'.

as emissaries of a greater enemy than themselves, as the heretics whom Paul foretold for the last days 'forbidding to marry and eating of meat', or as the disciples of Arius or Mani. The questions put to them were designed to confirm these expectations. Answers which failed to do so were often disbelieved in favour of the more trust-worthy and authoritative assertions of the fathers of the Church. By this means the disparate, fragmented, inarticulate heresies of the eleventh and early twelfth centuries were converted from their untidy, and generally rather insignificant selves into fragments of a larger picture – the picture of the monster by which their adversaries believed themselves to be threatened. And it was very largely the many-headedness of that monster, the expectation that if a head were lopped off in one diocese new ones would appear in its stead in several others, which lay behind the elaboration of the general appa-ratus of legislation and inquisition. The movement towards the per-secution of heresy, therefore, was very far from being a simple response to the appearance, or even the multiplication, of the heretics themselves. On the contrary, though the heretics were real enough, and increasing in number as the twelfth century wore on, the signifi-cance which they assumed in the life and concerns of the Church was very largely a function of its own development.

Leprosy: The Problem of Diagnosis

The present state of knowledge is quite inadequate to form a serious estimate of how far the growing fear of leprosy in the twelfth century was a response to a true increase in the incidence and virulence of Hansen's disease. In the first place, the length of time which the disease takes to develop – between two and seven years from first infection to the appearance of clinical symptoms is normal – makes the mechanism of its transmission still extremely obscure. In the second, while it is clear that individuals vary greatly in their suscep-tibility to infection it is not at all clear why. Hence, while we have categorical archaeological evidence that lepromatous leprosy was present in early medieval Europe we have no certain basis for assess-ing how contagious it was. Current opinion is that the degree to which individuals resist Hansen's disease depends upon previous exposure to it or to related tuberculosis bacteria which seem to confer immunity to leprosy. It also appears that the less virulent forms of leprosy arise not from changes in the bacterium but from variations in the degree of the patient's susceptibility. So it would follow that a population in which leprosy has been present for some time, and in which tubercular infections are common, is probably less vulnerable to leprosy and when infected more likely to succumb to the less virulent forms of the disease (which leave no archaeological trace) than to lepromatous leprosy. As to the means of transmission, it is thought that the infection may arise either from bacilli concentrated in the skin lesions themselves or in the exhaled breath, but that the degree of infectiousness is low, so that prolonged physical contact is usually necessary for infection to take place.

If these hypotheses are correct it is possible to construct an epidemiology of leprosy in medieval Europe which is consistent with them. It would run something like this. *Microbacterium leprae* reached some parts of the Roman world, including Egypt, France and England, towards the end of antiquity but did not become widespread, presumably because the concentration and movement of population were insufficient to encourage its diffusion. Leprosy can remain endemic in isolated communities for long periods, as it did in parts of Scandinavia between the seventeenth and nineteenth centuries.[5] The rapidly growing and urbanizing population of the high middle ages therefore had a low degree of resistance and was vulnerable to a great epidemic which seized Europe in the twelfth and thirteenth centuries. An example of the vulnerability of a newly exposed population may be provided by Hawaii, where leprosy was first recognized in 1835, 686 cases were diagnosed in the next thirty years, 3119 between 1866 and 1886, and 7217 from 1886 to 1915.[6] In Europe, the disease reached its peak around the middle of the thirteenth century, and developing resistance was greatly enhanced by the increased frequency of tubercular infections which seems to have marked the period after the Black Death.[7] Hence lepromatous leprosy had become a rarity in most regions by the fifteenth century and was virtually extinct by the seventeenth.

This account has the great attraction of consistency with the literary sources, upon which the previous chapter's discussion of leprosy in the high middle ages was very largely based. However, apart from the speculative character of its medical premises, it leaves some

[5]   Richards, *The Medieval Leper*, pp. 84–97.
[6]   Cochrane and Davey, *Leprosy*, p. 75.
[7]   W. H. McNeill, *Plagues and Peoples*, pp. 164–6.

awkward historical questions unanswered. The most fundamental is the almost complete lack of archaeological confirmation. The most striking feature of the archaeological record is that after the seventh century there is silence for several hundred years, and that the number of leprous skeletons identified from the very period when we postulate the height of the epidemic is tiny – from the British Isles, for example, seven.[8] Yet the Carolingian world of the ninth century, when the river valleys of northern Europe were extremely densely populated and there was a good deal of regular military and commercial contact between them, should have been very vulnerable if our hypothesis is correct. So, for the same reasons, should Wessex at the end of the ninth century and the beginning of the tenth, when the kingdom was expanding into the south-west where earlier traces of leprosy have been found. Both of these regions have been relatively extensively excavated. More broadly, the place of Italy in this scheme of things raises obvious questions. If rapid population growth, overcrowded conditions and a great deal of travel stimulated an epidemic in the twelfth century that is where it should have shown most dramatically. On the other hand, to argue that Italy might have built up resistance earlier than northern Europe through its closer and more continuous contacts with infected regions of Egypt and the Middle East would lead us to expect archaeological evidence of widespread infection in the earlier middle ages, which is lacking.

It may be that these gaps in the evidence are there simply because no one has yet sought to fill them. Very few cemeteries datable between the ninth and thirteenth centuries have been excavated and far fewer skeletons from that period examined than would be necessary to legitimate an argument from silence. But the fact remains that the only archaeological evidence – impressive though it is in itself – which testifies to the existence of lepromatous leprosy on a substantial scale in Europe in the high middle ages comes from the cemetery of one leper hospital in a rather peripheral region, St Jørgens at Naestved in Denmark.[9] Similar sites have not been excavated elsewhere, and effective segregation would be one possible explanation of the absence of leprous skeletons from other burial

[8]   Manchester, "A Leprous Skeleton of the Seventh Century', p. 209.
[9]   Møller-Christiansen, *Bone Changes in Leprosy; Leprosy Changes of the Skull*; for a general account of Møller-Christiansen's work, Richards, *The Medieval Leper*, pp. 112–20.

places.[10] Nevertheless, so long as that remains the case the assertions of the literary evidence will have to be taken with a very generous helping of salt.

Isidore of Seville, whose *Etymologiae* served as a general compendium of information and advice, lists *lepra* as one of the 'diseases which are seen on the outside (*superficie*) of the skin', along with erysipelas, scabies, elephantiasis (the most specific classical term for leprosy), cancer and a variety of venereal diseases, boils, goitres and so on. This, and the seeming interchangeability of many of these terms in common use, has tended to foster the impression that he and his successors did not distinguish at all clearly between them. Further reflection makes this rather patronizing assumption seem less clear than once it did. By far the greatest proportion of the occurrences of these terms do not appear in clinical or social contexts, where specific ailments of specific individuals are in question, but in expository, allegorical or moral ones – in biblical exegesis or sermons for example – where literary variation would take priority over diagnostic consistency. That in the course of a few lines Eckbert of Schönau (writing *c*.1163) calls heresy a poison, leprosy and a cancer does not necessarily mean that the infirmarian of his abbey would have failed to distinguish between patients suffering from those three conditions.[11] Conversely, the very fact that painful and hideous disfigurements were the constant afflictions of those who lived in these centuries makes it the more probable that careful and minute distinctions were made between them (though doubtless not in what we would consider a scientific way), and less probable that panic or revulsion would arise simply from a particularly horrible appearance or smell. After all, upon what subject do most of us lavish more minute attention, more exhaustive and regular comparison and consideration, than our own bodily distresses and ailments?

These rather abstract considerations may encourage us to give some weight to the impression conveyed by several eleventh-century

[10]   Richards, ibid., pp. 118–19, discusses a rare exception, a female skeleton which, alone among the 633 at Øm monastery, also in Denmark, shows the bone changes typical of lepromatous leprosy; his suggestion that it may have been buried before the decree of 1179 (or, strictly, its implementation) is a reasonable one.
[11]   Eckbert of Schönau, *Sermones XIII contra Catharos*, I, *PL* 195, col. 13.

writers – Eadmer's description of the noble 'deserted even by his own men despite the dignity of his birth, on account of the foulness of so great an affliction', is a good example[12] – that the leprosy which they described was something new and shocking, and not just a particularly unpleasant case of scrofula or ulcers. Plainer indications of precision in diagnosis are harder to come by, but not wholly lacking. William of Tyre recognized the onset of the disease in his 9-year-old pupil, the future Baldwin IV of Jerusalem (1161–85), when he saw that a game involving pressing their nails into each others' arms made all the boys cry, except Baldwin.[13] It is a famous example of what seems to have been a widespread understanding of the loss of sensation at the nerve ends, which is one of the early and reliable symptoms of Hansen's disease, and could be tested in various ways. That 69.5 per cent of the skeletons excavated at the Naestved leper cemetery, and all nine of those sufficiently well preserved for diagnosis at the smaller cemetery of St George's leper hospital in Stendborg, show the bone erosion characteristic of lepromatous leprosy (but not necessarily to be found in the skeletons of all its victims, since many would die of other causes before the disease was so far advanced) suggests that there at least the diagnosis was not entirely haphazard.[14]

These remarks should evoke caution, not the suspension of criticism. One question which they bring sharply to mind is that of the relation between practice in the diagnosis and treatment of leprosy and the theory expounded in medical textbooks. Theodoric of Cervia (1205–98), for instance, noticed correctly that in what is now recognized as an early stage of infection (indeterminate leprosy) lesions often appear and then quickly heal again; but his belief that the ability of the patient's blood to dissolve salt rapidly was another early symptom is as baseless as some of his contemporaries said it was. More generally the tendency of Theodoric and other medical writers to list possible symptoms of leprosy at great length – spots and wounds of various colours and sizes, damage to eyes, nose and voice,

---

[12]   Above, p. 50, n. 77.
[13]   Shahar, 'Des lépreux pas comme les autres: L'ordre de Saint-Lazare dans le royaume latin de Jérusalem', 37.
[14]   Møller-Christiansen, *Leprosy Changes of the Skull*, p. 42; Andersen, *Medieval Diagnosis of Leprosy*, pp. 82–5; Richards, *The Medieval Leper*, p. 120.

depilation, shiny skin, swellings, lesions and so forth – would certainly, if followed slavishly, have led to the diagnosis as lepers of many who suffered from other conditions than Hansen's disease.[15] However, these treatises are no sound guide to practice. The academic medicine of the high and later middle ages, after all, is commonly scouted for its remoteness from actual patients. It was booklearning and little else. Two of the witnesses to a donation to a leper hospital at Troyes in 1151 are described as *medicus*, and one of them was a master,[16] but they are unlikely to signal any direct liaison between the hospitals and the schools. The diagnosis of lepers for the purpose of confinement was commonly carried out by ecclesiastical or secular officials – the magistrates of Amiens, the bailiffs at Picquigny, the abbot at St Quentin – or by a jury of laymen among whom would be a number of lepers.[17] These juries did not begin to be displaced by doctors until the fifteenth century, and by that time the epidemic, if that is what it was, was nearly over. The whole question of how lepers were identified and their diagnosis confirmed is of central importance, and our ignorance of it is still almost total. It will be answered not from the treatises of academic doctors, but from the patient and piecemeal collection and careful assessment of anecdotal evidence from chronicles, miracle collections and court rolls.

Before leaving the textbooks we must notice another tendency which they show strongly, and apparently more so with the passage of time. Most of the clinical symptoms which they describe would permit, or require, a high degree of subjectivity in diagnosis, and might have a marked social content. Thus Guy de Chauliac (1363) lists among the certain symptoms of leprosy in addition to loss of hair and swelling of the lips, 'stinking breath, raucous voice and a fixed and horrible stare', which are indeed probable consequences of Hansen's disease but must also depend a good deal for their identification on the perceptions and even the preconceptions of the observer. Guy goes on to name among sixteen 'equivocal symptoms', along with wasting of muscles and skin, insensibility at the extremities, an oily appearance when water is dropped on the skin, bad dreams, a short temper and a tendency to impose oneself on the

[15] Brody, *Disease of the Soul*, pp. 34–40.
[16] Mesmin, 'The Leper Hospital of St. Gilles', p. 35.
[17] Brody, *Disease of the Soul*, pp. 63–4.

company of others.[18] Leprosy is still considered a disease which it is easy to diagnose mistakenly. Guy de Chauliac's list, which could readily be duplicated, shows how easily difficult or anti-social traits might be represented as resulting from it.

It is an acceptable working hypothesis that the explosion of anxiety in the twelfth century had its basis in a real epidemic of lepromatous leprosy, to which the population of north-western Europe was at first highly vulnerable. We are greatly in need, however, of archaeological information, to establish how extensive the epidemic was and to help to assess the effectiveness of segregation.

It is also important to collect and examine systematically material relating to the diagnosis of leprosy and the segregation of lepers, to assist a better estimate of the likelihood of Hansen's disease having been confused clinically with other conditions, and to explore the social dimensions of these procedures. There are some indications that it was at least possible to distinguish Hansen's disease with a fair degree of consistency from other disabling and disfiguring conditions, including venereal ones. But it is also easy to see how the suspicion of leprosy might fall on those who incurred the disapproval or displeasure of their neighbours, or became a burden to them. Every account of the leper makes him a repository of fear and suspicion. 'Evil, crafty habits appear, patients suspect everyone of wanting to hurt them'; 'they have bad habits of life . . . many of them burn with desire for coitus [in fact this is the opposite of the truth] . . . they gladly have intercourse with the healthy, but if a healthy person who is also unacquainted with their ailment such as a child looks them in the face their faces are troubled, and they despair'[19] – understandably enough, we might think. It is not far-fetched to observe that the diagnosis of leprosy was capable of providing a far-reaching and flexible principle upon which almost anybody might be excluded from the community on the basis of a minimal consensus that they ought to be, as accusations of witchcraft did in seventeenth-century Europe or, some argue, certification of insanity may do in the United States today. Equally, the regime revealed by the statutes of leper houses, in which men and women were separated, fornication, drinking, gambling and chess prohibited, attendance at mass, food, clothing, and movement inside as well as outside the house

18 Bourgeois, *Pas-de-Calais*, p. 18.
19 Brody, *Disease of the Soul*, p. 51.

minutely regulated, and the whole enforced by a stern code of punishment, points beyond concern with the disease itself to wider social
anxieties – however rationalized by analogies between the leper and
the enclosed religious.[20]

The barrage of legislation against lepers in the late twelfth and
early thirteenth centuries and the substantial investment in institutions for segregating them need to be considered as social, and not
merely as medical or even charitable measures. In this light, modern
medical knowledge of the disease, still so very far from complete, is
perhaps less helpful than Susan Sontag's observation, arising from
her brilliant discussion of attitudes to tuberculosis in the last century
and cancer in this one, that diseases which have not succumbed to
scientific understanding tend not only to generate metaphors of
general decay but to be regarded as arising from many causes – 'Lepra
cometh of dyvers causes,' as Bartholomaeus Anglicus remarked, 'for
the evil is contagious and infecteth other men' – and as being symbolic, or even punitive of viciousness or weakness on the part of their
victims.[21] The analogy with AIDS, which has become epidemic in
Britain and North America while this book has been in preparation,
is no less instructive for being so obvious. Hence, it is particularly
worth adding in our context, the victims of such diseases are especially vulnerable to identification as scapegoats.

The Jews: Assimilation and Rejection

The history of the Jews in the early middle ages is a great deal less
obscure. The great dispersal created substantial Jewish communities
in many cities of the Roman world, and not only in cities, for there
are references to Jews settled as *coloni* both in the eastern and in the
western parts of the empire.[22] The protection of the law and the
emperors did not prevent the emergence of widespread anti-semitism,

---

[20]   Ibid., p. 78. The resemblance of the regime there described to that of a
nineteenth-century workhouse is underlined by the installation of a clock
at the leper hospital at Arras in 1241 (Bourgeois, *Pas-de-Calais*, p. 95) – a
very early date for a device closely associated with the public regulation of
hours of work: cf. Landes, *Revolution in Time*, pp. 71–4.
[21]   Sontag, *Illness as Metaphor*, especially pp. 47–75; Bartholomaeus Anglicus is quoted by Brody, *Disease of the Soul*, p. 55.
[22]   Jones, *Later Roman Empire*, p. 944.

and there were forced conversions in the fifth and sixth centuries. There is no reason to think that the decline of the western empire led to a deterioration in the position of the Jews. Anxious to be Roman in all things, Theodoric the Ostrogoth maintained their privileges in Italy, and visited severe punishment on the culprits when synagogues were burned in Rome and Ravenna. On the other hand, he seems not to have enforced the prohibitions, including those on bearing arms and holding high office.[23] Without entering in detail what has been a vigorously debated question we may say that much the same seems to have been true in the Visigothic and Merovingian kingdoms. While hostility towards Jews was sometimes practised by the populace, and extortion by the kings when they were strong enough, the Jewish communities were by and large too well established and too well protected to be profitably attacked, even if there were any real reason for assuming a widespread or consistent desire to attack them.

When Pepin III conquered the Narbonnais (768) he confirmed both the alodial rights of Jewish landholders and the authority which they were entitled to exercise over Christians in consequence.[24] His successors followed his example. Charlemagne relaxed limitations on the rights of Jews to give evidence in court; Louis the Pious not only refused to enforce the prohibitions on the exercise of civil and domestic power over Christians by Jews and permitted his Jewish subjects to convert, and circumcise, their servants, but forbade the baptism of slaves owned by Jews without the consent of their masters.[25]

We have already seen how Louis' protection of Jews against all justice but his own had disastrous consequences for them in the long run, and it is equally probable that his brusque dismissal of complaints on these and similar matters fuelled the growth of anti-semitic sentiment. Several Jews held influential positions at court during his reign, and there was a substantial Jewish community at his capital at Aachen. Jews played a valuable role both in the defence of the Empire in frontier areas where they were settled, such as that around Barcelona, and financially and commercially.[26] Jewish mer-

---

[23]   Bachrach, *Early Medieval Jewish Policy*, pp. 29–30.
[24]   Ibid.; pp. 66–7.
[25]   Ibid., pp. 84–107.
[26]   Ibid., pp. 70–1, and, with qualifications, Wallace-Hadrill, *The Frankish Church*, pp. 397–8.

chants were granted widespread exemptions from tolls and other inhibitions on their trade – including the trade in Christian slaves. This was one of the prohibitions which Bishop Agobard of Lyons sought in vain to have enforced by the emperor. He also complained that Jews were permitted to employ Christian labour, with the result that their employees worked on Sunday after resting on Saturday, ate meat and wine produced by Jews and feasted with their Jewish households during Lent. On the other hand, the emperor had forbidden the market at Lyons to be held on Saturday, to protect the interests of Jewish traders.

It does not seem that Agobard's campaign, which he sustained for several years in the face of imperial displeasure, was moved by personal hostility to Jews, of whom he remarked that 'since they live among us we should not be hostile to them, or injure their life, health or wealth'.[27] His demand for the canons to be upheld was taken up by the west Frankish bishops, led by Hincmar of Reims, in a series of councils between 843 and 846, which restated the ban on the building of new synagogues, the holding of civil offices and dignities by Jews, marriage between Jews and Christians and so on, as well as advocating the removal of Jewish children from their parents in order that they could be baptized. That the emperor took no notice may in the long run have been less important than the reinvigoration of the ancient disabilities which was provided by this series of what would later be taken as authoritative statements, and particularly by the firm identification which it made for the future between enforcement of the prohibitions against the Jews and the cause of church reform. It is, for example, very much in the tradition of these councils that we find Bishop Ratherius of Verona complaining in 965 that his clergy and people did not treat Jews with appropriate hostility.[28]

The worries of Agobard and Ratherius also confirm, however, that by their time Jews were very fully integrated in the community. It may, indeed, be mistaken to assume that it had once been otherwise, for the probability is that the great majority of Jews in Frankish Gaul were descended from converts rather than migrants of the diaspora;[29] that is also probably true of western Europe in general. Jewish landholders and agricultural workers were not uncommon around 1000;

[27]   Bachrach, *Early Medieval Jewish Policy*, p. 98.
[28]   *PL* 136, col. 536.
[29]   James, *Origins of France*, p. 101.

they have been identified among the tenants of Tegernsee in Bavaria, held alodial lands in the villages of the Maconnais and were quite numerous in the Languedoc, Catalonia, Provence and southern Italy.[30] In the towns Jewish artisans were found in all trades, if especially in those like dyeing and weaving which had links with international exchange: at Macon this was reflected in the 'custom' levied on them in 1051 of exacting payment of pepper and imported textiles. At least in the Mediterranean regions Jews sometimes played a part in public life, joining in the ceremonial welcome provided for Otto III by the city of Rome in 996, participating in the government of Capua and Benevento, and fighting alongside Alphonso VI at the capture of Toledo in 1085.[31] Jewish doctors were much in demand by the great, and Jews were prominent at the courts of Christian Spain and in the Languedoc. They were assumed, according to Abelard's *Dialogue*, to observe the dietary prohibitions of their religion,[32] but it seems plain that that did not prevent them from living among Christians in town and country, speaking the same language – for Yiddish and other Jewish vernaculars did not begin to develop until the thirteenth century and beyond[33] – and giving their children Latin forenames as well as Latinized versions of Jewish ones. In the Rhineland Jewish children learned Hebrew in the synagogue, for religious purposes, while in Spain it seems that teaching was conducted both in Hebrew and in the vernacular.[34] During the twelfth century anxiety to preserve the integrity of Judaism and its law led to the establishment at Vienne of a group called the Marufia, charged with maintaining orthodoxy by expelling those who infringed the

[30] Fossier, *L'enfance de l'Europe*, p. 501; Duby, *La société maconnaise*, pp. 119–21; Baer, *Jews in Christian Spain*, p. 40; J. P. Poly, *La Provence et la société féodale*, p. 230; Mundy, *High Middle Ages*, pp. 94–5.
[31] Roth, *Jews of Italy*, p. 69; Wickham, *Early Medieval Italy*, p. 150; Fossier, *L'Enfance de l'Europe*, p. 590.
[32] Abelard, *Collations*, ed. Marenbon and Orlandi, pp. 20–3, 66–9. Poliakov, *History of Anti-Semitism*, vol. I, pp. 13–15, points out that the maintenance of dietary prohibitions and other forms of religious separation did not prevent Indian Jews from becoming ethnically indistinguishable. But it would be difficult, if fascinating, to compare the influence of the caste system with that of Western social structures in this respect.
[33] Poliakov, *History of Anti-Semitism*, p. 164n.
[34] Grabois, 'Ecoles et structures sociales', pp. 939–40.

law from the Jewish community.[35] The followers of Rabbi Judah Hab-Hasid (1146–1217) insisted on social and commercial as well as religious segregation from Christians, arguing for instance that a Christian should not be given a drink from a cup over which a Jew had made benediction, and that Christian ritual objects should not be accepted in pawn.[36] These developments obviously form a counterpart to the growth of anti-semitism among Christians, but they also imply that Peter Damiani was not alone in the belief which made him reluctant to write a treatise against the Jews in the middle of the eleventh century, that 'they have now almost ceased to exist'.[37]

The growth of anti-semitic sentiment and behaviour and the reiteration and renewed enforcement of the canonical prohibitions in the twelfth century had the effect of eroding social integration and reducing Jews to a marginal position, with the vulnerability that that entailed. We need not become bogged down in discussion of the priority of processes which evidently reinforced one another; by forbidding Jews to carry weapons in 1096, for example, Henry IV deprived them of one of the defining attributes of freedom, and made them more liable to social isolation as well as physical aggression. But in two important respects it is possible to trace the signs of growing restrictiveness on Jews and their activities sufficiently to suggest that persecution tended to create rather than to result from what was later regarded as Jewish exclusiveness.

In the Carolingian period and immediately after it there is nothing to suggest that Jews were particularly associated with usury. Indeed the Jews of the Maconnais frequently found themselves obliged to resort to money-lenders and mortgage their land to them. It is only after the first crusade that the identification of Jews with money-lending begins to appear. In prohibiting the burial of usurers in Christian cemeteries the second Lateran Council of 1139 both repudiated usury as unchristian, and acknowledged that many of its practitioners were Christians. It was in lamenting this fact that St Bernard of Clairvaux, in the 1140s, seems to have been the first to use the verb *judaizare* in the sense of 'to be a money-lender', rather than 'to advocate or make converts to Judaism'[38] – a sense which, in

35 Fossier, *L'enfance de l'Europe*, p. 590.
36 Katz, *Exclusiveness and Tolerance*, pp. 93–105.
37 *PL* 145, col. 61, quoted by Little, *Religious Poverty*, p. 44.
38 Mansi, 21, col. 529; Little, *Religious Poverty*, p. 56.

another sign of the times, there was no longer need to express, as there had been from time to time in the eleventh century. Nor was the change a sudden one. It is clear that the largest and best connected money-lenders in England, nationally and internationally, were Christians until as late as 1164, when Henry II seems to have transferred his business rather abruptly to Jews, for reasons which remain unclear;[39] his contemporary Pope Alexander III was another substantial customer of Christian usurers, including Englishmen and Flemings.

As R. B. Dobson has observed, 'Jews probably replaced Christians less because they were offering a new economic service than because they performed a well-established service more efficiently than their Christian competitors.'[40] But there is no doubt why they set out to do so. As the Jew in Abelard's *Dialogue* (*c*.1125–6) put it:

> Confined and constricted in this way as if the world had conspired against us alone it is a wonder that we are allowed to live. We are allowed to possess neither fields nor vineyards nor any landed estates because there is no-one who can protect them for us from open or covert attack. Consequently the principal gain that is left for us is that we sustain our miserable lives here by lending money at interest to strangers. But this just makes us more hateful to those who think they are being oppressed by it.[41]

The fate of the Jewish landowners and cultivators of the early eleventh century is not recorded, but is obvious enough. The subjection of alodial proprietors to serfdom by sheer force in the middle and later decades of the eleventh century, especially in north-western Europe, is now quite familiar. The formal illegality of their tenure and their special dependence on the counts (as the agents of the crown) made Jews particularly vulnerable to it, as Abelard's Jew pointed out. At the death of a Jew the lord who claimed to be his heir (having usurped the count's powers) need simply retain the land that fell to him, instead of regranting it to the Jew's descendants. One who was brutally reminded of that vulnerability, in this case at

[39]   Richardson, *English Jewry*, pp. 50–63.
[40]   Dobson, *Jews of Medieval York*, p. 9.
[41]   Abelard, *Collationes*, p. 20, trans. Payer, p. 33. The case for dating the *Dialogus c*.1125–6 is that of Mews, 'On Dating the Works of Peter Abelard', pp. 122–6.

the hands of the count himself, was Mar Rueben bar Isaac of Rouen, 'rich in gold, silver and cultivated lands'. He was ambushed in the forest, about 1033, and his only son killed by the attackers, along with his servants; he went to the Count (Robert I of Normandy) for justice, to be told, 'You are old and you have no son. All your possessions henceforth will be mine.' So Mar Rueben became one more wandering Jew, and died in Jerusalem a few years later.[42] Presumably this is why so many Jews appear in the service of lords, as bailiffs and financial agents, towards the end of the century. It is also reasonable to speculate that some at least chose the alternative of conversion, and still more that the expulsions of Jews from this place or that which we hear of from the middle of the tenth century onwards were accompanied by the confiscation of land and capital goods. There is no need to suppose that Philip Augustus was the first to think of that device when he expelled the Jews from his demesne in 1182, readmitting them on terms which effectively confined their livelihood to money lending.

The exclusion of Jews from craft and merchant guilds, and so from the trades in question, was axiomatic by the end of the twelfth century, but perhaps not absolutely so at its beginning.[43] A Jew was admitted, though exceptionally, to a London guild in Henry I's reign. That London still had Jewish goldsmiths and vintners at that time probably reflects the incompleteness as yet of the guild's monopoly of the trades rather than the Christian monopoly of the guilds, which were primarily religious associations in name and by origin. But either way the effect of the development which lay ahead was to exclude Jews from every comfortable or respectable means of making a living. What remained was money-lending, and the sorts of petty trade suggested by the order of Henry II's reign which forbade them to deal in religious articles and bloodstained clothing, together no doubt with the essential but unmentionable occupations of city life connected with the disposal of waste and sewage which fall to the lot of every reviled caste.

The restriction of occupation in itself would have tended to produce a concentration of habitation. Early references to Jewish quarters – the first turns up at Vienne in 849 – are of no great significance when occupation and family ties ordinarily governed where people lived.

[42]   N. Golb in Foreville, *Les mutations socio-culturelles*, pp. 152–3.
[43]   Richardson, *English Jewry*, p. 27.

Toulouse had a Jewish quarter in the eleventh century, for instance, but there were Jews who did not live in it.[44] In mid twelfth-century London Jews and Christians still bought houses from each other and lived as neighbours. The events of 1190 notwithstanding, Jewish property was still widely dispersed through the city of York in the 1220s in a manner which, as Edward Miller remarks, 'does not suggest any great tension at this period between the Jews and their Christian neighbours'.[45] The first area reserved exclusively for Jews and walled to show it – another poisoned privilege – was provided by Bishop Rudiger of Speyer in 1084 'so that they could escape the insolence of the people'.[46] It was intended, like many of its successors in Germany and south-western France especially, as an inducement to settle. The one at Perpignan (1243) seems to have been the first in which residence was obligatory for Jews of the city.

The ghetto *tout court*, with its gates locked by night so that Jews could not wander among sleeping Christians, did not appear until the later middle ages, but the principle of residential segregation of Jews as Jews, rather than as members of this or that family or trade, was established during the twelfth and thirteenth centuries. In this, as in all things, death imitated life: it was from a slightly earlier date than this that separate Jewish cemeteries were established at Macon, Tours and Worms, and in the middle of the twelfth century Geoffroi de Courlon resented Louis VII's permitting Jews to establish their own cemeteries and leper houses.[47] It is a reminder that the process of definition and classification which we have followed was not one which applied to Jews, or for that matter lepers and heretics, alone. For Christians, too, this was an age of classification, and it was in the eleventh century that cemeteries began to imitate the precise and sharp distinctions which were being rapidly and harshly established among the living.

[44]   Mundy, *Liberty and Political Power*, p. 325, n. 2.
[45]   Richardson, *English Jewry*, p. 8; Miller, 'Medieval York', p. 48.
[46]   Parkes, *The Jew in the Medieval Community*, pp. 160–1.
[47]   Fossier, *L'Enfance de l'Europe*, p. 594; Chazan, *Medieval Jewry in Northern France*, pp. 32–3. This does not necessarily imply that Jews and Christians had previously shared burial places, though I do not consider that so improbable as it seems at first sight. The question of burial practices in the eleventh century is one to which I hope to give further attention; its interest is underlined by Fossier, *L'Enfance de l'Europe*, pp. 329–35 and D. A. Bullough, 'Burial, Community and Belief', pp. 177–201.

Rhetoric and Reality

The assimilation of Jews, heretics and lepers into a single rhetoric which depicted them as a single though many-headed threat to the security of Christian order was not simply the continuation of an earlier tradition. Certainly classical and patristic texts and precedents provided a basis for the process of classification and the procedures and punishments whose elaboration we have traced. But they did so not of their own volition, as it were, but because they were turned to by those who sought solutions to present needs. Authority answered questions, but only the questions that were put to it; and the resultant apparatus of confiscation, deprivation and punishment was, by the thirteenth century, far more elaborate and far more comprehensive than its counterparts in the classical world.

Neither can the development of persecution during the eleventh and twelfth centuries be accounted for simply by reference to changes in the number, quality or nature of the victims. If in the case of heretics and lepers it is often hard to distinguish reality from perception that of the Jews is decisive, because it shows not simply a veil of ignorance between antiquity and the high middle ages, but a clear change of direction after about 1000. The balance of the evidence is quite firmly that between the seventh and the tenth centuries Christian authority in Western Europe treated Jews notably less harshly than it had done before or would do again; that the Jews were assimilated into Christian society to a considerable degree; that the assimilation was continuing – in some respects right up to the twelfth century; and that it was reversed by the growth of persecution. The long agony of European Jewry therefore (and this is a conclusion that runs counter to venerable traditions in Jewish as well as Christian historiography) has not perhaps its most distant origins but certainly its direct and major sources in events that took place in Western society in and around these two centuries.

The behaviour and social demeanour of Jews, as of lepers and heretics, were inextricably entangled with the way in which they were perceived and treated. This is not simply a matter of distinctions which are not made by the sources, though obviously it is a problem which the sources magnify enormously. As hostility narrowed the opportunities available to them Jews were forced ever more relentlessly into certain roles, that of the money-lender *par excellence*. The characteristics of the part then became those of the actor. The

Stereotyping

distinction between reality and perception is hard to maintain if reality only has one form.

Of course it never did. Nevertheless, the fates of all the victims, so diverse in their own natures and histories, come together here, in the creation of a stereotype which blended reality and fantasy into a whole that was consistent, coherent and terrifying. In the new year of 1024–25 Bishop Gerard of Cambrai began to interrogate the suspects before him. His questions were not based on the reports which had reached him about their teachings and convictions, but on Paul's prediction that in the last days heretics would appear 'seared in their conscience, forbidding to marry and the eating of meat'. So the answers which he elicited enabled Gerard to understand the phenomenon before him as a fulfillment of the prophecy and present it accordingly, at the modest price of attributing to the 'heretics' doctrines much more radical and much more coherent than those which they had in fact avowed. Over the next two centuries, and especially from about 1160 onwards, the same techniques and expectations led to the creation of 'the medieval manichee'. It came to be universally believed among Catholics (or at any rate among bishops) that there was a single highly organized dualist church, emanating from Bulgaria, which had lain concealed since antiquity and whose numerous and persuasive emissaries to Latin Christendom were dedicated to the destruction of the Church and of man on earth, and the restoration of Satan's kingdom by means of unrestrained sexual licence, the abandonment of procreation and the renunciation of Christian belief.[48]

Labeled all heretics as one and same beliefs – and same motives – to destroy the Church & Christendom

The reality, as we have seen, was quite otherwise. Heretics differed greatly from each other in their beliefs, backgrounds and motives. Very few of them possessed either the capacity or, for all we know, the inclination to expand their anxieties and aspirations into a coherent alternative to Catholic faith and practice. Even the Cathar churches, when they did appear in the West, were divided into tiny and quarrelsome sects, their organization patchy and their links with Bulgaria tenuous in the extreme. The harshness of their beliefs and the mildness of their lives might win them adherents, but they could not begin to measure up to the formidable portrait that the inquisitors painted of them. And, it should be added, the Cathars were not the last; in their turn Waldensians, Poor Franciscans, the Brethren of the Free Spirit and many others all went through the process of

[48] Moore, *Origins of European Dissent*, pp. 9–20, 243–6.

having not only their numbers but the dissoluteness of their behaviour, the coherence of their history and beliefs, the universality of their organization and influence, vastly exaggerated by the orthodox, and suffered greatly in consequence.[49] Still greater cruelty and more far-reaching oppression arose in just the same way from the alacrity with which priests, ministers and magistrates all over Europe, Protestant as well as Catholic, began in the fifteenth and sixteenth centuries to seize upon scattered expressions of popular belief in magic and sorcery as confirmation of their own nightmare of a Satanic conspiracy to overthrow Christendom, and the recruitment of countless human agents for the purpose.

Here is the crucial distinction. The medieval heretic was a reality; the medieval manichee was a myth. Heresy was varied in its origin, incoherent in its convictions, inarticulate in its forms; the myth which the bishops made of it was clear, simple and universal. Individual Jews and Jewish communities, each with their own particular conditions, traditions, tensions and difficulties, their own relations, good or bad, with their Christian neighbours, were welded into a single, coherent stereotype of 'the Jew'. And when our knowledge is greater we may equally find that many who were afflicted by a shifting variety of medial and psycho-social conditions, some no doubt highly contagious and others quite imaginary, were brought together in the single, universal image of 'the leper'. Nevertheless, the antithesis between the real and the imagined threat is too simple for our case: the construction of the stereotype on a basis of reality gave it a real and potent existence of its own.

Male Homosexuals

The three groups of people whom we have considered so far by no means exhausted the potential applications of the stereotyping process. Another example will show how, in the course of developing its machinery of persecution, the West not only isolated and exposed existing or at any rate previously identified minorities, but invented a new one. It is provided by John Boswell's fine account of the treatment of male homosexuality.[50]

---

[49] For examples, Merlo, *Valdesi e valdismi medievali*, pp. 9–42; Lerner, *Heresy of the Free Spirit*, pp. 1–34.
[50] Boswell, *Christianity, Social Tolerance and Homosexuality, passim*.

Boswell is able to show that both in classical antiquity and in biblical and patristic thought erotic relations between men were not distinguished *per se* from other varieties of sexual behaviour or preference. In some forms or contexts it might be scorned or censured. The Romans regarded the acceptance of the passive role by men (though not by boys) as worthy of contempt, but it was not alone in that. When the fathers of the Church cautioned against erotic relations between men, or men and youths, they did so within the context of their advocacy of chastity in general, and not on the basis or with the implication that this particular form of unchastity was unnatural or especially heinous. Indeed criticism of homosexual behaviour, which did begin to become commoner in late antiquity, was if anything more evident in pagan than in Christian circles. Nor is there any sign of special antipathy or opprobrium in the early middle ages. The biblical condemnation of sodomy was interpreted, by Hincmar of Reims for example, as referring to any sexual engagement which would not result in procreation, and Hincmar considered 'against nature' not only those acts but also sexual intercourse with forbidden women, including nuns and close relations or their wives. Burchard of Worms (d.1025) classified homosexual behaviour as a kind of fornication, and not one of the most serious; he described anal intercourse with a married man as a grave sin, but it carried a lighter penance than adultery, and no penance at all if between unmarried men.

Boswell argues that the peculiar horror which has been associated with male homosexuality in Western culture and the correspondingly violent condemnation of it were products of the twelfth century. The charge of sodomy (which, as we have just seen, was less specific in its implication than it has become since) was sometimes associated with simony in the rhetoric of the reform movement, though in practice the simony of Bernard, who bought the abbacy of Montmajeur from the archbishop of Arles a little before 1079, was considered a much graver matter than his sodomy.[51] In the main the accusation was more likely to be levelled against reformers than by them, perhaps by way of retaliation for their attack on clerical marriage. Peter Damiani launched a famous attack in his *Liber Gomorrhiani*, but in this matter entirely failed to persuade his fellow reformers of the seriousness of the sins which he berated so graphically. For example,

[51] Poly, *Provence et la société féodale*, pp. 257–8.

Urban II declined to be greatly perturbed by the election of a clerk named John, popularly known as Flora, to the bishopric of Orléans on the nomination of his lover, Archbishop Ralph of Tours, in spite of the indignation of Ivo of Chartres. And Ivo's opposition, to which we owe our knowledge of these and other details, seems to have been based on John's political rather than his sexual proclivities.[52]

Peter Comestor (d.1197) was the first influential scholar and teacher to interpret biblical injunctions against sodomy as referring specifically to homosexual intercourse. The Third Lateran Council of 1179, which we have encountered so often, became the first general council of the Church to legislate on it, ordaining that clerks found to have committed 'that incontinence which is against nature, on account of which the wrath of God came upon the sons of perdition and consumed five cities with fire', should be deprived of office or confined to a monastery for penance, while laymen should be excommunicated.[53]

The real impetus of the attack on homosexuality, however, did not come from the Church; the Fourth Lateran Council actually reduced the penalties prescribed by its predecessor. Gregory IX instructed the Dominican inquisition to extirpate homosexuality from Germany, likening it to 'the foulness of leprosy', and sketching a lurid picture of the torments awaiting its practitioners in the next world. But almost a century earlier the kingdom of Jerusalem had promulgated a legal code which ordained death by burning for sodomites, clearly meaning male homosexuals. No legislation of the kind appeared in the West before a series of codes prescribing death, usually preceded by torture, dismemberment or castration, was promulgated in Spain, France and many Italian cities from the 1250s onwards. By 1300 places where male sodomy was not a capital offence had become the exception rather than the rule.[54]

How consistently and universally such laws were enforced is, of course, quite another matter. However, apart from the obvious fact,

[52] Boswell, *Christianity, Social Tolerance and Homosexuality*, pp. 210–14; *Yves de Chartres: Correspondence*, pp. 282–305.
[53] Ibid., pp. 277–8. The Council of Reims, 1049, 'pari modo damnavit et sodomitas' (Mansi, xix, col. 792), but, as Boswell demonstrates, pp. 203–6, there is no basis for interpreting the term at all precisely at this time: Pope Leo IX was not enthusiastic for the persecution of male homosexuals.
[54] Ibid., pp. 288–93.

illustrated by the misfortunes of Edward II in England and the Knights Templar in France, that by the beginning of the fourteenth century sodomy had become disreputable enough for the imputation of it to be (as it has remained) a powerful political weapon, renewal of such legislation, prescription of even more savage punishments, and infliction of them upon those successfully accused were commonplace throughout Europe in the later middle ages.[55] The opinion of the Anonimo of Genoa (*c*.1300) that sodomy 'is so filthy and grave that anyone who commits it deserves death by fire'[56] was generally held and frequently acted upon. As with leprosy, the terror of discovery implanted in this period persists even in modern times.

The history of the persecution of sodomy differs from that of our other examples in a number of ways, and not least in that it developed distinctly later. Lurid tales of sexual assault had long held an honoured place in moral reflections. In the tenth century the nun Roswitha of Gandersheim gave a vivid account of the rape of a Christian boy by a Moorish tyrant. The association of pederasty with Moslems which remained prominent in Western literature for so long gathered pace, as might be expected, in the early part of the twelfth century. Once again we find Guibert of Nogent, who had also proclaimed heretics indifferent to the sex of their partners, in the van of the stereotyping process, though his animosity was probably more against the Moslems than the sodomites. But in general it is not until the thirteenth century, especially with the proliferation of associations for the glory of the Virgin and the suppression of heresy, sodomy and usury in the Italian cities, that the persecution of homosexuals was really under way – or to put it more accurately, that the accusation of homosexuality became an acceptable and accepted basis for persecution. In the essential characteristic which was ascribed to them, a degree of lasciviousness that menaced good Christians, their children and even their wives, male homosexuals were obviously and easily assimilated to the stereotype of the common enemy along with the Jews, heretics and lepers with whom, as several of the texts quoted remind us, they rapidly became identified in rhetoric and invective.

[55]   Goodich, *The Unmentionable Vice*, pp. 82–5.
[56]   Quoted by Martines, *Power and Imagination*, p. 118.

Female Prostitutes

Prostitutes appear to constitute another group whose classification and subsequent treatment followed the same pattern. They have been a good deal studied in the later middle ages,[57] but there is no systematic scholarly discussion for our period. Prostitutes figure prominently in the gossip and morality tales of monastic writers. Guibert of Nogent has them crowd around Thomas of Marle, whom he has already introduced to us as a patron of heretics and Jews, and William of Malmesbury illustrated the licentiousness of William IX of Aquitaine, the troubadour, with the story that he used to amuse his fancy with a project to fill his castle at Niort with a community of prostitutes of which the most notorious would be abbess, another famous courtesan prioress and so on.[58] It was an obvious parody of the great monastery at Fontevrault, founded by Robert of Arbrissel in 1100, of which Duke William was a patron, so his mockery need not be taken too seriously. But it was directed at a real preoccupation of the reformers, and no doubt suggested by the fact that Robert of Arbrissel himself specialized in the redemption of prostitutes and was famous for the number of them who followed him about the countryside: one of the four houses which made up Fontevrault was dedicated to St Mary Magdalene, and to the use and salvation of these women. Robert's associate Vitalis of Mortain, who founded a monastery at Savigny a few years later, with a companion nunnery nearby, was said by his biographer Stephen of Fougères (writing some half-century later) to have advocated marrying prostitutes to redeem them as a work of spiritual merit.[59] If so he anticipated not only the fashionable preacher Fulk of Neuilly at the end of the century and Pope Innocent III, but his own less respectable contemporary Henry of Lausanne, who scandalized the clergy of Le Mans by organizing a series of marriages between the prostitutes and young men of the town during his brief revolutionary reign there in 1116.

Instances of enthusiasm for redeeming prostitutes among the leaders of the reform are easily multiplied. The difficulty is to know what they

[57] For references see Otis, *Prostitution in Medieval Society, passim.*
[58] Guibert, *Autobiographie,* iii, xiv, p. 398; William of Malmesbury, *De gestis regum Anglorum,* v, p. 469.
[59] *Vita B. Vitalis,* p. 13.

meant by it. Prostitution at all carefully defined is not only essentially an urban phenomenon, but necessarily a cash-based one; indeed the relationship between the prostitute and her client could serve as a paradigm of the anxiety so widely expressed in these centuries that money dissolved traditional personal ties and obligations and substituted for them impersonal one-way transactions which contributed nothing to the maintenance and renewal of the social fabric.[60] But the cash economy had not developed so rapidly as to make prostitution in that sense a widespread phenomenon in one of the most backward regions of Western Europe by the last decades of the eleventh century. A suggestion that these 'prostitutes' were the cast-off concubines of newly celibate priests similarly overestimates the rapidity and enthusiasm which which celibacy was embraced by the country clergy, even at the behest of preachers so eloquent as Robert and Vitalis. It would be foolhardy to propose a solution until we have the careful study of the texts and vocabulary of this period which would enable us to distinguish between morality and reality, and to establish whether there are any significant differences of meaning between the teeming synonyms of words like *pellex*, *meretrix* and so on. It is a useful pointer that *meretrix*, the commonest Roman term for 'prostitute', seems in the early middle ages to have come to describe any woman who behaved scandalously, so that later in the twelfth century it was necessary to qualify it with the word *publica* to restore the older and precise meaning of a woman available for cash.[61]

In the meantime, it is best to suppose that the development reflected in the entourage of the preachers had more to do with changing structures of lordship and kinship in the countryside, and with the hardships of a decade marked by famine, than with the familiar phenomenon of urban prostitution which comes clearly into view in the cities of Northern Europe in the second half of the twelfth century. Henry II laid down regulations for the conduct of brothels in London at Bankside in 1161, and Philip Augustus made it one of the first acts of his reign to prohibit Parisian prostitutes from plying their trade in the cemetery of the Holy Innocents. The group of masters at the University of Paris whose deliberations on social problems at this period have been preserved saw the principal ethical problem raised by prostitution as being whether it was right for the

---

[60]   Cf. Otis, *Prostitution in Medieval Society*, pp. 154–5.
[61]   Ibid., p. 16.

church to profit, through alms, from their earnings, and concluded (we might read without surprise) that it was.[62] The question had been prompted by the offer of a group of prostitutes to contribute a window in honour of the Virgin to the rebuilding of Notre Dame, as representatives of other trades were doing; it was not accepted, but the way was prepared for the receipt of less embarrassingly obtrusive charity in the future. When a member of this group, Robert de Courçon, was named papal legate in 1213 he laid it down that women who were 'named by legal confession, conviction of witness or notoriety of facts' as prostitutes should be excommunicated, expelled from the city and treated according to the customs that applied to lepers – an analogy that had already been suggested by the exclusion of prostitutes from mass at Notre Dame a little before 1200. Prostitutes were also removed beyond the walls of Toulouse in 1201, by decision of the consuls, and the same provision was laid down in the statutes of Carcassonne a few years later;[63] it was a policy widely followed in the first half of the thirteenth century, but one which often implied – and in practice must always have entailed – that the conduct of the trade in the fields or suburbs beyond the walls was accepted.

The treatment of prostitutes thereafter often resembled that of Jews. By the end of the thirteenth century the profitability of the trade was very widely exploited by princes or municipal authorities through licensing systems and firmly protected monopolies, but from time to time fits of public morality, often precipitated by disaster, brought imprisonments and expulsions; by the end of the middle ages, at least in the south-west of France, the red-light district was walled and guarded like the ghetto, and residence in it was compulsory.[64] The place of prostitutes themselves among the outcasts is regularly proclaimed in fiction, rhetoric and regulation. In London and many other cities they were joined with Jews and lepers in being forbidden to handle goods on display for sale – especially food – and were always liable to be driven off the streets, particularly during holy seasons. At Perpignan they were compelled to suspend their business during Holy Week and confined to the leper hospital, until

[62]   Baldwin, *Masters, Princes and Merchants* I, 133–7; II, 93–5.
[63]   Otis, *Prostitution in Medieval Society*, p. 17.
[64]   Ibid., pp. 25ff; 'Prostitution and Repentance in Late Medieval Perpignan'.

the poor house came to be preferred as providing not healthier but better guarded accommodation. Arnold of Verniolles drew the threads of anxiety together as well as anyone when he explained to the inquisitor Jacques Fournier that he had feared himself infected with leprosy when his face became lumpy after he had been with a prostitute – so he took to sleeping with boys instead.[65]

The Enemy Defined

The argument might be pressed further, at the cost of outrunning present knowledge even more than we have done already. Guibert of Nogent (again) tells several stories against usurers, one of whom (evidently not a Jew) was visited by the Devil;[66] usurers were excluded from communion and Christian burial by the Second Lateran Council in 1139, and associated with Jews and prostitutes as prime objects of the preaching campaign of Fulk of Neuilly in Northern France and Normandy in the 1180s, of urban societies for the suppression of heresy and sodomy in thirteenth-century France and Italy, and of the inquisition in fourteenth-century Florence.[67] Heresy was often likened to madness; that during this same period mutes and idiots came to be excluded from inheritance in English law presupposes another process of classification and identification.[68] The definition of outlawry was central to English legal development in the Angevin period. As the use of money became more general the poor themselves – that is, the involuntarily poor – were more starkly defined by the lack of it, and became the focus of growing anxieties.[69] All of these cases and no doubt others exemplify not a series of distinct developments leading independently to the persecution in greater or lesser degrees of this or that pre-existing and objectively defined category of people, but aspects of a single and far reaching process of social reclassification. It might be described in these words, borrowed from Edmund Leach:

[65]   Le Roy Ladurie, *Montaillou*, p. 145.
[66]   Guibert, *Autobiographie*, iii, xix, 450.
[67]   Webb, 'The Possibility of Toleration'.
[68]   Pollock and Maitland, *History of English Law*, 1, 481.
[69]   Cf. Boswell's remark that 'the poor . . . became the objects of massive legislation and considerable antipathy on the part of the establishments of many countries' in the later middle ages: *Christianity, Social Tolerance and Homosexuality*, p. 271 and n.

Although our ability to alter the external environment is very limited, we have a virtually unrestricted capacity for playing games with the internalised version of the environment which we carry in our heads: we have great freedom to carve up the external world into named categories, and then arrange the categories to suit our social convenience.[70]

In these first two chapters we have seen how during the eleventh, twelfth and thirteenth centuries, Jews, heretics, lepers, male homosexuals and in differing degrees various others were victims of a rearrangement of Leach's 'internalised version of the environment', which defined them more exactly than before and classified them as enemies of society. But it was not only a matter of definition. In each case a myth was constructed, upon whatever foundation of reality, by an act of collective imagination. A named category was created – Manichee, Jew, leper, sodomite and so on – which could be identified as a source of social contamination, and whose members could be excluded from Christian society and, as its enemies, held liable to pursuit, denunciation and interrogation, to exclusion from the community, deprivation of civil rights and the loss of property, liberty and on occasion life itself. All this was by no means a simple or a single process. It had a long and terrible history before it, with a period of major growth between the middle of the fifteenth and the middle of the seventeenth century and another, it is hardly necessary to add, in the twentieth. It became, in short, part of the character of European society, and one which began here in the eleventh and twelfth centuries, with the persecution of heretics, Jews and lepers. The question to which we must now turn is, why? What social convenience dictated this rearrangement of categories? What necessity was the mother of this singularly durable and adaptable invention?

[70] Leach, *Culture and Communication*, pp. 35–6.

CHAPTER 3

PURITY AND DANGER

The Fear of Pollution

The rhetoric of persecution provides an obvious first clue to its motive. The threat which the victims present is omnipresent, and so highly contagious as to be virtually irresistable. It is contained especially in sexual menace and represented most vividly by it. The dreary stereotypes of unconforming and oppressed minorities which have become so familiar in more recent centuries are prefigured in the assertions that Tanchelm and Henry of Lausanne attracted women to their sects by seducing them. Henry's paramours were said to have included the wife of a knight, with whom he disported himself during an interlude in his subversion of Le Mans; according to the chronicler he was formidably equipped for the task, as Jews were said to be, and also lepers, whose extremities were swollen by their foul disease. Less often stressed, but no less significant, is the habitual description of those who carry the threat as wandering and rootless people confined by no boundaries, subject to no restraint of custom or kin, without visible means of support or a settled place in society. This is the language of fear, and of the fear of social change.

The fear of pollution protects boundaries, and the fear of sexual pollution, social boundaries in particular. In recent years historians have found one application of this generality especially illuminating. In her famous exploration of the relationship between *Purity and Danger*, Mary Douglas has shown how anxiety about sexual power may be a means of expressing or focusing nervousness of those whose

[handwritten marginalia: Much like any (taboo) other unknown & prohibited practice or thought]

[handwritten marginalia: Envy??]

functions or value in a society give them much greater importance than is reflected in their status or influence.[1] The foundation of Douglas's thesis was provided by her study of the Lele of the Kasai, in the Congo, who attached very great importance to being able to control sexual access to their daughters and granddaughters, but did not exercise a sufficient degree of direct physical coercion over them to be confident of doing so with unfailing success. A Lele woman could exploit this contradiction between the values and the institutions of her people with the implicit threat that if she were excessively ill-treated by her husband she might run off with someone else, thus depriving him of his potential daughters, and with them the prestige and bargaining power that would sustain his dignity in old age. So women possessed highly developed skills of coquetry and manipulation to enable them to make the most of these opportunities, while men endeavoured to control them through a stern code of sexual purity.

Anxieties of this kind are very commonly directed against women in societies which, in one way or another, give them both high value and low status. Twelfth-century Europe was one such society. The same anxieties are also easily identified in the fears projected against other groups similarly placed, especially groups which are clearly defined by race or caste as occupying an inferior position while performing essential functions. Such people present the danger that by asserting their real power they may subvert a social structure which is founded on the premise of their impotence.

Pollution fear, in other words, is the fear that the privileged feel of those at whose expense their privilege is enjoyed. Marked sensitivity to the possibilities of sexual pollution may therefore suggest that the boundaries which the prohibitions in question protect are threatened, or thought to be. Conversely (what may in practice amount to the same thing) if new social boundaries are being established it will be appropriate to consider whether heightened vigilance over sexual matters may be one means of securing them.

The Powerful and the Poor

The scale of the transformation of European society in the eleventh and twelfth centuries can hardly be exaggerated. In the countryside

[1] Douglas, *Purity and Danger*, especially pp. 140–58; *The Lele of the Kasai*, especially pp. 68–84, 113–27.

the completion of the manorial, or as it is more often called on the continent, the seigneurial economy gathered those who worked the land into a single, homogeneous servile class uniformly subjected to their lords, who in turn consolidated themselves into a single, hereditary and legally privileged nobility which advertised its essential coherence, despite the enormous variety in the fortunes and power of its members, by a universal adherence to the title, values and code of the knight. The towns, growing extremely rapidly, created a system of markets which exchanged the products of the countryside for those of long-distance commerce and urban manufacture, and transformed Europe from a society of gift exchange into a money economy, with profound results for its entire structure of values and social custom. Over both town and country kings, popes and nobles extended governmental institutions of new force, permanence and intimacy, substituting for the occasional presence of an itinerant monarch or bishop on the way from one estate to another networks of permanent officials to do their justice, raise their taxes and enforce their will. Historians have become so familiar with all this as to take it for granted, but in sum it was the most profound and most permanent change that overtook Western Europe between the invention of agriculture and the industrial revolution.

It is not difficult in principle to identify the relationships between the multifarious social changes which these developments precipitated and the various groups who became the targets of persecution. The most universal anxiety is that which is typically expressed in Baldri of Dol's description of the followers of the alarming, though eventually beatified, Robert of Arbrissel, as heedless of social boundaries, including 'men of every condition, women both servile (*pauperes*) and noble, widows and virgins, old and young, whores and spurners of men...turning away neither the poor nor the weak, the incestuous nor the depraved, lepers nor the helpless (*impotentes*)'.[2] Around all such passages, and they are very common, a simple description hovers with menacing ambiguity: *pauperes Christi* such people claimed to be, whether itinerant preachers, mendicants and their followers or lepers, but the very description evoked the sinister possibility that in reality they were somebody else's poor.

That points directly to the most elementary and farthest reaching of all the reclassifications which constituted the social revolution of

[2]   *PL* 162, col. 1053, 1055.

the eleventh century.[3] If the sharp and clear distinctions between Catholic and Manichee, between the leprous and the clean, even between the Christian and the Jew, originated very largely in the minds of the observers, the great division between *pauperes* and *potentes* (or, as they modestly learned to call themselves, *milites*) was founded very firmly indeed in external reality. The collapse of public authority which occurred so dramatically in Northern France in the 1030s radically simplified the many varieties of freedom and subjection on the one hand, of nobility and privilege on the other. At the same time that they reorganized their family structures to defend the integrity of their estates, the nobles asserted their physical control over the countryside, claiming and exercising authority as trustees or usurpers of the royal power to tax and command all free men: the power of the *ban*. In that guise 'customary' rights to demand tolls and dues in every imaginable circumstance, from passing a bridge, grazing a goat or baking a loaf, to demanding attendance at their courts and labour services on their lands, broke down ancient distinctions between the servile and the free and subjected all who lacked the strength to resist it to an impartial regime of subjection and extortion. By 1100 the broadest, the deepest and the most unbridgable of all social gulfs was that between those who possessed the *ban* and those who were subject to it.

The spiritual ideal which animated the great reforms of the eleventh century was that of *paupertas* – not poverty, as we conventionally translate it, but powerlessness. Certainly it meant the avoidance of possession, and possession in the twelfth century more and more often meant money and what could be bought with it. But in the eleventh century possession was land and the power over those who cultivated it – a power being asserted with rapidly increasing brutality and effectiveness. In these circumstances the renunciation of noble privilege was naturally demanded of those who joined the new monastic orders, and was an absolute prerequisite of holiness or the claim to it. Giovanni Gualberti's espousal of the religious life was marked by his repudiation of '*terrenas honores, falsaque divitias*' – landed property and false riches – to which his family and rank made

---

[3] This account of eleventh-century social change is essentially that of Duby, most recently expounded in *The Three Orders* and *The Knight, the Lady and the Priest*; for fuller discussion, Moore, 'Duby's Eleventh Century'.

him heir. The sanctity of the parents of the Patarene leader Ariald was attested by their refusal to allow their servants to ride down other people's standing corn, or to use the power which they possessed to abuse their neighbours.[4]

It was to the *pauperes* – to the poor in this sense – that all the great preachers of this age of great preachers addressed themselves, whether subsequently acclaimed as Catholic like Gualberti, Robert of Arbrissel and Bernard of Clairvaux, or reviled as heretical like Ariald, Henry of Lausanne and Arnold of Brescia. It was from the acclaim of the *pauperes*, who flocked to their sermons, proclaimed their miracles and followed them through the countryside, that they derived their power. The Gregorian revolution itself, prefigured by the revolt of the Patarenes in Milan, and given force and impetus by popular risings at papal instigation against 'corrupt' and 'simoniac' bishops all over Europe, provided the most momentous and unnerving example of it. Whether as the resounding orator surrounded by adoring crowds of the decades around 1100 or the humble and inconspicuous Cathar *perfectus* making circuit of his followers in the towns and villages of Lombardy and the Languedoc a hundred years later, the successful preacher represented unlicensed, uncontrolled power. Therefore he must either recognize the authority of the Church, and so by implication the legitimacy of secular power and the social order, or be extirpated.

Similar anxieties are visible elsewhere, and could be used by an accuser either to rationalize his own privilege and defend it against those less fortunately situated, or to attack those whose power or status he wished to challenge. Jews were particularly vulnerable on both counts. Lester Little and Alexander Murray have shown how by around 1100 money was increasingly identified – and not altogether wrongly – as the great engine of social change, and therefore the great symbol and servant of pollution.[5] The figures of Dives, often represented as a money bag, and later as a Jew, came to epitomize greed, lechery and dirt. All the distresses and abuses of rapid economic growth, the fragmentation of communities, the swarms of rootless and workless migrants huddling in streets and gutters, the

---

[4]   Moore, 'Family, Community and Cult', pp. 53–5; *Origins of European Dissent*, pp. 263–83.
[5]   Little, *Religious Poverty*, pp. 3–41; Murray, *Reason and Society*, especially pp. 59–71.

accumulation of great fortunes which rewarded extortion and exploitation carried out by men of no family or background – all these were seen as the doing of money and of those who owned and trafficked in it, the Jews and usurers who could most easily be represented as both its masters and its servants. 'Many a social tie,' Maitland wrote, 'the tie of kinship, the tie of homage – is being dissolved by the touch of Jewish gold; land is being brought to market and feudal rights are being capitalized.'[6]

The dislocations associated with rapid economic change and particularly with the growth of cities are familiar enough in several periods of European history. In this one, however, money stands for an additional dimension of change. Its coming into regular, day-to-day use for the first time since antiquity involved replacing a system of exchange which was ruled by the ethics of the gift to one which conformed to the values of the market-place. It was not simply a matter of using money instead of barter; that change, indeed, would not be completed for many centuries to come. But whereas in the gift economy which is so clearly displayed in the world of Beowulf or Gregory of Tours it is the fact of exchanging gifts which is critical in establishing the relationships of the parties, and not the nature of the objects themselves (except that, broadly speaking, they reflected in their munificence or modesty the social standing of the giver), the common use of money provides a common standard of value in which the worth of all goods and services can be precisely reckoned. Money becomes the measure of all things, and the means by which new wealth can be amassed in entirely new ways, often at the expense of those who have enjoyed security and pre-eminence in the past.

At the beginning of our period a market in land was created. By 1000 dramatically increasing land prices in the areas around the Mediterranean cities which first saw the effects of the boom were encouraging a rapid movement of population into the towns, helping to break up families which had been based on the possession and joint cultivation of particular estates, introducing new causes for quarrels and disputes, and above all assisting the rise in wealth and power of those who dealt in money or could turn their dues and services into it, against those whose fortune was in rents and services in kind. This was the world of avarice, the object of fear, disgust and repudiation by an eloquent procession of preachers and moralists,

[6] Pollock and Maitland, *History of English Law*, 1, 475.

from Peter Damiani in the eleventh century through Valdès in the twelfth to Francis of Assisi and beyond – a world in which, as it seemed, money had usurped the place of love, loyalty and valour.

Where money reigned supreme, the growing and increasingly menacing presence of the poor pointed to the necessity of providing for their control and, if necessary, their confinement or expulsion from the community. From one point of view, though only from one point of view, growing anxiety about prostitutes might be seen as a manifestation of the rising concern about crime and order which was first comprehensively displayed in England, in the stringent provisions of the Assize of Clarendon (1166) for the examination and inspection of those who were held to be of ill repute. And long after the disease itself was acknowledged to have died out the network of regulations and institutions for the segregation of lepers provided the hospitals, prisons, poor houses and madhouses of early modern Europe, and the principles upon which they were run.

Deviance and Authority

All this might suggest that the appearance of persecution in Western Europe provides a striking illustration of classical deviance theory as it was propounded by the father of sociology, Emile Durkheim. On his view the purpose of defining individuals or groups as deviant (the idea of deviance embracing both crime as formally delineated by law and other kinds of behaviour generally held to violate social norms and values) is by excluding some to reinforce the unity of the rest.[7] The exercise is particularly necessary at times of rapid social change and increasing differentiation, when the redefinition of social values and the reaffirmation of social unity is called for.

So far as it goes this would be hard to deny. It is in the inferences that we draw from it that danger lies. For example, it is apparently on the assumption of some such process that heretics are supposed to have 'aroused intense feelings of fear and hatred among the mass of the people because they dissociated themselves completely from all the values on which society was based'.[8] This is an assertion for which, as we shall see, there is no evidence whatsoever in our period. It was offered by Bernard Hamilton in its context as an inference

[7]   Cf. Lukes, *Durkheim*, pp. 160–3.
[8]   Hamilton, *The Medieval Inquisition*, p. 25.

from certain events, and not as an explanation of them, but if gen-eralized it easily assumes the appearance of explanation nevertheless. Similarly, the views with which we have already taken issue, that 'those who bore authority in the church were agents with very limited powers of initiative. They were not free agents',[9] and that 'the atti-tude of the clergy was shaped by the society in which they lived',[10] are indeed Durkheimian in regarding the people who carried out persecution and the institutions through which they did so as 'embodying and applying collective beliefs and sentiments of "society" as a whole' rather than considering the possibility of their having 'distinctive interests and goods that might conflict both with one another and with the wider social consensus'.[11] The difficulty with the theory and with its application is that it leaves unanswered, except by somewhat mystical reference to *représentations collectives*, the crucial question, whence does this reaffirmation of values arise?

Once a pattern of persecution has been established and its victims identified that question becomes so difficult to answer as almost to lose its meaning, and loses also much of its urgency. If the belief that Jews, sodomites or witches exist and are contagious and dangerous is firmly established and universally acknowledged then popular opinion may indeed demand that the instruments of persecution should be energetically applied by those who control them, and will if necessary be turned against any slackness on their part. In that case it becomes effectively impossible to distinguish between society and its agents, at least until such time as the necessity of persecution begins to be questioned. Thus anti-Protestant rioters in sixteenth-century France or anti-Catholic rioters in eighteenth-century England expressed a consensus which was already embodied in their laws and social institutions, so that to speak of the persecution for which they

[9] Southern, *Western Society and the Church*, p. 19.
[10] Hamilton, *The Medieval Inquisition*, p. 33.
[11] Lukes and Scull, *Durkheim and the Law*, p. 4; for Durkheim's rejection of the distinction between society and its agents, ibid., p. 45. An interesting and explicit attempt to apply Durkheimian deviance theory to another example of persecution in an emerging society, that of heretics, quakers and witches in seventeenth-century New England, is Kai Erikson, *Wayward Puritans*. Erikson writes of 'the community' throughout, but in fact focuses almost entirely on the magistrates and their actions, though citing much which suggests, especially in relation to the Quaker persecutions, that they were not always confident of popular support.

called as originating in the people rather than the institutions or *vice versa* would make, on the face of it, very little sense.

That may help to account for Durkheim's indifference to the distinction, at least in this connection. He lived in an age which could still congratulate itself on the progress which it had made in disposing of these relics of a barbarous past, and his interest was in understanding the functioning of society as he found it, which he held would be distracted rather than assisted by consideration in a historical way of how it came to be so. Nevertheless, the question is not only of evident historical importance but of some theoretical interest, since upon it must turn in considerable measure the view which we form of the relationships between those who exercise power and those over whom it is exercised.

An alternative understanding of the extension of the powers of government which is inherent in the growth of persecution may be suggested by the development of the criminal law.

Durkheim's view of the conception of criminality in primitive societies appears to rest on an assumption of progress very similar to that which for so long prevented historians from feeling the need to account for the emergence of persecution. He believed that societies progress from a retributive to a restitutive conception of criminal justice: from a legal system which reserves its heaviest sanctions for the maintenance of impersonal, and especially religious values to one which gives priority to protecting individuals against injury and damage, tending increasingly to treat religious and moral matters as part of a private domain.[12] We are now in a position to see (as indeed was Maitland) that this is, if not the opposite of the truth, at any rate another example of the dangers of trying to measure change against too short a chronological scale. It is a familiar characteristic of segmentary societies, including those of early medieval Europe, that their legal codes are concerned precisely with the compensation of particular injuries to particular people, identifiable individuals, and that disputes are resolved by a process of mediation between the parties involved, face-to-face, which produces an agreed settlement, often a compromise of some sort, rather than a verdict imposed from above that one is in the right and the other in the wrong.[13] Order is main-

[12] Lukes and Scull, *Durkheim and the Law*, pp. 259–62.
[13] For what follows I am especially grateful to Roberts, *Order and Dispute*; for the distinction elaborated below see especially pp. 115–53.

tained not by a ruler and his agents – if the ruler has a role it is largely a symbolic one, and he exercises little day to day authority – but through the community, and generally through the family or clan.

When rulers begin to assert themselves, and to create a recognizable apparatus of state, the earliest developments always include the appearance of a hierarchy of specialized agencies for the enforcement of order – judges, police forces, and so on – and law itself becomes coercive, imposing from above a pattern of guilt or innocence in accordance with codes promulgated by the central authority, rather than mediatory, seeking agreement or compromise. Hence the state can be seen in one perspective as an aspect of the division of labour, the expression of a new specialization, and in another, as Max Weber defined it, as a monopoly of legitimate violence. The new system of authority will seek to define and assert itself by attacking the old, that is, the family or clan which formerly exercised the power that the state now seeks, and notably by suppressing the systems of feud or vendetta which, in one form or another, generally provided the sanctions on which kin-based systems of order depend. As Lucy Mair put it, writing of Africa, 'feuding is one of the first activities which colonial governments make it their business to suppress'. We need no reminder that the same was true of their European forerunners in the high middle ages.[14]

One aspect of this transition from segmentary society to state is particularly pertinent to our concern. In the ordinary way face-to-face communities recognize and regard as criminal only specific injuries to specific individuals or groups. A wrong is indentified and dealt with when and if the person who has been injured or his representative chooses to take the matter up by way of the socially approved means of redress. By contrast, as the state begins to emerge its rulers seek to assert and extend their authority by creating what are in effect victimless crimes, offences against abstractions such as 'the ruler', 'the state', 'society' or 'morality'. Familiar examples of the process can be seen in the infiltration of such categories into the Germanic law codes of the early middle ages.

Furthermore, the ruler and his developing institutions of order will themselves seek out and punish these new offences, even though no

---

[14] Mair, *Primitive Government*, p. 52. Conversely, medievalists will recall Wallace-Hadrill's famous conclusion that 'feuding in the Carolingian world had a long future before it': *The Long-Haired Kings*, p. 146.

particular individual may feel or express a grievance.[15] This is precisely the transition which took place in the attitude to heresy in the
second half of the twelfth century, from reacting to dramatic and
aggressive expressions of anti-clerical sentiment to actively seeking
out those who were disseminating heretical beliefs, on the premises
that they must there to be found, and that any failure on their part
to make their whereabouts and activity obvious only confirmed the
insidious cunning with which they concealed themselves. The change
becomes clearly visible after the council of Reims in 1157, which
prescribed imprisonment, branding and exile for 'the most wicked
sect of the Manichees who hide among the poor [*imperitissimos*] and
under the veil of religion labour to undermine the faith of the simple,
spread by wicked weavers who move from place to place, often
changing their names and accompanied by women sunk in sin'.[16]

The council of Reims caught a rising tide not so much of ecclesiastical as of secular vigour. Within a few years a group of heretics,
including a young girl whose steadfastness in her faith moved and
disturbed the onlookers, were caught and burned at Cologne after
neighbours noticed their failure to appear in church on Sundays;
Alexander III was trying to restrain the vigour of Louis VII against
some alleged heretics who had been found by his brother Archbishop
Henry of Reims; and the most aggressive pioneer of government of
his generation, Henry II of England, had the opportunity to make a
stern example of the handful of '*Populicani*', who found their way
across the channel.[17] 'They could not hide for long,' says William of
Newburgh, 'for they were tracked down by men curious to know to
what foreign sect they belonged, and were arrested, detained and
held in public custody.' In due course they were tried at Oxford
before the king himself, condemned and branded; 'their clothes were
cut off as far as their belts, and they were driven from the city with
ringing blows into the intolerable cold, for it was winter. Nobody
showed the slightest mercy towards them, and they died in misery.'

These '*Populicani*' provided, in chapter 21 of the Assize of Clarendon, the occasion of the first secular legislation against heresy.
Although the single old woman whom they were said to have converted seems a modest enough trophy of their iniquity the surprise

---

15   Roberts, *Order and Dispute*, pp. 142–3.
16   Mansi, 21, col. 843.
17   Moore, *Birth of Popular Heresy*, pp. 80–4.

sometimes expressed that this innovation should have appeared in England, which was otherwise quite innocent of popular heresy, is misplaced: the legislation reflected the vigour not of the heresy, but of the legislator. When Frederick II chose to exhibit a similar though much more voluble ferocity half a century or so later he needed not even a single old woman by way of justification, and was content with a simple assertion that heresy had entered his kingdom of Sicily. No other evidence has survived of its having done so to any significant extent.[18]

The observation that the development of legal processes and institutions for the persecution of heretics, Jews and others was the work of kings, popes and bishops hardly requires laborious demonstration. However, in directing our attention towards the political and governmental framework of persecution it has the merit not only of proposing a specific identification of the source of change, but of evoking a persuasive theoretical context for it, in a conflict of the kind which Max Weber associated with the establishment of the universal religions. 'The great achievement of the ethical religions', he wrote, 'was to shatter the fetters of the kinship group...[by establishing] a superior community of faith and a common, ethical way of life in opposition to the community of blood, even to a large extent in opposition to the family.'[19]

'A superior community of faith and a common, ethical way of life in opposition to the community of blood' admirably describes what are commonly regarded as the highest achievements of the religious and intellectual movements of the twelfth century, the reform and renewal of the institutions of church and state driven by a fresh and universal commitment to Christian faith and values. Weber's words were written to describe developments which he associated with the

[18] Powell, trans., Liber Augustalis, pp. 7–10. The inquisitor Anselm of Alessandria, writing c.1270, mentions a French Cathar who stayed in Naples about a hundred years earlier, and the Cistercian visionary Joachim of Flora (d.1199) thought that there were Cathars in Calabria. He is not generally believed: see Dupré Thesider, 'Le catharisme languedocien et l'Italie', p. 304. The most respected inquisitorial authority on Cathar organization in thirteenth-century Italy, Rainier Sacchoni, does not mention the Regno in his list of Cathar churches, c.1250 (Moore, *Birth of Popular Heresy*, p. 138).

[19] Weber, *Religion of China*, p. 237, quoted by Bendix, *Max Weber*, p. 139.

emergence in classical China both of the bureaucratic state and of an economy in which the exchange of goods and services for cash played a regular and substantial part. He specifically observed an association between the activity of the state and the vigour of persecution: even though 'from early times religious edicts of the emperor had made the persecution of heresy a duty...tolerance gave way to the persecution of heresy [only] when the conflicting claims and ideas of Taoism or the religious practices of Taoist or Buddhist priests appeared to become a political threat to the prevailing order'.[20]

Persecution and 'the People'

The question whether it is more appropriate to envisage the rulers and magistrates of the twelfth-century West as expressing, in a Durkheimian fashion, an instinctive and collective determination to preserve social unity, or as embodying a Weberian progression towards the establishment of a bureaucratic state, therefore depends in considerable measure on the extent to which the emergence of persecution was the result of popular hostility to its victims. So far as most of them are concerned evidence is simply lacking. Even in the case of leprosy, for example, we should need to review a much greater variety of materials much more systematically than has yet been done to suggest any worthwhile conclusion. That a few individuals like the Abbot of St Omer and Bishop Aelfward found themselves forced into retirement on the grounds that they were lepers means nothing without knowledge of their personal circumstances, such as whether their subordinates had other reasons for being glad to be rid of them. An assertion of popular demand for segregation like the petition said to have been made to the bishop of Tournai by the inhabitants of Péronne in 1118 may, in isolation, represent no more than a conventional formula, but even if it is taken at face value more cases are needed before anything can be built on it.

There is every reason to suppose that once the conviction of the contagiousness of leprosy was established it nourished popular antagonism to sufferers, or at any rate avoidance of them. It is obvious that the leper soon became the object of detestation and terror which long outlasted any basis that such sentiments may have had in the facts, for it seems certain that by the time of the Black

[20] Bendix, *Max Weber*, pp. 133–4.

Death the European population had accumulated sufficient resistance to the bacterium to make leprosy one of the least rather than one of the most contagious of diseases. But whether those emotions were aroused by the appearance of the disease itself and its visible effects on the sufferer rather than by the interpretation of it which was formed and disseminated by bishops or doctors is an entirely different question, and one which there is no present means to answer. Indeed in agreeing with Rotha Mary Clay that 'popular opinion of the contagious nature of the disease developed strongly towards the close of the twelfth century'[21] it is hard not to wonder, even so, whether it is only a chance bias in the evidence which makes it so much easier to find clear expressions of the horror of leprosy in the period among the socially eminent, whether in the form of the brutalities of a Henry II or a Philip Augustus, or the piety of Queen Matilda or a Hugh of Lincoln.

We are better placed to assess the situation of heretics and Jews. Even so it is important to insist upon what is sometimes overlooked, that popular sentiment and behaviour are not to be identified either with monastic opinion or with that of the laity in general. It is easy to be lulled by the vivid, gossipy quality of much monastic writing into forgetting that the chroniclers represent a section of society with strong interests, traditions and prejudices of its own – obviously with respect to heretics, but also very markedly with respect to Jews. They did not always coincide with those of authority, certainly, but that does not mean that they can be taken as those of 'the people'. Even less is it justifiable to identify 'the people' with the laity in general. In our sources (as in conventional social analysis) the word *populus* referred very precisely to the unprivileged and illiterate, whose interests and outlook were entirely distinct from those of the privileged, in the world and in the Church, and very often sharply antagonistic to them.

That observation made, the over-familiar assertion that 'medieval man' feared and resented any deviation from his simple Catholic faith is remarkably difficult to justify. On the contrary, the reason why preachers of heresy were denounced, pursued and extinguished by whatever means availed was precisely the fear that they would undermine the faith of the *simplices*, and with it the social order. Ecclesiastical observers habitually exaggerated the number, intellectual

<hr>

[21] Clay, *Mediaeval Hospitals*, pp. 52–4.

sophistication and organizational coherence of heretics, but there is
every indication that their nervousness of the capacity of heretical
preachers to excite social disruption was well founded. Wherever
they appeared in Europe from the eleventh century to the Reformation those who denounced the power, the corruption and the claims
of the Church were assured of a warm popular reception, provided
that their own claims seemed to be supported by their demeanour
and manner of life. When they succeeded in putting down roots and
establishing regular institutions and religious services – as the Cathars
did in the Languedoc and in Lombardy between the late twelfth and
late thirteenth centuries – they picked up a good deal of support,
sometimes faithful and passionate, though no longer quantifiable.
That is by no means to say, of course, that left alone heresy would
have swept the Church away, or even detached a large proportion of
its following. It might as easily have become equally complacent,
corrupt and extortionate, just as Guillaume Bélibaste, the Cathar
perfect of Montaillou, was as devious, as ignorant and as lecherous
as any priest.

It is necessary to make this very obvious point only because the
contrary is so frequently asserted. It was a distinguished scholar who
mentioned 'the popular demand for inflicting the death penalty for
"aberration from the faith" and the popular insistence on executing
it in public' as the reason 'why Frederick II in decreeing death for
the heretic laid down that the execution must be public'.[22] There are
indeed a few cases which seem to lend credibility to the notion that
heretics were burned by public demand, but on inspection their
number shrinks rapidly. It was the King of France who burned the
clerks of Orléans in 1022, the nobles of Milan who insisted that the
heretics from Monforte must be burned, against the (formal?) protest
of the Archbishop, and the servants of the bishop whom he had

[22]   W. Ullmann, introducing his selection from Lea, *The Inquisition of the
Middle Ages*, p. 31. Examples could easily be multiplied; the extent to which
popular hatred of dissent is taken for granted is such that as careful and
sceptical a scholar as Edward Peters can be found asserting that 'although
violence was certainly exercised against heretics and dissidents during this
period . . . it was more often than not exercised by lay people, usually by
mob action', and that 'the first stirrings of violence against dissidents were
usually the result of popular resentment' (Peters, *Heresy and Authority*,
pp. 165, 189). *Per contra*, Moore, 'Popular Violence and Popular Heresy
in Western Europe, *c*.1000–1179', but see below, pp. 117–23.

denounced as simoniac who dragged Ramihrdus of Cambrai to his funeral pyre in 1076. 'The faithful' (*fideles*) of St Gilles, according to Peter the Venerable, were responsible for putting Peter of Bruys on the bonfire which he was making of a cross there (c.1139), but even if this means 'its people' rather than 'its vassals' they had a strong commercial incentive for doing so – their dependence for a living on the pilgrimage trade to their great church, which Peter had denounced.[23] In any case Peter the Venerable's words suggest something more in the nature of an affray than a trial. This reduces to three – at Soissons in 1114, Liège in 1135 and Cologne in 1143 – the number of cases where it does seem that heretics were burned by genuine popular action and against clerical resistance; to them may probably be added a fourth, at Liège again, in 1145. It is a small sample, circumscribed in time and place, to provide a basis for a large generalization. Closer inspection reveals another factor common to the four cases. All of them involved a conflict between popular jurisdiction, which had condemned the accused by traditional methods, and bishops or abbots who wanted to ignore these verdicts and reserve the trials to ecclesiastical tribunals. We shall return to the conflict about jurisdiction later; for the moment it is sufficient to note that what was at stake on these occasions was not the question of heresy *per se*, but that of how and by whom it was to be dealt with.

In short, these incidents, which have made an impression out of all proportion to their number and distribution, provide no true evidence of general popular antipathy to heresy as such. By the same token, it need hardly be added that the frequent involvements of those labelled as heretics in the civic conflicts of thirteenth-century Italy do not do so either. To argue that they did it would be necessary to show both that the conflicts themselves were essentially religious in nature, and that the side asserting Catholic orthodoxy was usually popular in character. Neither proposition is likely to be seriously entertained. On the contrary, there seems on at least some occasions to have been genuine popular opposition to the burning of heretics, at Parma in 1279 and Bologna in 1299 for example, while the gradual adoption of imperial and papal decrees against heresy was often quite clearly the result of political and diplomatic considerations.[24]

---

[23] *Tractatus contra Petrobusianos*, p. 5.
[24] Webb, 'The Possibility of Toleration', pp. 91–113; Moore, *Origins of European Dissent*, pp. 237–9.

The case of the Jews is more complicated. There are, as we have seen, occasional indications in the eleventh century of casual hostility towards them, most obviously in the 'Jew striking' of the *midi*, the observations of the Jew in Abelard's *Dialogue*, or the occasional prohibitions which it was thought necessary to issue against assaults on Jews and their festivals. It is impossible to say how widespread or frequent such occurrences were; in this case that very few are recorded tells us nothing in itself. However, in view of the evidence of substantial and increasing social integration of Christian and Jew in the centuries before 1000 it would be perverse to assume deeply rooted or endemic popular anti-semitism in that period. In the eleventh and twelfth centuries the situation of Jews was distinguished from that of other victims of persecution by their relationship with holders of authority. When Guibert of Nogent accuses Count John of Soissons of associating with Jews he reflects the role which they often filled as financial agents or managers of the lords, a role which obviously attracted much unpopularity. From the popular as opposed to the monastic point of view, one might say, the grievance was not so much that the Count associated with Jews as that the Jews associated with the Count. As J.H. Mundy has put it, 'almost every medieval movement against princely or seignorial power attacked Jews'.[25] The more they were excluded from other occupations and forced into dependence on the princes the more true that became. Such opprobrium, like that which attached to the money-lender and his activities, was not necessarily anti-semitic in itself, but as it contributed not only to the misery but to the stereotype of the Jew it was increasingly so in its consequences.

How far this generally diffused though not easily measured anti-semitism contributed to the development of persecution (which it obviously helped to sustain in the centuries to come) is a different question. It does appear that Jews often felt their situation to be a precarious one, especially when religious excitement or anxiety was in the air. Jewish chroniclers believed, for example, that in 1146 only the intervention of Bernard of Clairvaux averted a repetition of the events of 1096 when the enthusiasm of the monk Ralph for the second crusade led him to call for the killing of Jews in Europe. Nevertheless, this is another area where we must be careful with our language. The massacres of 1096 themselves were the work not of

[25] Mundy, *Europe in the High Middle Ages*, p. 91.

'the people' but of crusading armies composed of mounted knights and led by nobles. At Mainz, the townspeople at first supported the Jews against the crusaders, though some of them joined in the killing and looting later; at Worms the Jews handed their valuables for safe-keeping to their Christian neighbours when they heard of the killings; at Cologne they went to gentiles for refuge. The motives of the crusaders themselves are not entirely clear, and some were doubtless personal: Emicho of Leiningen, whose army carried out the first attacks, was apparently somewhat unbalanced. But a prominent objective was undoubtedly supplies and loot, inevitably demanded by a large but poorly organized and unprovisioned army on the march, and another, for some of the leaders at least, was the protection money which their threats and previous deeds enabled them to extort from Jews on their route.[26]

The York massacre of 1190 also appears, on the excellent authority of Roger of Hoveden, to have had its origin in a conspiracy by local notables to liquidate their debts along with their creditors.[27] We have already noticed that the hangings at Bray-sur-Seine the next year were inspired by the military interest of Philip Augustus in asserting his presence there, and the burnings at Blois twenty years earlier by court intrigue apparently ignited by jealousy of the Count's Jewish mistress, Polcelina.

The Enemy Discovered

Once violence broke out many were prepared to join it, sometimes with great savagery. Apart from the obvious interest of those who incited the riots in encouraging disorder and confusion the urban populations of the twelfth century were not usually averse to opportunities of looting and mayhem that came their way, whether the victims were Jews or not. But that is not the same thing as regarding popular anti-semitism as the principal cause of the violence. It existed, certainly, though we cannot estimate its extent. The best we can do to understand its role in the misfortunes of the Jews is probably to examine one particular and crucial episode which is extremely fully, though also extremely partially, documented. In doing so we shall

[26] Riley-Smith, 'The First Crusade and the Persecution of the Jews'.
[27] Dobson, *Jews of Medieval York*, pp. 26–28, 33–37; Miller, 'Medieval York', p. 47.

make extensive use of G. I. Langmuir's recent re-examination of the text.[28]

Thomas of Monmouth's account of *The Life and Miracles of William of Norwich* was composed in several stages between 1149 and about 1173. Its purpose was to vindicate William's sanctity and promote his cult by demonstrating that he had been ritually murdered by the Jews of Norwich, and that a variety of miracles had occurred at his tomb.

Thomas was a Welshman, as his name implies, who arrived in Norwich as a monk at the cathedral priory a few years after William's death. He heard the story of the allegation that a Christian boy had been murdered by Jews, and began to look into it. His interest may have been aroused by a story told by one Wicheman, that on his deathbed a prominent citizen of Norwich named Aelward Ded had confessed to having recognized as a body the contents of a sack being carried by a Jew whom he met near the place of William's death and on the same day, saying that he had been persuaded by the Jews not to report it. Thomas sought out William's mother and her brother, his uncle, who had made the original accusations. They were repeated to him in fuller and more circumstantial form, no doubt encouraged by his sympathetic ear as well as the passage of time and the polish of many repetitions. So Thomas concluded that the Jews had done William to death. As to how or why, his witnesses had nothing to tell him. But another relative newcomer to the cloister was a converted Jew named Theobald, who told Thomas – with what degree of prompting there is no means of guessing – that every year the Jews of Spain met at Narbonne and cast lots to decide in which country a Christian would be put to death for revenge for the ills that had befallen their race since the death of Christ. Then the leaders in the chosen country would cast lots in their turn to nominate a city upon whose Jews the duty of performing the sacrifice would fall: in 1144 it had fallen on Norwich.

This is the first appearance of what became the foundation of the myth of Jewish conspiracy. Whether or not Theobald was real, and whether (as Langmuir thinks) Thomas of Monmouth actually invented the rest of the details for which he claimed to have uncovered circumstantial evidence – the crucifixion of William, the nature of his wounds and so on – or found them in versions of such stories

[28] Langmuir, 'Thomas of Monmouth'.

already circulated or recorded in the writings of the fathers of the Church, we have here the effective creation of the story that Christian children were ritually murdered by Jews.

The relationship of Thomas's story to what actually happened in Norwich in and after 1144 is quite clear. It was not until some years after William's death that any credence was attached to the accusation of Godwine and Elviva that the Jews were responsible for William's death. Indeed, we only have Thomas's word for it that they made the accusation at all, though it is probably fair to argue that writing only five or six years later he could hardly have made it up altogether. According to Thomas the bishop had called on the Jews to answer the charge, the sheriff had forbidden them do so, and despite some murmurings among the people that, for the time being, was that. Only six years later, under the aegis of Thomas himself, who provided out of the resources of his own reading and imagination not only the account of William's death but most of the evidence for it, was the 'martyrdom' proclaimed and the development of the cult launched, with the assistance of a new bishop. Even then there were many in both town and cloister who declined to believe in it.[29] We owe it to the memory of the prior, Brother Elias, to recall that his scepticism particularly incensed the saint and his promoters.

Popular prejudice against the Jews may have been among the elements which combined to make the story of St William of Norwich, but if so it played a very small part. The accusations made by Elviva and Godwine might have assumed some importance if they had been taken up by the bishop and the sheriff, and they may have provided the inspiration for Thomas of Monmouth's imaginative, skilful and unscrupulous reconstruction, but in themselves they had neither weight nor durability. For all we know to the contrary there may have been many other occasions when similar accusations against Jews came to nothing for lack of influential support, but we should not use that to suggest that anti-semitism was widespread or particularly virulent at the humbler levels of society when so little real evidence of it has survived. On the other side we would have to weigh the fact that even by the end of the thirteenth century Edward I carried out his expulsion of the Jews from England entirely for his own reasons, and without any suggestion of pressure to do so from

[29] On this aspect see also Ward, *Miracles and the Medieval Mind*, pp. 68–76.

his subjects. When Philip IV of France followed his example a few years later there were among the poor some at least to complain that the Jews had been much milder in their dealings than their Christian counterparts.[30]

Thomas of Monmouth's story may be compared with another which arose only a few years before it. In 1143 two sects of heretics were found at Cologne, brought to the attention of the authorities by quarrels between themselves. On interrogation the leaders of one of them revealed that they were missionaries of a church which had lain hidden in Greece since the time of the martyrs and had its own pope and its own bishops. The sect distinguished between those who had been baptized into it – the *electi* – and the believers (*credentes*) and auditors (*auditores*) who had not yet attained that condition. The elect would not eat meat or anything made from it or otherwise produced by procreation; to preserve secrecy they would attend mass, wearing veils, but would only pretend to take the sacrament because they had their own, which they celebrated daily. This, from Prior Eberwin of Steinfeld, is the first complete account we have of the appearance in the west of Bogomil missionaries from the Byzantine lands, with all the essentials of organization and doctrine that made up the myth of 'the medieval Manichee'.[31]

Another example occurred slightly earlier. In 1114 the Bishop of Soissons accused two men, Clementius and Everard of Bucy, of preaching heresy. These two lived under the patronage of Count John of Soissons, to whom we have already been introduced by Guibert of Nogent as an exceptionally brutal and rapacious lord, and as a lecher, a patron of Jews and a user of their services as sorcerers and pimps. Lisiard found it difficult to make much sense of the interrogation, because Clement and Everard seemed to be dullwitted and illiterate. Clement, for instance, offered in defence of his heresy Christ's saying 'Beati eritis...', which he took to mean 'Blessed are the heretics.' Getting nowhere, the bishop called in Abbot Guibert to see if he could make sense of them. And, triumphantly he did. In response to his question about the theology of baptism the accused said, 'In God's name do not expect us to search so deeply', and

---

[30] Richardson, *The English Jewry*, pp. 231–3; Poliakov, *History of Anti-Semitism*, 1, 80–1.

[31] PL 182, cols 676–80, trans. Moore, *Birth of Popular Heresy*, pp. 74–8; Moore, *Origins of European Dissent*, pp. 168–22.

avowed their belief in each article of faith as Guibert went through them. But Guibert knew better. 'I then remembered that line to which the Priscillianists formerly agreed; that is "Swear, perjure yourself, but do not reveal the secret".' This enabled him to recognize Everard and Clement as Manichees and, by consulting Augustine's account of them, to fill out his own with a very complete statement of their rejection of Catholic teaching and sacraments, refusal of meat, abhorrence of procreation and so on. Better still, he was able to add on the same authority a detailed description of how they met secretly at night to conduct wild orgies, and baked the ashes of the children born of them into bread which they used as a sacrament. It was, in fact, the story already told of the heretics of Orléans by Paul of St Père of Chartres, and ultimately derived from the accusations levelled at the early Christians themselves by their Roman persecutors.[32]

In each of these stories we see the shaping of the stereotypes of the Jew and the heretic (the 'medieval Manichee') which justified their persecution. The common elements are plain. At Norwich and at Cologne dispute among the unprivileged, accompanied by accusations of wrong-doing in a religious context, reached the attention of the ecclesiastical authorities. We do not know how Lisiard of Soissons came to hear about Clementius and Everard, but their association with John of Soissons and the enthusiasm with which they were put to the ordeal after Guibert's interrogation (at least according to Guibert's own account) point at least to the possibility of some sort of communal resentment associated with them. Both Thomas of Monmouth and Guibert of Nogent drew on their knowledge of literature and of a wider world to identify the people and the allegations before them as part of a great conspiracy against Christendom, filling in gaps in the evidence, and even manufacturing further evidence in support of the conspiracy theory. Eberwin's story seems to be one stage further along in the process, since he is reporting events in which he was apparently not a direct participant, but the same learned elaboration of fragments of charge and counter-charge which reached the ears of authority as a result of communal tension is close to the genesis of his account.

It would not be difficult to multiply similar examples, especially of the construction of 'the medieval Manichee'.[33] But it is hardly

---

[32] Guibert, *Autobiographie* iii, xvii, 428–34; Moore, *Origins of European Dissent*, pp. 67–8, 166–7.
[33] Moore, *Origins of European Dissent*, pp. 243–6.

necessary to do so, for we have here instances of another process which was to become familiar in the annals of persecution in Europe. It is precisely the way in which Norman Cohn and Richard Kieckhefer have shown the priests, ministers and magistrates of early modern Europe interpreting accusations of sorcery among the peasantry, of storm-raising or casting the evil eye, as confirmations of their nightmare of a satanic conspiracy, and launching the great witch craze to extirpate it.[34] In short, despite the simple piety which we are encouraged to imagine at the heart of everyday life in the Europe of the cathedrals, and despite the invidious position which Jews unquestionably occupied in its political and financial structures, it seems necessary to conclude that heretics and Jews owed their persecution in the first place not to the hatred of the people, but to the decisions of princes and prelates. In neither case have we found grounds to justify a description of the persecutors merely as the agents of society at large, at least if our conception of society is one which includes the great majority of its members.

[34] Cohn, *Europe's Inner Demons*, especially pp. 245–55; R. Kieckhefer, *European Witch Trials*; see also the works of Larner and Peters cited below, ch. 4, nn. 42, 43.

CHAPTER 4

POWER AND REASON

Trial by Ordeal

Guibert of Nogent's account of the interrogation of Clementius and Everard of Bucy was considered in the previous chapter as an example of the way in which learned officials elaborated the statements and assertions of simple people so that they could be interpreted as evidence of far more comprehensive and sinister threats to the faith. The same story is often cited as a vivid example of trial by ordeal, which it is, and of popular detestation of heresy as such, which it is not.

The charge upon which Clement and Everard were brought before Bishop Lisiard of Soissons was that they held meetings outside the church, and were said by their neighbours to be heretics. 'When they were examined about their beliefs (by the bishop),' Guibert says, 'they gave most Christian answers, and yet they did not deny their meetings. But since people like these always deny the charges against them, and at the same time seduce the hearts of the foolish in secret they were assigned to the judgment of exorcised water.'

While the ordeal was being prepared Guibert examined Clement and Everard in the exchange discussed above, and remembered from his knowledge of the Priscillianist heresy that heretics would always protest their innocence. Unfortunately, although rumours of Clement's heretical teachings had reached both Guibert and Lisiard, nobody who had actually heard them preach was available to give evidence, so Guibert advised the bishop to proceed with the ordeal. The rest of the story deserves to be quoted in full:

The bishop celebrated mass, and they received the sacrament from his hands with the words 'May the body and blood of Christ put you to the proof this day.' Then the reverend bishop and Archdeacon Pierre, a most honest man who had spurned the things which they had promised him if they were not subjected to the ordeal, led the way to the water. With many tears the bishop recited the litany and pronounced the exorcism. They swore on oath that they had never believed or taught anything contrary to our faith. Clement was thrown into the vat and floated like a stick. When they saw this the whole church was overcome in rejoicing. Nobody present could remember seeing so large a crowd of both sexes as was attracted on this occasion. The other fellow confessed his error but did not retract, and was locked up with his convicted brother. Two other notorious heretics from the village of Dormans had come to watch, and were held with them.

We then went to the Council at Beauvais to ask the bishops there what should be done with them. But the faithful people, fearing softness on the part of the clerks, went to the prison, seized them, and lit a fire outside the town on which they were burned. Thus the people of God acted with righteous zeal to prevent the spreading of this cancer.[1]

The nature and workings of trial by ordeal have been widely discussed in recent years.[2] Most of its principal elements are clearly portrayed in this story. Although the accused were said to have been publicly active for some time, no witnesses to their crimes were available. The object of the trial, therefore, was to establish the credibility of their denial, as the oath which they took immediately before their immersion underlined. The use of water is associated with humble social standing; in England, according to Glanvill,[3] villeins went to the water and freemen to hot iron. The ordeal itself was carefully prepared and surrounded by an elaborate ritual framework, though it may be noticed that Guibert does not refer to it as 'the judgment of God' and says nothing to suggest his personal acquiescence in the view that a divine judgement was taking place, for all his warm approval of the outcome.

Less obviously at first sight the story illustrates what Peter Brown in particular has emphasized as the essential features of the ordeal.

[1]   Guibert, *Autobiographie*, iii, xvii, 434.
[2]   For general accounts see Gaudamet, 'Les ordalies au moyen âge', pp. 99ff., and Bartlett, *Trial by Fire and Water*. The discussion which follows is also greatly indebted to Brown, 'Society and the Supernatural: A Medieval Change'; Hyams, 'Trial by Ordeal' and Morris, *Judicium Dei*.
[3]   *Glanvill*, p. 173.

The verdict of the water was not unambiguous; it had to be interpreted. And the interpretation was pronounced not by the bishop, or any other judge or official, but by the assembled people, the community at large. The assertion that Clement 'floated like a stick' – that he was unhesitatingly rejected by the water – can hardly represent any objectively defined or measured degree of buoyancy on his part: for how long did he float before the verdict was announced, and with what degree of immersion, and how was it affected by the manner in which he was bound and weighted? When heretics were put to the water at Vézelay (c.1165) there was some dispute afterwards as to whether one of them had been received by the water.[4] The ambiguity was the same as that which attended the decision to be taken when the hand of someone who had carried the hot iron was unbound after three days, whether or not they were healing cleanly.

In Clement's case Guibert clearly implies that the verdict was unanimous, though he could hardly expect his readers to suppose that the heretics from Dormans (if such they were) observed the proceedings with quite such unbounded joy as the rest. But that was not always the case with those who were accused of heresy. At Ivois near Trier a few years later a priest named Dominic William was vindicated by the form of ordeal appropriate to his station when he affirmed his orthodoxy with a mass, and continued to preach his heresy afterwards. The alleged heretic who was acquitted by the water at Vézelay later in the century was one of two who been put to the ordeal at their own request. Two parish priests, Albero, of Mercke near Cologne, and Lambert le Bègue, of Liège, asked to be allowed to vindicate themselves against charges of heresy with the hot iron in the 1160s: both had got into trouble with their ecclesiastical superiors, whose laxity and corruption they had criticized, but were beloved by their parishioners for their humility and devotion.[5] The English anchoress Christina of Markyate demanded the hot iron when her virginity was impugned, but the Jews of the city declined to clear themselves of the murder of William of Norwich by it.[6] Since

---

[4] Moore, *Birth of Popular Heresy*, p. 56; cf. Bartlett, *Trial by Fire and Water*, pp. 39–40.

[5] Moore, *Origins of European Dissent*, pp. 187–9, 191–3.

[6] *Life of Christina of Markyate*, pp. 62–3; Thomas of Monmouth, *The Life and Miracles of William of Norwich*, pp. 47–8. Exemption from the ordeal had been a normal privilege of the Jews since the ninth century: Bartlett, *Trial by Fire and Water*, p. 54.

the ordeal was a judgement of the community those who were confident of their standing in the community (or at any rate more confident
of that than of their standing in law) might well prefer it to the justice
of their hierarchical superiors, even if charged with heresy. This was
not the case with Clement. He had tried to bribe the Archdeacon to
keep him from the ordeal, having been exposed to the danger in the
first place because his neighbours complained of his behaviour. Evidently he was not a popular man. That he was under the protection
of the rapacious and cruel Count John of Soissons seems a good
enough reason for that. The joy which proclaimed his flotation
did not, therefore, represent an evaluation of his theological
soundness.

Apart from the circumstances of Clement's particular case,
however, yet another tension is illustrated here. We have noticed that
though Guibert approved the outcome of the trial he did not expressly
endorse the procedure. A few pages earlier he had described the
defeat in trial by combat, another form of ordeal, of a merchant who
had correctly accused a ruffian called Anselm of stealing jewels from
the church of Laon. There Guibert says categorically that 'no canon
approves this law of combat'.[7] In this he expresses the hostility to
the ordeal which was being voiced more and more by churchmen, as
it would continue to be until the ordeal was abolished by the Fourth
Lateran Council in 1215.[8] The avowed objection was that it was
irrational, and no doubt it was, but it was also, as we have seen, an

[7]   Guibert, *Autobiographie*, iii, xv, 418.

[8]   Bartlett, *Trial by Fire and Water*, pp. 34–69, demonstrates decisively,
against the view of Brown and Hyams, that ordeal was brought to an end
by deliberate clerical opposition, embodied in the legislation of Lateran IV,
and did not 'wither away' through any general erosion of confidence in its
operation. Hyams' argument on this point ('Trial by Ordeal', pp. 103–4)
appears to rest on a distinction between 'thinkers and intellectuals' on one
hand and 'doers and writers' on the other, which is quite at odds with the
view taken here, in the footsteps of Clanchy, Murray, Stock and others,
that the *literati* of the twelfth century should be viewed pre-eminently as a
single class, ultimately serving the same interests and causes (for better or
worse) whether they happened to find themselves agents at any particular
moment of 'church' or 'state'. Equally, Hyams' description of the church as
'an improbable engine of radical change' implies, if seriously sustained, an
understanding of its activities in the eleventh and twelfth centuries dia-
metrically opposed to that maintained in these pages.

expression of authority vested in the community, and one that did not always produce results of which the rulers approved. The famous occasion on which an English jury solemnly affirmed that the hands of some Saxons who had been put to the hot iron on the charge of stealing the king's deer were healthier after the ordeal than they had been before, and provoked William Rufus to burst out 'Is God a just judge? Damn whoever thinks it!' had many humbler parallels.[9] Max Gluckman observed that in Africa the colonial regimes 'virtually eliminated the blatant public use of ordeal and divinatory techniques in the assessment of charges of witchcraft and sorcery, or in the determination of guilt in "not proven" accusations'.[10] So did the clerks of our period, and for very much the same reasons. If the ordeal offended their sense of decorum it also undermined their control of events.

In that context the action of the people of Soissons as described by Guibert takes on an additional dimension. The power of collective sentiment once evoked could not be safely flouted. Bishop Lisiard's decision to refer the case to the Council of Beauvais amounted to a repudiation of the community's verdict in favour of an appeal to the abstract justice of the clerks. The action of the crowd therefore vindicated a local decision against the encroachment of a distant and alien authority. Though we know nothing of the details it was also the case at Cologne in 1143 that the heretics who were burned by a crowd against the wishes of the clerks had been condemned by the water before the clerks tried to take them into custody, and it appears that at Liège in 1135, and again in 1145, though no ordeal was employed because the accused confessed, the traditional form of

[9] Eadmer, *Historia Novorum*, pp. 101–2. Hyams, 'Trial by Ordeal', p. 116, interprets this as expressing resentment of the susceptibility of the ordeal to 'clerical management' rather than to religious scepticism, unlike Bartlett, *Trial by Fire and Water*, pp. 96–7. In the context of this story Hyams is surely right. Once again, however, what follows from it depends on one's view of the sociology: it appears to me that in this case it was the English and not the clerical status of the actors, including in all probability those who arranged the ordeal, that thwarted the king's will, just as it is the English and not the clerical sympathies of Eadmer that inform the satisfaction with which he reports it.
[10] Gluckman, *Politics, Law and Ritual*, p. 174; Hyams makes the same analogy: 'Trial by Ordeal', p. 118.

public trial was first invoked and then repudiated by the ecclesiastical authorities.[11]

The trial of Clement of Bucy also helps to illustrate, and in a small way to resolve, one of the central points at issue in current discussion of trial by ordeal. The form which his ordeal embodied was a collective one, the judgement expressed on him that of the community. But Robert Bartlett has established quite clearly that the ordeal was not popular or local in origin, but royal and centralizing.[12] It was a device of the Carolingian monarchy to enhance its ability to intervene in the enforcement of order, which spread through Europe with Carolingian power and influence, and was jealously guarded and vigorously used, as a regalian right, by kings themselves and the secular and ecclesiastical officials upon whom it devolved from them. It was most likely to be invoked where there was a shortage of evidence or of witnesses, where the accused were strangers with no standing or support in the community, and where the nature of the crime alleged made the accusation difficult to substantiate – all circumstances which frequently applied where heresy was in question.

In this case Bishop Lisiard had resorted to ordeal because he was unable to produce witnesses that heresy had been 'publicly avowed', and the demeanour of the accused in their interrogation hardly amounted to its being 'pertinaciously defended' as a conviction under canon law would have required. Guibert's assertion that there 'was a lady whose mind Clement had addled for a year and a deacon who had heard other wicked statements from his mouth' fails to obscure these deficiencies in the case against him. What secured Clement's conviction – as his attempt to bribe his way out of the ordeal shows that he expected – was not niceties like these, but the general opinion that people had of him. Thus, while the fact that it was Lisiard who ordered the trial illustrates Bartlett's point that the ordeal was a

---

[11] Moore, 'Popular Violence and Popular Heresy', *Origins of European Dissent*, pp. 258–61.

[12] Bartlett, *Trial by Fire and Water*, pp. 9–12, 36–41 and *passim*; conversely the pursuit of exemption from ordeal by urban communities (ibid., pp. 54–6), for whatever reason, militates against any description of the ordeal as a form of popular justice. My suggestion (above, n. 11) that the use of ordeal in trials for heresy involved a conflict between clerical and traditional popular jurisdiction is therefore erroneous – but a conflict of sentiment might have similar results.

regalian institution and not a popular one, designed to bolster central
authority, we are also reminded that the power upon which it relied
for its effectiveness was that of collective sentiment. This was, from
the bishop's point of view a somewhat unpredictable weapon, deliv-
ering on this occasion (but not, we have seen, on all) the verdict he
wanted, at the price of depriving him of the power of sentence.

way to intervene in the enforcement of order – to shift the power of sentence into the hands of the king

Authority and the Community

When the consensus upon which its communal procedures relied
coincided with the objectives of the authorities the ordeal provided a
powerful weapon. The difficulty arose, as Rufus had mentioned,
when the views of the community were not those which the ruler
wanted to hear. The English Assize of Clarendon of 1166 offers a
notable example of how that obstacle might be overcome. Its first two
clauses provided for 'twelve of the more lawful men of each hundred
and four of each vill to affirm whether there were any in their district
who were accused or notoriously suspect' of various crimes since the
beginning of Henry's reign – exactly the procedure which the papal
mission of 1178 used to identify heretics in Toulouse. Those named
would be brought before the royal justices, and put to the ordeal if
they deemed it appropriate. But the fourteenth clause added that
'those who shall be tried by the law and absolved by the law, if they
have been of ill repute and openly and disgracefully spoken of by the
testimony of many and that of lawful men' should be exiled or outlawed. Thus while the opinion of the neighbourhood was called upon
and the communal device of trial by ordeal employed, the king's justices reserved to themselves the right both to dismiss charges against
those brought before them without putting them to the ordeal and to
proceed against those who had been put to it and vindicated. In this
way traditional procedures were still more firmly harnessed to the
royal will, and the ordeal itself took a long step towards what it
eventually became, a form of judicial torture designed to produce a
confession and quite divorced from the judgement of the community.[13]

[13] Douglas and Greenaway, *English Historical Documents*, II, 408–10;
Hyams, 'Trial by Ordeal', pp. 121–3; Bartlett, *Trial by Fire and Water*, pp.
65–9; cf. E. Peters, *Torture*, pp. 45, 58–9, where Henry II's measures are
also seen as representing a retreat from the independent and unpopular
exercise of prosecutory powers by royal officials in his grandfather's reign.

The abolition of trial by ordeal was therefore an example of the attack upon the community as the source of justice and order – albeit a source of which the attackers themselves had previously made effective use – which Max Weber pointed out as characteristic of emerging bureaucratic regimes. At the same time the Assize of Clarendon deployed two of the instruments which superseded it. The inquest, by which an official was empowered to place men on oath to answer questions about their neighbours and neighbourhood, breaks surface in the Carolingian period. It was clearly associated from the outset with the use of reputation as a test of legal standing. In the twelfth century the elaboration of judicial theory, and particularly the revival of Roman law, made this combination an extremely powerful and flexible one for the extension of legal power over wide areas of life and activity. It is hardly necessary to dilate on the long future which awaited the inquisitorial procedure, whose essence in all its applications is that it allows authority to launch investigations on its own account against a crime or offence whose presence it suspects, instead of having to wait for one person to accuse another before moving into action. This is exactly the point which we have already noticed as critical in the transition from systems of justice associated with segmentary societies to those typical of centralized states, and as critical in the evolution of European persecution from the middle of the twelfth century onwards.

Less familiar, but as Edward Peters has laboured to teach us no less important, is the convergence between the general and weighty importance attached to the maintenance of good reputation in Germanic society (as indeed in most segmentary societies) and the very precise elaboration of the Roman idea of legal infamy which was worked out by the civil and canon lawyers of the twelfth century.[14] Its kernel, much expanded between the second and fourth centuries AD, but not formally embodied in Roman law until the codification of Justinian, lay in the idea that certain forms of behaviour and certain ways of life were so demeaning to the individual as to imperil his legal status. Infamy diminished or destroyed the credibility of a man's testimony, depriving him of the protection of the courts, and exposing him to the torture which was otherwise held inconsistent with the dignity of a free man. It might be incurred not only by conviction for various crimes, but by involvement in heresy or sexual scandal, and by Justinian's time its penalties included exclusion from

[14]   Peters, *Torture*, pp. 30–1, 44–5.

public office and impairment of the rights of inheriting and transmitting property by will.

The contribution of these principles to the mentalities and mechanisms of persecution which were traced in the first two chapters hardly needs further commentary. As Peters has insisted, the legal preparation and background of the bull *ad abolendam* of 1184 is in effect a comprehensive application of the principle and penalties of legal infamy to those suspected of heresy and abetting heretics. The method of detecting them was the *inquisitio* in its successive developments. The law of infamy also opened the way to the use of torture in its proceedings. Beyond that, the entire range of persecution which we have considered might be described in the same way, as the transformation of the procedures and disabilities associated with legal infamy into an instrument of universal application, which could be brought to bear at will upon any situation or any group of people whom it might be desired to subject to it, including groups conceived and defined especially for the purpose.

If the part played by the principles of centralizing and rationalizing legality in the evolution of persecution is self-evident the reason for their adoption is self-explanatory. Just as trial by ordeal expressed the authority of the community in its judicial role, popular heresy represented, not exclusively but more than any other single force, the assertion of collective values and communal independence against the subordination of religion first to seignurial and later to bureaucratic power. In each case it was agreed on all sides that it was largely immaterial whether the power was exercised in secular or ecclesiastical guise by baron or pre-Gregorian bishop, royal clerk or papal judge delegate. The main religious message of the heretical leaders was the repudiation of innovation in daily patterns of life and worship. Their political message, far more devastating, was their own independence of the structures of established power. They looked for their authority to those who heard them. Recognition or acclamation of their leadership therefore amounted at best to communal autonomy, at worst to rebellion. 'We have a father,' the people of Le Mans said to Bishop Hildebert when he returned from Rome to find the city under the rule of Henry of Lausanne, 'a bishop and defender greater than you in authority, fame and learning.'[15] That was why

[15] *Gesta Pontificum Cenomannensium* in Bouquet, xii, 54–5, trans. Moore, *Birth of Popular Heresy*, p. 34; cf. *Origins of European Dissent*, pp. 270–2; 'New Sects and Secret Meetings', pp. 54–7.

obedience was the test of the heretic, and why those who exercised authority in the name of higher powers felt it increasingly urgent to seek out and destroy the disobedient in heart.

Heresy differed from other objects of persecution (apart from Judaism, which did not overtly bid for popular approbation) in being identifiable with personal leaders and possessing its own structures of explicit authority. That placed it at the forefront of challenge, and therefore of persecution. But it was far from being the only way in which collective judgement and opinion asserted themselves. On the contrary, the identification of powers and functions which might be transferred from the community at large to the organs of the bureaucratic regime was a long and slow process, intimately related to the division of labour as well as the distribution of power. That is an enormous subject, of which we cannot attempt even a limited taxonomy here. One small example of it is that during the fifteenth and sixteenth centuries the identification of lepers, in our period usually carried out by local juries which often included lepers among their number, was taken over by medical practitioners.[16] That in turn was a relatively minor aspect of the attack conducted during those centuries and beyond on the performance of 'medical' functions of healing and curing by uneducated, unqualified and in effect – since their possession of a clientele could arise in no other way – popularly selected persons. This attack was one of the functions served by the witch craze. As Christina Larner demonstrated most entertainingly, though it was carried out in the name of reason, like the attack on trial by ordeal, it can by no means be described simply as the substitution of a more rational practice of medicine for a less rational one.[17]

The attack on heresy was only one aspect of the analogous concentration of 'religious' functions in the hands of an increasingly professional clergy which took place in our period. Another, which in effect applied the same principle to the dead as the licensing of preachers did to the living, was the gradual transference of the process of canonization from popular to clerical and eventually to papal control during the twelfth century. Two brief examples will illustrate its motives, and their direct relationship with the concentration of power in the hands of the privileged, in the name of reason.

[16]   E.g. Bourgeois, *Pas-de-Calais*, pp. 86, 102–3, 110, 115, 134, 163.
[17]   Larner, *Witchcraft and Religion*, pp. 141–52.

Brian Stock has recently demonstrated how Guibert of Nogent's dislike of the cult of relics, once hailed as an early triumph of reason over medieval superstition, was not the result of any scepticism about relics as such, but arose from his identifying their cult, quite correctly, as a mechanism for conferring sanctity by popular acclaim rather than by the approbation of the literate. Guibert's distaste is seen elevated to the point of doctrine as it were, two or three generations later, when William of Canterbury remarks that reports of miracles emanating from the poor should be discounted because they were always liars – *mendacos mendaces*. Thus the community had become incapable by definition of exercising the religious judgements which in simpler forms of society express and articulate its values and embody its decisions.[18]

The Triumph of Reason

The attacks on particular *loci* of communal power which are represented by these forms of persecution and allied processes are generalized in the campaigns of moral repression with which newly instituted regimes so often establish their legitimacy, proclaim their adherence to traditional values, discredit their enemies and consolidate their hold on the instruments of power. Such drives tend to be directed not only against recognized forms of moral laxity, like sexual pleasure or conspicuous consumption, but also against stereotypical public enemies who may serve as the focus of rhetoric and the object of attack. A few years ago Christina Larner argued with brilliant effect that the witch hunts in Scotland between the 1590s and 1660s must be understood in that light, as one of the means by which the Calvinist regime consolidated itself;[19] other examples come easily to mind, from Cromwell's England to Khomeini's Iran.

As befits the epoch of the foundation of the modern state, the eleventh and twelfth centuries are rich in opportunities for the illustration of that generality. It is plainly no accident that the kings and popes whose names have cropped up most often in these pages are those most firmly identified with vigorous and imaginative innovation in the arts of government. We have seen Henry II of England

[18] Stock, *Implication of Literacy*, pp. 244–51; Ward, *Miracles and the Medieval Mind*, p. 96.
[19] Larner, *Enemies of God*, pp. 40–59 and *passim*.

legislate to control prostitution in London early in his reign, and seize the chance which the wretched *publicani* hailed before him at Oxford provided to proclaim himself a scourge of heresy. In the context of his policies these are of a piece with the wider campaigns in which he used the disorders of his predecessor's reign and the alleged misdeeds of ill-disciplined clerks to assert his own claims to authority against those of aristocracy and episcopacy respectively. Philip Augustus, with less of the real substance of governmental power immediately at his disposal, was loud from the very beginning of his reign in attacking Jews and driving lepers and prostitutes off the streets. Louis IX 'marked the establishment of royal legislative initiative'[20] in 1254 with an ordinance prohibiting gaming, blasphemy and usury and condemning prostitution, at a time when his brother Alphonse of Poitiers had at last consolidated his hold over the county of Toulouse after the death of Raymond VII, last of the line of St Gilles, in 1249. Frederick II, who surpassed them all in the loftiness of his claims, expressed corresponding and superfluous ferocity against heretics, brought usury under civil control, and enacted stern penalties for blasphemy, pimping and procuring.

The new order which this moral fervour proclaimed asserted itself not only through a number of emerging nation states – not all of them successful – and the nascent papal monarchy, but also in municipal government and even through the households of lay and ecclesiastical nobles. Nevertheless it was a single regime. Its foundation, laid everywhere in Western Europe during these centuries, though with some variations of pace and procedure, was the replacement of payment in service and kind by payment in cash, and of oral process by written instrument. It was, as we have seen, the expression of fundamental changes in social and economic organization. And its establishment required another change, no less profound: the replacement of warriors by literate clerks as the agents of government and the confidants of princes. It is among these clerks that we see most clearly how the emergence of the state represented a new stage in the division of labour, a specialization or professionalization of government – and it is among them, the agents as well as the theorists of persecution, that we will find its origin and *raison d'être*.

The rise of the *literati* in the courts of the eleventh and twelfth centuries was the subject of much contemporary comment, most of

<hr/>

[20] Otis, *Prostitution in Medieval Society*, pp. 19–20.

it unfavourable. The clerks who surrounded the thrones of kings and magnates, lay and ecclesiastical, were regarded as upstarts by the nobles who felt their natural position usurped. The feeling was often returned: Walter Map told Ranulf Glanvill that some royal justices were harsher than others because as the sons of serfs they relished the opportunities which their new position gave them to behave oppressively towards barons.[21] The rivalry was no less intense in the cloister than at court. Orderic Vitalis' legendary disdain for 'new men raised from the dust' is widely shared by monastic writers. Later in the twelfth century Jocelin of Brakelond describes the mutual distrust of literate and illiterate monks at St Edmund as they plotted and manœuvred over the appointment of a new prior, regarding each other respectively as illiterate clodhoppers and arrogant trouble makers.[22] It is a portrait in gossipy miniature of the way in which traditional monastic virtues of calm and humility came to be identified with aristocratic sanctity, in opposition to the harsh and worldly values of the clerks.

As that implies the clerkly skills of reading, writing and reckoning were seen by those of more traditional outlook, nobles, scholars and monks alike, as the vehicle of social ambition, the path to power and influence of men who were not fitted by birth or character to possess them. Literacy increasingly cut across familiar social boundaries. A promising lad who attracted the attention of a priest or bishop might be sent to school through his patronage, as John of Salisbury tells us he was, probably exaggerating the humbleness of his origins. The court itself could provide an education in its skills which might, but need not, be made more formal in the schools later. As Michael Clanchy observes, the three men who did most to enlarge the use of writing in English government in this period, Roger of Salisbury, Hubert Walter and Ralf Nevill, owed their education to their upbringing at court and were jeered at by university men for their lack of classical scholarship and the polish that came with it.[23] The *clericus* emerges from the jaundiced pages of the monastic chroniclers as a hard and narrow upstart, grasping and unscrupulous in the service of his master, exploiting every pretext of law and every resource of power to expand his master's prerogative and maximize his master's

---

[21]   Clanchy, '*Moderni* in Education and Government in England', p. 674.
[22]   Butler, *The Chronicle of Jocelin of Brakelond*, pp. 124–8.
[23]   Clanchy, *From Memory to Written Record*, p. 262.

income – and his own. And not only from the chronicles: 'In your service and in my own affairs,' the dying Nigel d'Aubigny wrote to Henry I in 1118, 'I have committed great sins and I have done few if any good deeds.'[24]

Of course, not all or even most of those who rose to wealth and power by way of great men's courts were born in the dust. But if the disruptive power of expertise did not draw all its beneficiaries from a single class it turned them into one, gave them their own loyalties and values, their own outlook and above all their own flag – reason – in whose names they claimed to rule. The antithesis between *clericus* and *laicus* no longer corresponded to the familiar distinctions between noble and non-noble or clerk and layman. The world of fantasy clung to the gallant knight and the learned clerk as ideal types. In the real world it came to seem no more incongruous to disparage an archbishop of Canterbury's culture by calling him a layman than to describe as *clericus* a knight or even a king who could read and write, or was notable for his sympathy for those who did so.[25] Such men everywhere relied on their quick wits, their support for each other and their shared familiarity with the new technologies of government, the counting of money, the sealed writ, the legal tag, to bring them the patronage and protection of those in whose hands they could place power of a quality undreamt of since the days of Rome, and with a far greater future before it.

To the *literati* the displacement of ordeal by inquest, the centralization and systematization of the process of canonization and of the acknowledgement of miracles and the power to perform them,[26] together with the reform of the church, the growth of both canon and civil law in theory and practice and the many other triumphs of their age and culture, represented the victory of reason over superstition and of truth over custom. Historians have generally been content to accept such judgements at their own valuation, perhaps adding another victory, of centralization over particularism, to the list. But these were also triumphs of the expert, of the clerks over the illiterate. Some contemporaries at least felt no doubt of the intimate relationship between the development of the machinery of royal and papal government and the sectional interests of their agents. 'Having

[24]   Southern, 'Henry I', pp. 220–1.
[25]   Clanchy, *From Memory to Written Record*, pp. 177–81.
[26]   Cf. Ward, *Miracles and the Medieval Mind*, pp. 167, 183 ff.

won themselves the favour of the secular prince they assert that all things are opened to them as of right because (as they say) the prince is not subject to law and what pleases the prince has the force of law', John Salisbury wrote,[27] generalizing Nigel d'Aubigny's equation of zealous service to the king with the advancement of his personal interests. Of this aspect of the question we need not say a great deal, for Alexander Murray has painted a brilliant picture of the world of ambition, and the emergence of the *literati* as a group whose common interests, common values and common loyalties were expressed in bottomless contempt for those who did not share their skills: 'O God who has sown discord between clergy and peasant, permit us by thy grace to live from their work, enjoy their wives, cohabit with their daughters and delight in their death.'[28]

This is the hostility of the *clericus* towards the *illiteratus, idiota, rusticus* – all words used regularly to describe those accused of heresy, and expressing perhaps the broadest and most universal of the stereotypes that, like those of heresy, of leprosy, of Jewry, the clerks constructed from the scattered fragments of reality they found to hand, with the help of the ancient texts with which their familiarity provided their badge of office, and in which they found both their authority and their instruments for persecution.[29]

The fear which was expressed in the language of contamination, directed against the poor in general and in particular against heretics, lepers, Jews, prostitutes, vagrants and others assimilated to them by the rhetoric of persecution, was the fear which the *literati* harboured of the *rustici*. No doubt it assisted many of them to identify themselves more securely with the privilege to which their skills had brought them access, by entrenching and justifying the exclusion of those who lacked them. No doubt, equally, persecution itself served to ward off the actual or imagined threats that might be represented by those whose real importance and potential power was not reflected in their condition and status. But persecution also had a more positive function. It served to stimulate and assist the development of the claims and techniques of government in church and

[27] John of Salisbury, *Polycraticus* vii, 20, trans. Dickinson, p. 307.
[28] Murray, *Reason and Society, passim*; the prayer is cited in the discussion of intellectuals' attitudes to peasants at pp. 237–44.
[29] Cf. Stock, *Implications of Literacy*, pp. 101–51, on the characterization of eleventh-century heresy as 'rustic'.

state, as well as the cohesiveness and confidence of those who operated it. It was the dark underside of the revival of the twelfth century,
and as such inseparable from the whole anatomy. Commenting on
the Fourth Lateran Council's abolition of trial by ordeal Sir Richard
Southern once remarked that 'by 1215 the essential steps had been
taken in making human justice and government an affair subject to
human rules and dependent on the efficacy of human agents'.[30] It is
not to deny the reality of the progress he described to observe that
he might as accurately have referred to clerical justice and government, clerical rules and clerical agents.

From Intrigue to Repression

The emergence of the bureaucratic regime, or the professionalization
of the exercise of power, had another face which we must contem-
plate before we leave it. It had to be determined not only over whom
but also by whom the power of government was to be exercised.
Indeed the latter question is logically prior to the former – and, as it
turns out, chronologically prior to it as well. Nor was the answer
nearly so much a foregone conclusion as our formation by the civilization which the victors in the struggle for that power moulded
tempts us to assume. The beginning of the conflict will be found by
returning, for the last time, to the shadowy and apparently uncon-
nected series of events which crops up in the chronicles of the few
decades on either side of the year 1000.

In 992 Sehok ben Esther, a convert from Judaism, hid a waxen
figure in the synagogue of Le Mans. He later unearthed it, claiming
that it was an image of the count, who was present, which the Jews
were piercing with pins in order to bring about his death.[31] It appears
that the accusation failed, though we do not know why. The charge
itself was common enough. About twenty years earlier an English
widow had been accused by a man called Aelsie of trying to kill him
by piercing a puppet which was found in her room; she was drowned,
her son was outlawed, and their land, which Aelsie had claimed
as his by right, was awarded to him by royal judgement.[32] The

[30] Southern, *The Making of the Middle Ages*, p. 103.
[31] Chazan, *Medieval Jewry in Northern France*, p. 12.
[32] Cohn, *Europe's Inner Demons*, pp. 153–4.

Carolingian court saw a number of similar episodes, especially during the intrigues around Louis the Pious. The influence of Bernard of Septimania over the emperor was attributed to sorcery, and in 834 Bernard's sister Gerberga was put in a barrel and drowned in the Saône as a witch by Louis' eldest son, Lothar.[33]

That example makes the significance of these incidents plain. Belief in magical powers and their use is widespread in many peasant societies, as it was in early medieval Europe. As the victory of Aelsie illustrates, it could provide a focus for a variety of disputes and conflicts. Witchcraft beliefs however, were not always endorsed by the upper levels of society. They were condemned as superstitious by the Council of Anse in 990 and by Burchard of Worms a few years later; much scepticism continued to be expressed occasionally thereafter, as when John of Salisbury dismissed them as the imaginings of 'a few poor women and ignorant men, with no real faith in God'.[34] When the belief in magical powers begins to be accepted by the privileged it is often found to illustrate not 'popular' supersitition in any general way, but the use of accusations of sorcery in the competition for power which surrounds the thrones of arbitrary rulers. This is particularly likely to happen when there is rivalry between traditional advisers and new aspirants to influence. In the context of the imperial court of the fourth century Peter Brown observed that 'sorcery beliefs may be used like radio-active traces in an X-ray: where they assemble we have a hint of pockets of uncertainty and competition in a society increasingly committed to a vested hierarchy in church and state'.[35] Edward Peters has shown exactly the same forces at work behind the outbreak of bizarre accusations at the Papal, French and English courts around the turn of the thirteenth and fourteenth centuries.[36] As we have just seen, the court of Louis the Pious provides other examples.

Sehok ben Esther's accusation against his former co-religionists would hardly sustain such an interpretation by itself; other

---

[33] Ibid., p. 150; Nithard, *History of the Sons of Louis the Pious*, i. v, trans. Scholz, pp. 135, 203, n. 5.

[34] Mansi, col. 102; John of Salisbury, *Polycraticus*, ii, xvii; Peters, *The Magician, the Witch and the Law*, pp. 71–8.

[35] Brown, 'Sorcery, Demons and the Rise of Christianity', p. 128.

[36] Peters, *The Magician, the Witch and the Law*, pp. 112–35; cf. Cohn, *Europe's Inner Demons*, pp. 180–205.

explanations of that particular episode are easy enough to postulate. Nor would the similar incident at Angoulême in 1028, when a woman was accused of causing the illness of Count William.[37] Though tortured she maintained her innocence, but three others confessed to having conspired with her in the manufacture and use of clay models of him which were found buried in the ground. By themselves even three or four more such episodes would hardly represent an impressive accumulation of Brown's 'radio-active traces'. In conjunction with the long series of intrigues and accusations which culminated (but did not end) in the heresy trial at Orléans in 1022, however, it is not unreasonable to see these sorcery accusations as manifestations of political tension, even though their context is now beyond recovery.

The affair at Orléans, as we have already seen, represented the climax of a long struggle for control of the bishopric of Orléans, in the persons of the rival nominees Thierry and Odalric, between the partisans respectively of Robert the Pious and his latest Queen, Constance, on the one hand, and Count Eudo of Blois on the other. The factions which R.H. Bautier identified at work there had already clashed over other strategic appointments. Robert's nomination of Leger, who remained one of his most constant supporters, to the archbishopric of Sens opened a long struggle with Count Renaud of Sens which ended after the latter's death with the division of his lands between the king and the archbishop; when he was driven from the city by a royal army in 1015 Renaud took refuge at the court of Blois. It is difficult in those circumstances to believe that Fulbert of Chartres' description of him as a heretic, or the general if imprecise allegation that he was a Judaizer, are more than part of the invective generated by these rivalries.[38] It is perhaps even more instructive to notice that Bautier's analysis of this series of interlocking disputes, which arose from the determination of Robert the Pious to secure his position by careful use of ecclesiastical patronage, takes us back to the oath abjuring heresy (of which there is not the slightest reason to suspect him) that was exacted from Gerbert as archbishop of Reims, some time before 999 – especially when we remember that Gerbert was also accused, behind his back, of dabbling in sorcery.

The trial at Arras in 1024 to which we have referred so often provides another very clear and complete illustration of the connec-

---

[37]   Cohn, *Europe's Inner Demons*, pp. 153–4.
[38]   *Letters and Poems of Fulbert of Chartres*, p. 50; Bautier, 'L'héréjsie d'Orléans'.

tion between conflict among the privileged and the pursuit of deviance among the populace at large. The elaborate superstructure which Bishop Gerard erected upon the very simple assertions of the 'heretics' who were brought before him is a fine example of the process which we observed in detail with Thomas of Monmouth and Guibert of Nogent, in which a straightforward and relatively minor expression of grievance or dispute among the unlettered is treated as evidence of a far more sophisticated and elaborate threat that had already been identified by the bishop himself. Furthermore, Georges Duby has placed Gerard's use of the incident in the clearly defined political context of the decline of the French monarchy whose powers Gerard thought were being eroded.[39] That is why he rebutted the heresy of the men of Arras in terms that identified it with the one recently detected and condemned at Orléans, and through it also with the entire series of charges and counter-charges of which the Orléans affair was part.

Together with the attacks on Jews in various parts of France in 1012–15, the arrest and burning in 1028 of heretics in a region over which the Archbishop of Milan intended to extend his authority, and the striking, if in themselves inexplicable circumstances of the curing of a leper at Arras in 1014 by a relic newly translated there by Bishop Gerard and Robert the Pious' going among the lepers at Orléans in 1023, these events must be seen even if they cannot all be easily understood as reflecting in their own ways the strains and dislocations in the social and political structures of the disappearing Carolingian world – as an accumulation of Brown's 'radio-active traces' around 'pockets of uncertainty and competition in a society increasingly committed to a vested hierarchy in church and state'. It is precisely with the consequences of increasing commitment to such a hierarchy that we have associated the growth of the mentalities and mechanisms of persecution during the next two centuries. By the same token both episodes and explanation direct our attention not only to the claimants to power themselves, the kings and bishops, but still more to those who made the claims on their behalf, who competed for power and wealth in their causes and at their courts, and who devised and operated the rationale and the processes of persecution. All the episodes have two points in common almost too obvious to be worth mentioning if they did not point so firmly to the intimacy of these connections. In the first place, their primary forum is the court – of the Count of

[39] Duby, *The Three Orders*, pp. 21–44.

Maine, the Bishop of Cambrai, the King of France – and not the street, the cloister or the popular assembly; and in the second they are preserved very largely in sources which owe both form and content to the political conflicts of which they were part.

Accusations of heresy arose in the eleventh-century West in the context of political rivalry, and they continued to serve similar purposes in various contexts and at various social levels; in the 1160s, for instance, Lambert le Bègue complained that he had been accused of heresy by fellow priests who were afraid that their own slackness and greed would be shown up by his vigorous and successful parochial ministrations, and there is every reason to think that his complaint was justified. But increasingly from the beginning of the twelfth century onwards the suspicion and accusation of heresy among the population at large was used as a means of suppressing resistance to the exercise of power over it, and of legitimizing the new regime in church and state; heightened vigilance for moral and physical health served the same ends. Before the century's end the new regime was in place. It was after 1180, Robert Fossier observes, that the new monarchies came of age; after 1180 that the growth of urban liberties was checked and the peasantry was finally subjected to a still firmer seignurial control; after 1180 that the segregation of the Jews was established.[40] And it was after 1180 that the transition was completed from the use of accusations of heresy and deviance, often arising from genuine social conflict, as an occasional expedient for the consolidation of power to the establishment of regular machinery for their detection and pursuit as one of the foundations upon which power was erected and maintained.

If the general progression is most clearly visible in the area where the institutions of the bureaucratic regime began to take hold soonest, northwestern Europe, it may also be traced, emerging rather more slowly, in the region which became the foyer of persecution par excellence, the Languedoc. The earliest references to heresy in the area are extremely vague, and there is little if anything to suggest that they were accompanied by action. The mission of St Bernard in 1145 was the first occasion upon which opinion was really mobilized to

[40] Fossier, *Enfance de l'Europe*, p. 599; for Duby, too, the last decades of the twelfth century saw the settling of north-western Europe into a new social and political order: see, most recently, *The Three Orders*, pp. 271 ff.

identify the region as being in particular need of attention. The decisive turning point came after Count Raymond V's appeal to the Pope and Philip Augustus in 1177 produced the mission of 1178, which in turn put the Languedoc at the top of the papal agenda. Both missions came at times when the city of Toulouse had taken important steps towards establishing its independence of the Count and his officers, and of crises in his relations with his most turbulent and aggressive vassals, the vicomtes of Béziers. If it is little more than speculation that Bernard's mission involved the declaration of a concerted boycott in Toulouse and that the lands of the vicomtes of Béziers, centred on Albi and Carcassonne, were the main focus of his preaching in the countryside, it is well established that these were the principal targets of the 1178 mission and its successors. In effect it was only after the political objectives of the Albigensian crusade had been secured by the Treaty of Paris in 1228 and the inquisition established in Toulouse in 1233 that the persecution of heresy began to be waged among the population at large.[41]

Such generalizations as these are always rash, and particularly so when scattered and fragmentary sources make them impossible to sustain in detail. They remain worth making not only because they provide a hypothesis whose criticism may improve our understanding of fundamental changes in these centuries which have been taken too much for granted, but because they correspond with the pattern of the great European witch craze a few centuries later. The mass trials at Toulouse and Carcassone which used to be believed to have resulted in some six hundred burnings in the middle of the fourteenth century have been exposed by Norman Cohn as the fabrications of literary forgers many centuries later, and it is now clear thanks to Richard Kieckhefer's careful examination of European witch trials that the earliest of them, from the early fourteenth century onwards, were political and courtly in character.[42] Only gradually during the

---

[41]   Moore, *Origins of European Dissent*, pp. 255–7, and more generally Wakefield, *Heresy, Crusade and Inquisition*.

[42]   Cohn, *Europe's Inner Demons*, pp. 126–46; Kieckhefer, *European Witch Trials*, pp. 10–14, confirmed by Peters, *The Magician, the Witch and the Law*, pp. 112–35. It may be noted that Keickhefer identifies the growing use of the inquisitorial procedure in municipal courts as a major factor in the rapid increase in witchcraft accusations from the later part of the fourteenth century (ibid., pp. 18–19).

fifteenth century did witch hunting begin to be directed against common people as the myth of the satanic cult was elaborated by magistrates and inquisitors. The significance of that pattern was further emphasized by Christina Larner, who found the same progression from courtly intrigue to mass repression in Scotland between the end of the sixteenth century and the middle of the seventeenth.[43]

The Enemy Destroyed

In the early middle ages as in the later, persecution began as a weapon in the competition for political influence, and was turned by the victors into an instrument for consolidating their power over society at large. The history of sodomy accusations, which began to be exchanged in court circles in the eleventh century but did not become a vehicle of general repression until well into the thirteenth, follows the same pattern. Although our knowledge of the cases is far too slight even to suggest making anything of it, it is a notable coincidence that the earliest accusations – and that is how they appear – of leprosy were levelled against important individuals well before anxiety about the general prevalence of the disease was being at all regularly expressed.

One more example will complete our discussion. In his important and unduly neglected exploration of magical beliefs and practices in the middle ages, *The Magician, the Witch and the Law*, Edward Peters showed that accusations of sorcery and willingness to believe in them appear once again as symptoms of the struggle for political power, and especially as the weapons of those who sought to gain it through their personal skills against the occupiers of positions designated by tradition. Such charges were much in evidence at the Carolingian court, especially in the reign of Louis the Pious, when it was said that every important man kept his own astrologer; they crop up again around the beginning of the eleventh century, as we have just noticed, and in the courtly literature of the twelfth; and they figure prominently in a number of sensational intrigues at the English, French and papal courts early in the fourteenth century, and quite regularly thereafter.

Perhaps the most valuable aspect of Peters' study is its demonstration of how the ways in which beliefs in sorcery and magic were

[43] Larner, *Witchcraft and Religion*, pp. 40–4.

revived, revitalized and taken into learned culture contributed vitally
to the evolution of legal principles and procedures, and to the growth
of belief in diabolic intervention in human affairs which helped to
prepare the way for the great witch craze. There are also indications,
however, that they contributed both substantially and directly to the
persecution of the high middle ages which is the subject of this book,
through the association that was made between sorcery and the Jews.
It is one of the successes of the stereotype which the thirteenth
century created of 'the Jew in the medieval world' – indeed it was
the crucial success – that the abject figure which it depicts, dirty,
downtrodden, sinister but contemptible, is not easily imagined as a
contender for political power. But Jews did, in fact, occupy positions
of very great influence at the Carolingian court, sufficient as we have
seen, to ensure that the emperors confirmed and extended the privileges of their people in spite of the vigorous and sustained opposition
of the Christian bishops. In southern Europe Jews continued
to occupy influential positions for much longer. That legendary
Christian hero the Cid had a Jewish treasurer at his court at Valencia
in 1094, and in 1135 Alphonso VII gave the command of the citadel
at Alcantara to Judah ben Ezra; Toulouse had a Jewish consul in 1180,
and his reliance on Jewish officials was one of the accusations against
Raymond VI to justify the Albigensian crusade; at Rome the famous
Pierleoni family had not been converted for many generations when
one of them was elevated to the papacy as Anacletus II in 1131.[44]

Jewish influence in the courts of northern Europe has not been
systematically reviewed, but we have already noticed that instances
of Jews acting as financial agents, and therefore probably general
advisers to kings and nobles are by no means uncommon around the
end of the eleventh century, at the time when stories linking them
with sorcery and the devil were beginning to appear. The allegations
made by Sehok ben Esther at Le Mans and the description of Renaud
of Sens at a Judaizer represent the first two examples of this connection. Similar stories attack Jewish doctors, whose skill was another
source of favour from the great, and therefore of professional jealously and hostility which culminated in the canon of the Council of
Béziers (1246), repeated frequently in the following centuries, forbidding Christians to use Jewish doctors on pain of excommunication.[45]

[44]   Fossier, *Enfance de l'Europe*, pp. 592–3.
[45]   Poliakov, *History of Anti-Semitism*, 1, 149 ff.

This is another example of the generalization of a form of persecution which originated in courtly rivalry. Since the patients of Jewish doctors inluded Alfonso VI of Castile, Henry I of England, Alfonse of Poitiers, and a long line of popes including Alexander III, it is not surprising that twelfth-century legends attributed the deaths of Charlemagne, Charles the Bald and Hugh Capet to their sinister ministrations.

The reason for all this is perfectly obvious, though it is not one which our Christian sources are at all anxious to stress. At least until the end of the twelfth century there can be no doubt that the Jews of Europe were culturally far superior to their Christian counterparts. Their twelfth-century renaissance was no less successful than the Christian movement which is generally described by that phrase in achieving a florescence of religious studies and stimulating the work of venerated philosophers and scholars of abiding influence. But that relatively familiar fact almost distracts our attention from the much more significant ones that the Jews had disposed of such learning for far longer and more continuously than Christians, that they had maintained a widespread and coherent educational structure from a far earlier date, and that in consequence the skills of literacy and numeracy were far more widely diffused among Jews than among Christians.[46] Charlemagne's inspiration (who would dare to suggest imitation?)which saved literacy for the West by making diocesan bishops responsible for the provision of elementary education in their churches had long been practiced in the synagogues, and continued to be, not only in the greatest centres but wherever Jewish communities were to be found. From twelfth-century Normandy, for example, Hebrew manuscripts attesting a lively religious and literary culture can be associated not only with Rouen but with places like Caen, Pont-Audemer, Falaise and Evreux.[47] By this time the larger communities added to the general provision for elementary education in the synagogues separate centres of advanced study and teaching; the one at Rouen has been identified, as a building comparable with the synagogue (which it stood oppo-

[46] For a general account of Jewish educational institutions in early medieval Europe see A. Grabois, 'Ecoles et structures socials des communautés juives dans l'occident aux IXe–XIIe siècles', in Gli ebrei nell'alto medioevo, ii, 937–62.
[47] N. Golb, 'Les Juifs de Normandie à l'époque d'Anselme', pp. 149–57.

site) in substance and grandeur.[48] One of Abelard's pupils described the result in these terms:

> If the Christians educate their sons, they do so not for God, but for gain, in order that the one brother, if he be a clerk, may help his father and his mother and his other brothers . . . But the Jews, out of zeal for God and love of the law, put as many sons as they have to letters, that each may understand God's law . . . A Jew, however poor, if he had ten sons would put them all to letters, not for gain, as the Christians do, but for the understanding of God's law, and not only his sons, but his daughters.[49]

As so often in these pages we have reached a point where speculation outruns present knowledge. A good deal could probably be added by patient collection from the Christian sources, and still more by their integration with the rich Hebrew sources of the twelfth century which remains manifestly imperfect in contemporary scholarship. Nevertheless, it is hard to evade the conclusion that the urgent and compelling reason for the persecution of Jews at this time – a persecution, as we have seen, which reversed the previous and well-established tendency to integration between the two cultures – was that they offered a real alternative, and therefore a real challenge, to Christian *literati* as the advisers of princes and the agents and beneficiaries of bureaucratic power. The papal court itself was using Jewish advisers in the eleventh century, and the papal household continued to be managed by Jews throughout the twelfth.[50]

In contemplating this possibility, which runs so strongly counter at least to gentile presuppositions about the nature of early medieval society, it is necessary once again to remember how revolutionary were the times with which we are concerned. In the middle of the ninth century Bishop Amolo of Lyons said that Jews won more converts than Christians because the rabbis preached so much better than Catholic priests.[51] Conversions to Judaism continued to occur well into the eleventh century; their cessation is another indication

---

[48] C. Varoqueaux, 'Découverte de vestiges médiévaux à Rouen'.
[49] Quoted by Chazan, *Medieval Jewry*, p. 52, from Smalley, *The Study of the Bible in the Middle Ages*, p. 78.
[50] Boswell, *Christianity, Social Tolerance and Homosexuality*, p. 274, citing Synan, *The Popes and the Jews in the Middle Ages*, pp. 79–80.
[51] Wallace-Hadrill, The *Frankish Church*, p. 401.

of the turn of the tide of intolerance rather than of any great improvement of the Church's power to outface the intellectual attractions of Judaism. And up to the eleventh century and beyond the comment of J. M. Wallace-Hadrill on Amolo's words remains applicable: 'It is only when we grasp how frail was the hold of organized Christianity and how various its practices that the reaction to Judaism makes sense.'[52] The religious reforms of the twelfth century, its intellectual renaissance, its elaboration of the procedures of law and government, represent in sum not only the establishment of a new regime, the transition from a segmentary to a state society of which we have made so much, but with it the imposition of a high culture, defining, uniting and perpetuating a dominant elite across the breadth of Latin Christendom. As always, the establishment of the high culture demanded the ruthless elimination of its actual and potential rivals. And of these the greatest was Judaism.

This leads us to a final and ironic twist in the tortuous path of the persecuting mentality. For, of course, that paragraph might have been expected to conclude, as its counterparts have done so often in the exposition of the history of Christian Europe, that 'the greatest of these was heresy.' From the moment of its appearance the intellectual sophistication and doctrinal coherence of popular heresy were greatly exaggerated by Catholic observers. Such attempts as popular preachers or enthusiastic priests made to give their followers direct access to the scriptures were quickly suppressed. From the middle of the twelfth century onwards the Cathar sects were inflated by commentators and inquisitors into a vast and well-coordinated international organization with a culture, a theology and even a pope of its own. The promulgation of these myths justified and encouraged persecution. But in the last analysis they could be promulgated quite safely precisely because they were not true. The Cathar churches simply did not possess the weight and power, historical, intellectual or organizational, to replace the Catholic church, though they might have inflicted a good deal of damage on it. Neither, in the high middle ages or for a long time to come, did the heresies which were native to Western Europe. Even the Waldensian, the greatest of them, amounted in reality to no more than a few scattered, insubstantial and even unrelated sects which owed most of their apparent coher-

[52] Ibid., p. 403.

ence of teaching and organization to the preconceptions and writings of the inquisitors themselves.[53]

What was false of the heresies was in all essential respects true of the Jews. They made no conspiracy, and had no political organization, certainly, but they did possess an ancient culture and religion, and truly formidable social and intellectual coherence. They would have been fully capable of taking the place to which the clerks aspired as the brains and muscles of the bureaucratic regime. That was a truth too dangerous for propaganda. On the contrary, it must be concealed as completely as possible. Christians stole the property of Jews, and murdered their children, desecrated their holy places and demanded their conversion by force, and therefore invented a mythology which owed its plausibility to the nightmare that one day the Jews might do as they were used to being done by. Equally, and for the same reasons, since Jews were in fact better educated, more cultivated and more skilful than their Christian counterparts legend must reduce them below the level of common humanity, filthy in their persons and debased in their passions, menacing Christian society from below, requiring the help of the powers of darkness to work evil far beyond their own contemptible capacities. For all those who were to be persecuted, we have seen, it was necessary first to create an identity. In the case of the Jews it was even more necessary to destroy one. In that respect as in others the persecuting society began as it would continue.

---

[53] Merlo, *Valdesi e valdismi medievali*, especially pp. 8–25.

CHAPTER 5

A PERSECUTING SOCIETY

The main argument of *The Formation of a Persecuting Society* was, and is, that the persecutions of heretics, Jews, lepers, sodomites and others in twelfth- and thirteenth-century Europe cannot be considered or explained independently of one another, as they almost always had been hitherto. The coincidences are simply too many to be credible. Whether we consider the chronology, the geography, the procedures of the persecutions, or the vocabulary and mentalities of the persecutors, the same patterns appear in every case. It follows that particular persecutions cannot be understood simply as a series of independent responses to real or imagined dangers. Nor can they be accounted for by the character, beliefs or behaviour of the victims. On the contrary, character, beliefs and behaviour could be, and if necessary were, invented – whether consciously or not – to facilitate persecution. Conversely, individual persecutions must be regarded as particular manifestations of a more general development or developments, and an explanation of them sought by reference to the persecutors, who unlike the victims were the same, broadly speaking, in almost every case, and to society itself.

Formation identified and offered for debate just such a general development, in the emergence of a new class of functionaries – clerics and courtiers – for whom persecution might serve the twin purposes of providing the means to extend the power and advance the interests of their masters, while consolidating their own position and undermining potential rivals. The systematic persecution of minorities in European history had its origin in the interests and concerns of this body of people, and not in the unregulated passions or prejudices of the population at large. It was they who identified and proclaimed the dangers with which the various groups of victims were held to threaten Christian society in the twelfth and thirteenth centuries, and they who prescribed the remedies; they who moulded the mentalities and devised the procedures which ensured that these patterns of persecution would endure in European society not just for the remainder of the middle ages, but until our own times.

It is necessary to insist that it does not follow, and was not claimed, that this amounted to a complete or sufficient explanation of every – or indeed any – episode or form of persecution in later centuries. I did not argue that, in the words of one of my most incisive critics, David Nirenberg, 'after its birth the persecuting mentality seems to transcend particularities of time and place'.[1] On the contrary, I wholly agree with him that such an assumption, by obliterating differences between particular groups of victims and the contexts and circumstances of their persecution, would greatly impoverish historical inquiry and understanding.[2] If anything in this book appears to suggest that it is in some way unnecessary or supererogatory to investigate every historical event with the close and sensitive attention to all its particularities – environmental, social, cultural, temporal, and so on – which Nirenberg's work exemplifies so well, either my prose or the reader's construction of it is at fault. What I did suggest, and hope to make more clear in this new chapter, is that part of the context of persecution in Europe since the twelfth century has been a rhetoric and a set of assumptions and procedures which made persecution both more likely to happen than it would have been otherwise, and when it happened likely to be more severe and sustained for longer. This was not necessarily or even usually true of the inter-communal and intra-communal violence which is Nirenberg's subject. And, it should be unnecessary to add, it was not equally true in every part of Europe, or at every subsequent moment in European history: intelligent historical discourse sometimes requires generalisation, and intelligent readers understand that generalisation is always qualified, implicitly if not explicitly.

[1]   Nirenberg, *Communities of Violence*, p. 5.
[2]   Ibid., pp. 242–3. It is fair to add, however, that since my concern was with persecution, and not with violence as such, the inadequacy of my model to explain the latter is neither surprising nor culpable. Also, that Nirenberg's brilliant account and analysis of the Jew-striking ritual (pp. 200–30) wholly supersedes mine (above, pp. 30–31).

It should also be emphasised at the outset that I did not identify either the persecutors themselves or the culture which produced them with the Church, as many commentators have supposed.[3] On the contrary, I argued throughout that the growth of secular power, and the pursuit of secular interests, constituted the essential context of the developments which are the subject of this book.[4] In the period with which we are concerned, notoriously, the government of the Church in western Europe was radically centralised, the aggrandisement of the Roman papacy in many ways (but not in all) mirrored that of the secular polities, and the 'papal monarchy' came to resemble its secular counterparts in its conduct, outlook and objectives a great deal more closely than many contemporary churchmen and women approved. How far the Church led these developments in general is a subject of perennial historical debate much wider than that conducted in these pages. As I shall argue further below, it played a significant role in the formation of the persecuting society, but not the leading one. However, the responsibility for making my meaning clear was mine alone. Apart from ordinary limitations of style and thought it was imperfectly discharged in this case because the idea of a persecuting society itself was, in 1987, a new one for me almost as much as for anybody else, and I had only begun to think through its meaning and implications. This chapter attempts to do so further, and, accepting that the phrase 'persecuting society' has become widely used, to consider a little more fully what it may legitimately suggest about the Europe of the twelfth and thirteenth centuries, and thereafter.

As far as it goes, and as far as I know, the first of my conclusions has not been seriously challenged in principle. That is to say, it has not been argued that the persecutions of heretics, Jews and many others were entirely independent of one another, or of wider developments in society and government. The second is more controversial, and more complex. The role of the literati is widely agreed to have been central. But important questions remain, especially about the extent to which 'bottom-up' as opposed to 'top-down' influences contributed to the growth of persecution, and about whether the literati can be treated as a single class, and if so how it should be

---

[3]   Including, for example, as careful and fairminded a scholar as John Van Engen, 'The future of medieval church history'.

[4]   E.g. above, pp. 37–42, 100–6, 127–32, etc.

defined. Many of the details of the argument, and of the implications asserted by me or others, of course, have been controversial and vigorously contested: the thesis would have been distressingly sterile if they had not been. Some of these issues are discussed in the Bibliographical Excursus to this edition.

To conclude, as I did in Chapter 2, that the silence of the sources about persecution before AD 1000 was the result of a real absence and not merely a defect of record is not to suggest that nobody was ever persecuted until after the millennium. That would be absurd as well as false. Rather, it suggests a distinction similar to the one which historians of slavery make between 'a slave society' and 'a society with slaves'.[5] The latter phrase implies simply the presence of slavery, irrespective of its scale and consequences. There have been many societies with slaves in human history, and in many of them slavery has been of minor importance, except from a purely moral point of view. But a slave society is something else altogether, one in which slavery is an essential feature, in the sense that fundamental necessities depend on it, directly and indirectly, and therefore society and culture as a whole are profoundly and pervasively affected by its presence and indispensability.[6] It would be impossible to imagine the Roman Empire or the ante-bellum South without slavery without immediately beginning to imagine also a series of other and profound differences in their organisation, *mores* and way of life. By this criterion it is generally agreed that there have been only a handful of slave societies in recorded history. This is not a matter of the number or proportion of slaves so much as, in the first place, of their role in the economy. Thus, most of those who use this terminology would not regard the Mamluk or Ottoman empires as slave societies, in spite of the militarily and politically significant role which was played

[5] Moore, 'A la naissance d'une société persécutrice'. Much of this paper is incorporated in the present chapter.

[6] 'A society in which slaves play an important part in production and form a high proportion of the population': Hopkins, *Conquerors and Slaves*, pp. 199–201, with references to an extensive literature. The implication of my analogy is not, of course, that persecution played a direct part in the productive process, but that 'there was enough of it about for it to be, of necessity, an integral factor in the society' (Finley, *Economy and Society in Ancient Greece*, p. 103). See more fully Turley, *Slavery*, pp. 4–5 and Chapter 3, 'Societies with Slaves and Slave Societies', especially at pp. 76–83.

in them by 'slaves on horseback'. As their personal circumstances and standing confirm, these were slaves in name only: their theoretical status was not essential to their actual role, and had in itself no important repercussions for other institutions and their workings. A slave society *needs* slaves, and it needs them to *be* slaves, in fact as well as in name. The perception that has driven this book since its inception has been the sense that somehow, for reasons which it seemed important to identify and understand, twelfth-century Europe – that is, of course, somebody or something in twelfth-century Europe – *needed* persecution, to the extent of expending much ingenuity and anguish to bring it about, though not necessarily (it is important to insist) with conscious intent.[7]

Most complex traditional societies, including at least some of those of early medieval Europe, were societies with persecution. There was nothing unusual in the principle of maintaining by force the dominance of the prevailing religion and culture. In China the persecution of heresy was a duty enjoined upon imperial authorities from very early times, though in practice enforced only occasionally, when a religious activity was perceived as a direct political threat. The persecution of Buddhism under the Tang dynasty, in the ninth century, is probably the best known example.[8] The persecution of both Christians and Jews in the Roman Empire was both intermittent and directly dependent on the political circumstances of the moment. In the Byzantine Empire, by and large, the long tale of conflict between imperial or ecclesiastical authority and the innumerable heresies generated by exuberant theological disputation seldom descended into sustained persecution. Even the reaction of the Emperor Alexius Comnenus to the discovery of Bogomils in Constantinople, *c*.1110, generally treated as one of the more severe episodes of persecution in Byzantine history, was mild by western

[7]   On this point I seem inadvertently to have misled, for example, Lipton, *Images of Intolerance,* p. 140, to whom my argument implied 'a conscious technique on the part of clerical or governmental elites for securing hegemony'; similarly Chazan, *Stereotypes,* p. 94: I intended rather to suggest something akin to the 'unconscious or semiconscious result of changes in how information was processed and disseminated' which Lipton not only expresses better than I had done but, in respect of the representation of Jews in the thirteenth century, traces with great insight.

[8]   Weber, *Religion of China,* pp. 213–19; Gernet, *History of Chinese Civilization,* pp. 294–6.

standards: only the leader was put to death. Bogomilism continued to be regarded as a dangerous heresy until the fall of Constantinople, but the measures taken against it were almost invariably spiritual and disciplinary.[9] Byzantine Jews were heirs to the same legacy of patristic obloquy and imperial legislation as their western counterparts. If that were enough to account for persecution they should have suffered during the early medieval centuries in proportion to the greater continuity and sophistication of the regime. This does not appear to have been the case. Jews and Jewish communities were always vulnerable to random and sometimes considerable ill treatment, and occasionally to persecution, as when under the Emperor Heraclius (610–41) or Basil I (867–86) a programme of forced conversion might serve a political purpose. Nevertheless, the legal status of Jews, though inferior, was not insecure, and they were subject to extra but not usually to arbitrary taxation.[10] These disabilities were not negligible, but neither were they sufficiently general or prolonged to alter the conditions of Jewish life fundamentally, or to undermine the relative political and economic well-being of Byzantine Jewry as sustained cultural, fiscal and physical persecution did to its western counterpart in the high middle ages.

In the absence of an ecclesiastical structure there could be no precise equivalent in medieval Islam to the Catholic conception of heresy. On the whole, respect for the prophet and observation of the essential obligations of the faithful were sufficient. As al-Ash'ari (d. 935–6) put it, 'I do not consider any who pray towards Mecca as infidels.'[11] As in the Christian west, it was not holding heterodox opinion that called for action, but disseminating it. 'Someone who makes propaganda for his view and leads people astray by his error must be stopped from doing this by whatever means', says Abu Bakr

[9] Obolensky, *The Bogomils*, pp. 197–205; Browning, 'Enlightenment and Repression'; Angold, *Church and Society*, pp. 468–501. Cf. Magdalino, 'Enlightenment and Repression'. Magdalino, to whom I am grateful for a copy and discussion of his paper, agrees that Byzantium did not become a persecuting society in the sense of this argument, but (p. 370) 'repression was on the increase, and it was a function of the professionalism of the sacerdotal clergy as they sought to gain, and retain, control of spiritual reform in the Church of Constantinople'.
[10] Starr, *Jews in the Byzantine Empire*; Sharf, *Byzantine Jewry*; Cameron, 'Byzantines and Jews'.
[11] Lewis, 'The Significance of Heresy in Islam'.

al Razi in the fourteenth century.[12] Consequently, in the Islamic world accusations of heresy might provide the occasion of conflict between rival schools of teachers or sufis, and sometimes the medium through which they competed for popular support. This may, as is often asserted, have smothered the intellectual creativity which had characterised the Islamic Golden Age of the ninth and tenth centuries, but it did not produce religious uniformity comparable with that of Latin Christendom in the high middle ages, or prevent the florescence of numerous traditions and sects, some of which were both widely diffused and long-lived. In principle, Christians and Jews were subject to restrictions similar to those which Roman law had imposed upon Jews, relating to the wearing of distinctively coloured clothing, exclusion from public office, prohibition of the public celebration of their rites at times or in ways which might be offensive to Muslims, and so on. The enforcement or reinforcement of such regulations occasionally provided the opportunity for a new or embattled ruler to display his piety and vigour, or for an impecunious one to replenish his coffers by taking fines to enforce and bribes to relax them, as the French and English kings did in the thirteenth century. Thus the Abbasid Caliph al-Mutawakkil (847–61).

> gave orders that Christians and dhimmis in general be required to wear honey-coloured hoods and girdles, to ride on saddles with wooden stirrups and two balls attached to the rear...gave orders to destroy any churches which were newly built and to take the tenth part of their houses...forbade their employment in government offices and on official business when they would have authority over Moslems...(and) forbade the display of crosses on their Palm Sundays, and of Jewish rites in the streets.[13]

Sustained comparison, as conducted by Mark R. Cohen, suggests that this was not simply a negative matter. Beyond the absence in Islamic society of many of the elements which combined to form the persecuting society in Latin Europe, Jews were protected from

---

[12] Abu Bakr al-Razi, *Ahkam al'Qur'an* (Istanbul, 1335–8), vol. 2, pp. 35–6. I owe this reference and translation to the kindness of Michael Cook.

[13] Cf. Lewis, *Jews of Islam*, pp. 3–67, quoted at pp. 48–9.

systematic persecution, in the period embraced by the present discussion, by the fact that, like other minorities, they were much less sharply segregated than they became in Europe from the social, economic and cultural patterns of wider society: though often in various degrees marginalized, they were not excluded. Conversely, William C. Jordan has pointed to the absence of such cross-cutting ties as a source of vulnerability for French Jews.[14]

In short, when particular instances are compared it appears that the occasions and the manner of persecution in Islamic society, and indeed in complex traditional societies in general, were likely to be much the same as in Latin Christendom. A well-documented example is provided by the great sorcery scare which swept China in 1768, when waves of persecution reminiscent of those of the European witch craze in the seventeenth century, directed against wandering sorcerers who might surreptitiously cut off one's pigtail, thus stealing one's soul, turn out to have been orchestrated by the Emperor himself, as a means of shaking up his civil service.[15] It would be tedious to continue: the point is obvious. But it is scarcely less obvious that, viewed over the long term, these persecutions were not part of a continuous and developing process of the kind that may be observed in European history. Persecution was not generally sustained against a particular religious or ethnic minority long after it had ceased to be capable of offering either political danger or substantial booty.

Perhaps more important, though the lack of comparative study and material must heavily qualify any suggestion of this kind, it does not appear that the variety of the victims of persecution was so great in other civilizations as it has become in the Latin west since the twelfth century. Nor, and this is perhaps the crucial point, does it seem that other civilizations evolved to such perfection the essential mechanism which made this continuous growth possible: the construction of a rhetoric and apparatus of persecution capable of being turned at will from one category of victims to another, including if necessary those invented for the purpose. This is what made the victims of persecution in the west for all practical purposes freely

[14]   Cohen, *Under Crescent and Cross*; Jordan, *French Monarchy and the Jews*, pp. 14–20.
[15]   Kuhn, *Soulstealers*.

interchangeable with one another,[16] and persecution itself a permanent and omnipresent feature of the social fabric, continuously expanding the range and scope of its activities.

The example of leprosy may clarify this point. Neither the characterisation of leprosy as divine retribution for breaches of the moral law nor the segregation of lepers as a sanitary measure was in itself peculiar to the western tradition, or indeed particularly unusual. Medieval Islam derived both its diagnosis and its treatments of leprosy from the same Galenic sources as western doctors did theirs, and isolation was practised certainly in some and probably in all parts of the Islamic world. Nevertheless, as Michael Dols showed, segregation was far less rigorous, and did not have the punitive aspect which was so cruelly apparent in the thirteenth-century west. 'The leper was segregated but not stigmatized', he said, making a distinction overlooked by several reviewers who objected to my inclusion of lepers among the persecuted of the medieval west. 'We do not find…any governmental regulation of lepers, any ritual for separating the leper from the community, any distinguishing costumes, or any communal persecution of the afflicted.'[17] Nor did he find the deprivation of legal and civil rights, including the rights of property, which by any test must be counted among the most fundamental acts of persecution. Scarcely less pertinent is the lack of stereotyping in Islam comparable to the western characterization of lepers as bad-tempered and over-sexed, and the absence of the leper as a stock character from Arabic, Persian and Turkish literature.[18] Since the function of such stereotypes was to assimilate the various categories of the persecuted to one another, suggesting that in the end they were simply different manifestations of the same essential menace, they provided an indispensable mechanism for transmitting, as it were,

[16] Chazan, *Stereotypes*, p. 83, says that Jews 'were not in fact perceived by their neighbours in precisely the same way as heretics, lepers and homosexuals' in the late twelfth century. I am quite sure he is right. My point, however, is that making them *rhetorically* identical placed them in the same category and created a rationale for their being treated accordingly by public authorities. How far this process influenced, or was influenced by, popular attitudes is another question, which is discussed below, pp. 178–80.

[17] 'The Leper in Medieval Islamic Society'; at pp. 914, 916. Cf. below, pp. 181–4.

[18] Ibid., pp. 912–13.

the virus of persecution from one time, place or set of victims to the next. For these reasons, and even though important new research on leprosy and leper hospitals in France and England suggests that much of the work on which I drew in 1987 exaggerated the harshness of prevailing attitudes to the disease[19] – or, perhaps, the extent to which the harshest attitudes prevailed – it remains appropriate to give those who suffered from it a place in this argument. Even if 'persecution' seems a simplistic description of their treatment, much both of its substance and of the attitudes associated with it was drawn from, and contributed to, the repertoire of techniques, institutions and ideas which constituted the persecuting society.

The lack of relevant comparative investigation makes it difficult to press this point about the exceptional creativity of the west in discovering victims for persecution very much further. Nevertheless, the case of lepers brings out what is also true of both heretics and Jews, though not to an easily measurable extent, namely the degree to which the identity of the victim was socially constructed, and persecution justified, or rationalised, largely in terms of the constructed persona. The point is even more clear when we consider the construction of sexual identities, and particularly in our period that of the male homosexual, and of the prostitute, who is the subject of an increasing though still insufficient literature.[20]

In short, we are presented with a contrast between two patterns of persecution. In the first, characteristic of agrarian bureaucracies in general, including those of classical and late antiquity in the west, persecution may be extremely savage, and is often trumped up for the sake of political advantage of one kind or another, or to increase the power of the centre over local communities. Nevertheless, while particular campaigns sometimes continue for many years,

[19] See especially Rawcliffe, *Leprosy in Medieval England*, forthcoming; below, pp. 181–4.
[20] Otis, *Prostitution*; Rossiaud, *La prostitution*. Both of these excellent studies, however, are based on record sources of the period since the thirteenth century. We still lack a full examination of the vocabulary and what evidence there is of the activity of prostitution during the emergence of urban society and the establishment of the cash economy. Though, as Christopher Brooke comments (*Europe in the Central Middle Ages*, p. 399), prostitutes have been simultaneously vilified and exalted in many societies, the chronology and extent of their assimilation into the broader pattern of persecution in Europe remain worth tracing.

persecution itself is occasional and intermittent. It ebbs and flows according (very generally) to the energy of rulers and to the variety and intensity of conflicts in which it has a role to play. In the second, which so far as I can see is uniquely European (at least until the twentieth century), a single set of mentalities (including, almost invariably, the demonisation of the accused) and mechanisms (including, almost invariably, inquisition, of which more below) has ensured, first, that in all the great persecutions from the Albigensian crusade to the present day each series of arrests, accusations and trials would itself provide the basis for the next, in an ever-widening circle of denunciations and confessions; and second, that as each particular persecution has run its course there have been others to replace it, so that while the victims have changed persecution itself has proceeded down the centuries, constantly expanding both the number and the variety of its objects.

This is why the persecution which developed in the twelfth and thirteenth centuries was a very much more serious matter than the occasional outbreaks of earlier periods. Europe has never been free of it since. There have been periods of greater and lesser intensity, of course, and great differences between different parts of Europe both in the groups that have fallen victim to persecution from time to time, and in the nature and extent of the protections that have been afforded against it. That is not a reason to conclude with the late Bob Scribner (1996: 43) that 'if the trajectories of several forms of intolerance were analysed and mapped in a comparative manner [at a local level] I suspect that it would become clear that sixteenth century society was not a persecuting society at all (nor, perhaps, when approached in the same manner were the middle ages or the modern period)'. The point seems equally applicable to any general characterisation of any society. I therefore take it as a methodological observation rather than as a specific objection to my model, which Scribner applied very fruitfully in this essay to show how many new groups – beggars, gypsies, spendthrifts, discharged soldiers and others – were made vulnerable in sixteenth-century Germany by being classified as outside the sacral community. It was the constant and universal availability of the mechanisms of persecution, not their constant and universal use, that was crucial.

The modern state has acquired a capacity to persecute beyond the dreams of the most ambitious medieval ruler, while industrial society has added new and dreadful forms of it, rooted in sources of conflict at communal levels which were not present in medieval society.[21] The present argument does not depend in any way on hypotheses about the continuity of ideas, either about the justification for or necessity of persecution itself, or about any of the victimised groups. It does not, for example, make any assumption as to the 'continuity' – or otherwise – of theories of religious coercion, or between 'medieval' and 'modern' anti-semitism. On the contrary, persecution in Europe has not required or depended on such continuities precisely because the patterns, procedures and rhetoric of persecution which were established in the twelfth century have given it the power of infinite and indefinite self-generation and self-renewal. The variety of the victims has been added to in every subsequent century (even during the Enlightenment the history of Freemasonry provides a textbook example of the process[22]), and their numbers have increased in most, both absolutely and proportionately. The exceptional character of persecution in the Latin west since the twelfth century has lain not in the scale or savagery of particular persecutions, or in the invention of accusations and whipping up of anxieties to suit the political needs or social jealousies of the accusers, but in its capacity for sustained long-term growth, though with occasional short-term and usually localised recession. I use the language of economics quite deliber-ately. The history of persecution exemplifies western dynamism with great vividness, though historians of that phenomenon generally prefer more comfortable examples. A quantitative tally of its victims, if such a thing were possible, would unquestionably show a rate and continuity of growth over the long term that would easily match any other index.

It is not asserted that all the characteristics of what might be called the European model of persecution were clearly present, let alone

[21]   It is hardly necessary to add that this comment does not deny the pres-ence or savagery of many sources of communal conflict in medieval society, such as those so movingly described by David Nirenberg in *Communities of Violence*. It would be superfluous to attempt a bibliography on the ques-tion why, nevertheless, industrial society has turned out to be *structurally* far more prone than traditional societies to generate such conflict – beginning, perhaps, with Arendt, *Origins of Totalitarianism* – but the observations of Gellner, *Nations and Nationalism*, especially at pp. 8–14, 61–87, are particularly pertinent.
[22]   Roberts, *Secret Societies*; note especially the observations on 'Histori-ans and Secret Societies' at pp. 23–31.

complete, with the upswing which is visible from just after the millennium. If the previous pattern had persisted the trend might have been expected to recede again, and indeed a case could be made that it did so for a time after 1100 or thereabouts. In the later decades of the twelfth century, however, the essential elements fall into place, and Europe can be seen as a persecuting society, rather than simply a society with persecution. The point may be illustrated, and much of the argument recapitulated, through a close examination of a single episode which in several respects marked a new, and, as it turned out, a durable ferocity on the part of authority towards heresy, or the allegation of heresy.

The twenty-first chapter of Henry II's Assize of Clarendon (1166) forbade 'anyone in all England to receive in his house or in his land or in a district under his jurisdiction anyone of that sect who were branded and excommunicated at Oxford...And if anyone shall so receive them he shall be at the mercy of the lord king, and the house in which they have dwelt shall be carried outside the village and burned.'[23] This chapter is famous as the first secular legislation against heresy in the west since antiquity, and the forerunner of a series of similar acts by other European monarchs in the following decades. The heretics to whom it referred were the 'rather more than thirty *Populicani*' who, in William of Newburgh's detailed narrative, had been examined by an episcopal synod towards the end of 1165, and handed for punishment to the secular arm. At the king's command they were 'branded on their foreheads...their leader receiving the ignominy of a double branding, on forehead and chin, as a badge of his pre-eminence. Their clothes were cut off as far as their belts, and they were driven from the city with ringing blows into the intolerable cold. Nobody showed the slightest mercy towards them, and they died in misery.'[24]

In its anti-sacramental and anti-sacerdotal character, and in the humble social standing of its members, 'simple and illiterate people, quite uncultivated rustics' (except for their leader, Gerard, who 'seemed to have some degree of learning'), this heresy was typical of many which had appeared in north-western Europe during the past

[23]   Stubbs, *Select Charters*, p. 176.
[24]   William of Newburgh, ed. Howlett, I, 131–4. For reference to other sources and discussion see Whitelock et al., *Councils and Synods* I, pt. II, 920–2.

century and a half. It was, on the other hand, quite untypical of those which reached a surviving record both in the feebleness of its efforts at evangelism, which netted one old woman who repudiated the sect the moment it was detected, and in the severity of the response it suffered. In the eleventh century those who were executed as heretics – at Orléans in 1022, Milan in 1028 and (most probably) Goslar in 1051– had been members of the nobility and higher clergy caught up in political conflicts within the elite.[25] Humble people, in the cases we know, were dealt with calmly and with restraint by the bishops. Those interrogated by Bishop Gerard of Cambrai at Arras in 1024/5, for example, confessed in effect to two of the most dangerous of ancient heresies, Donatism and Pelagianism. It is almost as revealing that Gerard did not use either word (and did not call them Arians or Manichaeans) as that he released them after requiring no more than that they should listen to a long sermon and subscribe a confession of faith: that is, he did not assert, either in interpretation of what they said or for rhetorical effect, that these people represented a resurgence of one of the great heresies of antiquity. Even by the 1140s, though executions like the burnings at Soissons in 1115, Liège in 1135 and 1145, Cologne in 1141, and Reims in 1148 were becoming more frequent, they were still confined to the leaders, to those who preached or were thought to preach heresy and sometimes violence against the church, its priests and property. In this respect the events of the 1160s betray a new and portentous development, reflected in the disquiet which was widely felt when in 1163 a young girl who refused to renounce her sect was burned at Cologne along with four adult men.[26] Although no blood was shed and no fire was lit, what William of Newburgh described as happening at Oxford in 1165 was the first mass execution of ordinary people on charges of heresy in the history of modern Europe.

The people who were burned at Cologne had been arrested after their failure to go to church on Sundays aroused the curiosity of their neighbours. In England Gerard and his followers 'could not hide for long, for they were tracked down by men anxious to know to what foreign sect they belonged'.[27] In contrast to the great heretical preachers of the previous generation, these groups had not forced

[25] Above, pp. 13–18.
[26] Simons, *Cities of Ladies*, pp. 22–3.
[27] *Chronica regia Coloniensis* ed. Waitz, p. 114.

themselves upon the attention of the authorities either by the violence of their anticlericalism, in rhetoric or in practice, or by the success of their evangelism. They fell foul of a new spirit, proclaimed by the Councils of Reims in 1157 and Tours in 1163, which maintained that heretics were lurking hidden among the people, and demanded that they and those who were suspected of supporting them should be denounced and subjected to severe penalties. In this we see not only a foreboding of the inquisition but, more generally, the transition on the part of authority from a reactive to an initiatory role.

The argument of this book has turned upon the distinction between a conception of justice which confines it to a passive role, mediating conflict between individuals and groups, avenging injuries and resolving disputes which are reported to it and so on, and an active, institution-building authority which seeks out offences on the assumption that they must have been committed, and which invents crimes, such as blasphemy, fornication or treason, which are offences not against identifiable individuals but against the system of law itself and the authority and values which it claims to uphold.[28] That distinction is clearly visible in the persecution of heresy. During the first century or so after the reappearance of popular heresy in the west isolated incidents – a pious conventicle here, a sermon against clerical avarice there – were identified as heretical and reported to the bishop, who could do little but confront the accused and, if he found them guilty, expel them from the diocese or hand them – in many cases, it seems, with genuine reluctance – to the secular power for punishment. King Henry II did not wait for the bishops to seek his help in that way: after the heretics had been arrested he 'was unwilling either to release or to punish them without discussion, and ordered an episcopal synod to meet at Oxford'.

According to William of Newburgh, writing some thirty years after the event, these heretics 'were believed to belong to the sect known as *Populicani*, who undoubtedly originated in Germany from an unknown founder, and who have spread the poison of their wickedness through many lands. Indeed so many are said to have been infected by this plague throughout France, Spain, Germany and Italy that they seem, as the prophet says, "to have multiplied beyond number".' His language is reminiscent of that of the Council of Tours (1163), which had spoken of a heresy 'that having emerged in

[28]   Above, pp. 102–4.

Toulouse spreads like a cancer to neighbouring regions and has now infected Gascony and many other provinces'.[29] Whatever the historical accuracy of those assertions the Council's tone was distinctly more melodramatic than that of most earlier reports. In particular, it based papal policy firmly on what over the centuries would become the familiar premise of the persecutor. Any public activity of heretics, irrespective of their number, demeanour or teachings, demonstrated the existence of a malignant and diabolically inspired universal conspiracy of which they were part. If, on the other hand, heretics did not openly proclaim their presence it was not because they did not exist, but because they were cunningly concealed by numerous and probably influential supporters, which made it all the more urgent to expose and extirpate them.

This mentality, though not entirely new, had not been general until now. The disposition of modern scholarship to describe all the simple and, for the most part, modest dissidents of the eleventh and early twelfth centuries as part of a single heresy is a historiographical inheritance from the inquisitors. It was not widely shared by strictly contemporary observers, most of whom showed little inclination either to regard the heretics they encountered with undue alarm, or to see them as part of a universal plot or conspiracy.[30] Gerard of Cambrai had erected a mighty rhetorical edifice upon the limited (though certainly radical) assertions brought to his attention in 1024/5, but was content to let those who had avowed them go free with a simple affirmation of faith; it was the *capitanei* of Milan, not Archbishop Aribert, who had insisted on burning the neoplatonists whom Aribert found at Monforte in 1028; and Wazo of Liège had been confident not only that it would be wrong, but that it was unnecessary to deal severely with the sectaries who had turned up in the diocese of Châlons-sur-Marne (1043–8). Even in the first half of the twelfth century, when the ability of Tanchelm, Henry of Lausanne, Peter of Bruys, Arnold of Brescia and perhaps Eon de l'étoile to excite large crowds up to or beyond the point of violence gave real grounds for alarm to the established authorities, the surviving reactions show little inclination to assimilate these preachers to any general or diabolic conspiracy. When the first reports of heretics from outside the Latin world begin to appear, in the 1140s and 1150s,

---

[29] Mansi XXI, col. 1177.
[30] Moore, 'The War against Heresy'.

their claims to be linked to groups that had survived from antiquity, and to be disseminating their sects widely in the west, were recorded soberly and without rhetoric or obvious embellishment by Eberwin of Steinfeld and Eckbert of Schönau, by far our most substantial informants.[31] There is a short, but nevertheless well-defined interval between these reports and the widespread acceptance, reflected towards the end of the century in William of Newburgh and others, of what might be called the conspiracy theory of popular heresy, and specifically of the dissemination of Catharism.

The language of William of Newburgh implies that the conspiracy did not embrace heretics alone, for the whole passage is imbued with the image of leprosy, to which the heresy of the *Populicani* is likened in detail, and which the Council of Tours had also invoked. This imagery was not new in the description of heretics and the threat which they represented, but it is used here much more systematically, and from this time forward more frequently, than formerly.[32] It reflects not only an increasingly sinister analysis of heresy, but a growing fear of leprosy. In the same decades we see the dissemination of the accusation of ritual murder against Jews following the killing of William of Norwich, *c.*1144.[33] In each case, as we have already seen,[34] we encounter a rhetoric of demonisation which represents those who are to be persecuted as inspired by the devil, and even directly in communication with him. The creation in this way of a single account of the victim as enemy of God and society, which might be transferred at will to any object, either a class of persons already existing, such as Jews, whom it might seem desirable or convenient to persecute, or a new one, such as sodomites or witches, which by an act of classification might be invented for the purpose, was a crucial stage in the development of the model of persecution

---

[31]   Though Uwe Brunn has recently argued that the content, as opposed to the tone, of these reports was rhetorically enhanced: 'L'hérésie dans l'archevêché de Cologne, 1100–1233'.

[32]   Moore, 'Heresy as Disease'.

[33]   Langmuir, 'Thomas of Monmouth', now significantly amended by McCulloh, 'Jewish Ritual Murder'. A number of other essays in Langmuir, *Antisemitism*, notably at pp. 197–208 and 263–81, illuminate aspects of the development of persecuting behaviour as part of the establishment of clerical culture.

[34]   Above, pp. 57–61.

that we are describing. It is hardly necessary to add that the model was to a considerable extent self-fuelling: those who were cast for persecution are depicted not only as the enemies of God and the family, but as outsiders, bereft of social ties and obligations, often rootless and wandering people, dirty, diseased and desperate – in short, as exemplifying the condition to which ostracism and persecution in themselves must eventually reduce them, whatever their initial vigour or prosperity.

A final point which emerges from William of Newburgh's account of the trial at Oxford is that we should not look immediately, exclusively, or even primarily to the papacy as the source of this taking of the initiative which marks the emergence of the new model of persecution. During the preparations for the Council of Tours Pope Alexander III received certain citizens of Arras who had been accused by Archbishop Henry of Reims and his brother King Louis VII of having fallen into the errors of the Manichees and belonging to the sect of the *Populicani*.[35] That they were not negligible people is attested equally by their offer of 600 marks to the Archbishop to drop the case and by their determination to secure justice at the papal court when he refused. The Pope's evident scepticism, despite his dependence on Louis VII for support against Frederick Barbarossa, who had driven him out of Italy, completes the impression clearly conveyed by a handful of fragmentary letters that we are dealing essentially with a political rather than a religious affair. As to the Council of Tours itself, we have no direct evidence of secular influence on its agenda or deliberations. But we should notice that it was held in the favourite city of Henry II, that (in marked contrast to his predecessor Stephen, who had forbidden English bishops to attend the Council of Reims in 1148) Henry sent an imposing delegation of obedient prelates, and that at this time it was greatly to his political advantage that the Count of Toulouse should be exposed as a protector of heretics.[36]

Not even the purest religious fervour would constitute a wholly satisfactory explanation of why Henry II should have thought it necessary, in the Assize of Clarendon, to act with such severity against heretics who were already dead. One possibility, no doubt,

[35] Bouquet, xv, pp. 790, 792, 799.
[36] Warren, *Henry II*, pp. 82–108; Barlow, *Thomas Becket*, pp. 84–6; Somerville, *Council of Tours*; Moore, 'Les albigeois'.

is that he knew from the experience of his continental lands how rapidly heresy might spread, and was determined that it should not do so in England. William of Newburgh's comments on that point might serve very well for any collection of texts designed to illustrate the general complacency of the English that providence has granted them immunity from so many of the evils which stalk the continental mainland. Another possibility is that the episode at Oxford provided Henry with a welcome opportunity simultaneously to proclaim his piety at a dramatic moment in his quarrel with Thomas Becket, and to make a salutary demonstration of the range and extent of his power. Whatever Henry's conscious motives may have been, however, few will have difficulty in detecting here a classic example of the invention or exaggeration of a danger to the 'common good' in order to justify the extension of the power of the state and the vigour of its application. We need only remember Philip II's treatment of 'his' Jews, or the legislation of both Henry and Philip against prostitution in their capital cities,[37] to make the point that action against heresy, real or alleged, fitted very well into the ambitions of monarchs for the aggrandisement of their realms and the extension of their power over an ever-greater range of their subjects' activities and concerns. Certainly they found it so when Count Raymond V of Toulouse, himself in need of a weapon against recalcitrant subjects, made his own use of the language of contamination in a famous letter to the Abbot of Clairvaux, in 1177, in which he described the ravages wrought upon his lands by the heretics, and the unwillingness of his greatest vassals to raise their swords against it.[38]

Even more than its sponsorship, the personnel and methods of the mission dispatched to Toulouse in 1178 at the urging of Henry and of Louis VII, and led by a papal legate, Cardinal Peter of St Chrysogono, proclaim its place at the birth of the persecuting society. Most of what needs to be said in the present argument is contained in one of its best known acts and one of its less known members. The mission entered the city in an atmosphere of hostility and suspicion, and after a few days asserted its presence by means of a highly

[37] Above, pp. 39–41, 90.
[38] Bouquet, xiii, 140. The authenticity of the letter is questionable, but it does seem clear that Raymond co-operated with the mission, and that the leadership of resistance to comital authority in the city and of the alleged heresy were substantially the same.

publicised sermon. Then 'the bishop and certain of the clergy, the consuls of the city and some other faithful men who had not been touched by any rumour of heresy were made to give us in writing the names of everyone they knew who had been or might in future become members or accomplices of the heresy, and to leave out nobody at all for love or money'.[39] This was the technique of the *inquisitio*. The word is conventionally translated by historians of English law as 'inquest', particularly when they write of its vigorous and effective use in the 1160s and 1170s by the officials of King Henry II – including some of those attached to this mission to Toulouse in 1178 – to extend and strengthen his government's capacity to reach into the English shires in pursuit of criminals and disturbers of the peace. Its most spectacular achievement in Toulouse was (according to one of the leaders of the mission, Abbot Henry of Clairvaux) to provide the basis for a confrontation with one of the most powerful citizens of the town, which led to his exposure as a leader of the heretics and public humiliation and denunciation: 'After a few days a very large number of names had entered this catalogue, and among them was that of the great Peter Maurand . . . We decided to begin our investigation with him, so that the rest of the heretics would be frightened when they saw [him] condemned.' Whatever the effect on the heretical community of Peter's collapse when confronted by the anonymous denunciations, it certainly appeared to the legate and his companions as the turning point of the mission. 'The story of what happened flew through the streets and squares of that great city . . . From that moment the word of God grew and multiplied, and the face of the city grew brighter as it escaped from the darkness of error into the shining light of truth.'

Henry of Clairvaux's account of the trial of Peter Maurand provides a classic description not only of the mechanism of an *inquisitio*, but of the social dynamics which made it effective. Just over half a century later, in 1231, Pope Gregory IX appointed members of the order of Friars Preacher (Dominicans) to carry out inquisition for heresy at Regensburg, and in 1233 in the dioceses of Toulouse, Montpellier and Valence, with power to act independently of their bishops. In the following decades, though intermittently and often in the face of determined local opposition, they and their successors became a familiar, feared and in both senses legendary part of the

[39] Roger of Hoveden, *Chronica*, ed. Stubbs, ii, 162.

fabric of European life. The scale of some of their operations –
between May 1245 and August 1256 the inquisitors of Toulouse took
depositions from 5,471 men and women from the villages of the
Lauragais, an area of some seventy kilometres square to the south
and west of the city[40] – and the intensity and durability of the conflicts in which they and their victims became involved soon wove the
activities of the inquisitors into the fabric of everyday life in the
regions where they were active.

The chilling dedication of the manuals in which they described
their techniques and characterised their quarry, and the sombre and
circumstantial detail of their voluminous records, which are still far
from completely explored, quickly established for the inquisitors a
sinister place in the European imagination. It was magnified and
dramatised by the passions and conflicts of later centuries, and they
occupy to this day a prominent place in the myths, as well as the
realities of European history.[41] They contributed fundamentally and
essentially to the perfection of the persecuting society, especially in
developing methods of interrogation which, as one historian has put
it, enabled them to 'make concrete the ideas, fears, and fantasies that
resided only in their own minds'.[42] Nevertheless, they were more
symbolic of that development than responsible for it. The inquisitors
'were always less numerous, and often less ardent than the judicial
servants of secular powers'.[43] Their essential techniques, including
the use of torture, were derived from Roman law, which from 1200
onwards was embraced and adapted to a rapidly increasing variety
of purposes by princes and civic authorities all over Europe. The
show trial mounted by the advisers of King Philip IV of France,
which for seven years from 1307 used every resort of torture, terror
– including the burning of 54 of its leaders in one day – and propaganda to depict the Knights Templar as a secret conspiracy of
sodomitical devil-worshippers, grimly attests the adaptability of
those techniques to persecution in our, and every, sense.[44]

The ambiguity of the word 'persecution', which evokes both the
pursuit of justice and the infliction of injustice, is not fortuitous. It

---

[40] Closely studied by Pegg, *The Corruption of Angels*.
[41] See Peters, *Inquisition* and below, pp. 176–8.
[42] Given, *Inquisition and Medieval Society*, p. 213.
[43] Peters, *Inquisition*, p. 57.
[44] Barber, *Trial of the Templars*.

derives from the nature of the process. Similarly, it would be hard to find a better example of the perils of translation than that provided by the resonances of the word *inquisitio* in the English-speaking world. As inquisition, especially as papal inquisition, absolutist and Roman, it stands for everything that the Whig and Protestant traditions which formed mainstream Anglophone historiography most disliked and distrusted about the medieval world and its inheritance. As inquest, it represents everything in which those same traditions most rejoiced, as the foundation of constitutional monarchy and the liberty of the Englishman under his idiosyncratic common law. As one of the greatest of English historians, F. W. Maitland, observed, it was 'not a little remarkable that two "inquests" or "inquisitions", one for the purpose of indictment, another for the purpose of trial [i.e. the coroner's jury and the trial jury] appear in the end the most emphatic contrast that Europe can show to all that publicists [Roman lawyers] mean when they speak of an inquisitory procedure'.[45] The two developments had begun, however, from the same place: in the universal premise of the legal revolution of the twelfth century that, in Maitland's words again, 'a system which left the prosecution of offences to "the party grieved" was showing its insufficiency'[46] – that is, its insufficiency from the point of view of the clerks and their masters for maintaining social order and doctrinal orthodoxy, and for penetrating and permeating the nooks and crannies of obdurate ancient communities and of new ones jealous of their liberties.

That sense of insufficiency became apparent when the Councils of Reims in 1157 and of Tours in 1163 demanded vigilance and action from laity as well as clergy, against not only heretics themselves (whose presence and activity was taken for granted), but those who were suspected of supporting them. The legal reforms promulgated by Henry II in his Assizes of Clarendon and Northampton were based on the same principle, when 'lawful men' were required on oath to denounce those of their neighbours 'accused or notoriously suspect' of various crimes and misdemeanours. It could scarcely have occurred to the party sent to Toulouse in 1178 to confine to the uses of either 'church' or 'state' the application of this formidable device, which was proving so effective and so adaptable. One of its members was Reginald Fitzjocelin, Bishop of Bath, who as the son of Bishop

[45] Pollock and Maitland, *History of English Law*, ed. Milsom, p. 656.
[46] Ibid., p. 658.

Jocelin de Bohun of Salisbury sprang from one of the leading Anglo-Norman curial dynasties, and had been in the household of Thomas Becket in the early 1160s, but active at the royal court ever since.[47] It would be supererogatory to attribute to him the adoption by the mission of the very technique (in written form) which he had seen pioneered by Henry II's justices. No such explanation is necessary, because Reginald's very presence illustrates the greater fact that the unity of curial culture in this period was far more important both in the present and for the future than the multiplicity of the titular authorities under which it flourished, or even than the distinction among those authorities between the secular and the ecclesiastical. So, in a more mundane fashion, does the presence in the party of John 'of the fair hands', bishop of Poitiers since 1162 and the most trusted of Henry's continental bishops. Once treasurer of York, and soon to become archbishop of Lyons, John was said as a young man to have made a pact of mutual support and advancement with two fellow clerks in the brilliant household of Archbishop Theobald of Canterbury, Roger Pont l'Evêque and Thomas Becket.[48]

The ability of men like these, both clerks and their brothers who had become knights, to move between secular and ecclesiastical courts, carrying with them common attitudes and values and a rapidly growing stock of expertise in the exercise of power, underlines the inadequacy of the idea of state formation to describe the changes which took place in eleventh- and twelfth-century Europe.[49] Valuable though it is as a concept, and important as a phenomenon, it was only one aspect – a secondary aspect – of the comprehensive reorganisation of the human and agrarian resources of north-western Europe and their subordination to a newly defined social hierarchy.[50] That hierarchy in turn was effectively under the practical and ideological direction of a clerical elite which constituted a new social

[47] T. Hunt, 'Fitzjocelin, Reginald', *Dictionary of National Biography.*

[48] Barlow, *Thomas Becket,* pp. 30–4. John was archbishop of Lyons, 1182–93; Roger Pont l'Evêque Archbishop of York, 1154–81.

[49] To insist on the unity of clerical culture in the respects discussed in these paragraphs is by no means to disagree with Miller, 'Religion makes a difference,' on the nature and importance of differences within it: see further below, pp. 189–90.

[50] For a full account of this transformation as I understand it see Moore, *First European Revolution.*

formation of the period. The key attributes of its members are well illustrated by those we have mentioned. They were overwhelmingly the younger sons, or descended from the younger sons, of knights; many, in the latter case, were the (illegitimate) sons of clerics. They were therefore the victims of the widespread adoption of primogeniture, in the eleventh and twelfth centuries, as the governing principle of inheritance. The dominance of the territorial aristocracy of the heartlands of Carolingian Europe (including, by conquest, England) had been preserved at their expense. They were compensated by more secure access to the incomes and offices of a reinvigorated and greatly enriched church, but only at the price of celibacy. Whether this prevented them from producing children was immaterial; what mattered was that it prevented them from producing heirs. Reginald Fitzjocelin may have received support and advice from his father, but not (except through the renewal of patronage) office or property. He depended on his wits; on the education which might make him a master of the new engines of power,[51] the abacus, the syllogism and the legal maxim; and on his ability to make himself valuable to his patrons.[52] It was therefore – and this, surely, is the secret of bureaucratic dynamism in western Europe – on the advancement of his patron's power and interest, and not on those of the biological family from which his antecessors had been so coldly driven forth, that his own advancement and security, and those of his children, must depend.

Men like Reginald were at the heart of every great development of this age. They were also perennially insecure, constantly competing for the favour of their masters, which brought office, eminence and wealth, constantly in terror of losing it, and with it all they had, to a jealous rival, an unlucky failure, a royal whim. My suggestion, in 1987, that they stoked anti-semitism because they feared direct competition for positions at court from better educated and more accomplished Jews was clearly wrong, as several reviewers maintained. I had no substantive evidence of such competition in northern

[51] Not, at this date, necessarily a formal education in the schools, though that was a rapidly growing advantage.
[52] Walter Map quotes the advice on career development which Jocelin, himself a product entirely of royal patronage, offered to his son: 'Be off quickly to the Pope...give him a good smack with a heavy purse and he will turn which way you will.' *De nugis curialium*, ed. M. R. James etc., pp. 68–9: once again the unity of curial culture is illustrated.

Europe and none has emerged since.[53] But the perception that
prompted it has been not only sustained but elaborated and enriched,
from the perspectives both of Jews and of Christians. It is now widely
agreed that the terrible events of 1096 did not signal a general
renewal or intensification of persecution for the Jews of Europe.
Their position was always precarious, and always being undermined
by the forces described in the preceding pages. In particular, the
prohibition on landowning, now strictly enforced in most places, and
the consequent constraints, ensured the chronic insecurity which
Abelard had evoked so movingly in his *Dialogue of a Philosopher
with a Jew, and a Christian.*[54] Nevertheless, for Jews the twelfth
century was a period of prosperity, expansion and cultural vigour,
and, on the whole, of relatively harmonious coexistence with Christian neighbours.

That may have had the effect, among others, of exposing Jews all
the more nakedly to the anxieties of the clerks, who also lived in a
condition of chronic insecurity, not only in their careers but in their
identity and their position in society. They were, as we have said,
new men, thrust from their families to make their ways as best they
could. Their prospect of position and respect in the world, their claim
to legitimacy in office and the exercise of authority which many of
them could not assert by birth, hung on their attainments, and ever
more directly on their education. The status and authority of their
education depended in turn on the position of the ablest and most
respected among them as the unquestioned guardians and inter-
preters of the Christian faith, whose logical foundations, teachings
and implications for every aspect of daily life they now hammered
out with a rigour and comprehensiveness undreamed of since the age
of the fathers. Every alternative source of religious authority, real or
potential – including the Eastern and Celtic churches and innumerable local cults and traditions, as well as heresies real and imaginary

[53] I note also the important distinction made for thirteenth-century Castile
by Teofilo Ruiz: 'Jews and Muslims also appear as royal agents, but the
actual running of the realm was firmly in the hands of the middling sorts':
From Heaven to Earth, p. 149.
[54] Quoted above, p. 80, but now better read in the edition and translation
of Marenbon and Orlandi, who (at pp. xxvii–xxii) incline to a slightly later
date for its composition – 1127–32 – than Mews's 1125–6 (1985,
122–6).

– must therefore be denigrated and if necessary destroyed. The Jews, however, presented a particular challenge. Not only did they deny the incarnation of Christ, and with it the doctrines (the Holy Trinity, the atonement) and the sacrament (the Eucharist) which were being placed at the very heart of the renewed Christianity, but they did so from the perspective of a history, a religious inheritance and a tradition of teaching and learning which Christians could only regard with respect – unless they could deny or discredit them utterly. That is why it was necessary, as we have said, to destroy the present identity of the Jews, as well as to invent a new one for them.[55]

In discussion of the agrarian transformation of Europe in this period it is commonplace to distinguish between economic growth by extension – of traditional methods of cultivation to new areas or regions – and by intensification – increasing the productivity of land already cultivated by means of technical improvement or enhanced efficiency. In the history of power persecution was part of the process of intensification. Its function (irrespective of the ideology and conscious personal motives of those involved) was to carry wherever and whenever might be desired the new political and cultural regime which accompanied the economic transformation. At first this only meant responding to actual resistance or overt and public opposition. But increasingly after the middle of the twelfth century kings and their advisers took the initiative against perceived and constructed deviancy, and in doing so increased the range, the variety and the effectiveness of central authority – that is, their own. Nothing illustrates the nature of the process better than the place of the *inquisitio* in the institutional development of the age. The confrontation at Toulouse in 1178 illustrated dramatically its power to break through the carapace of instinctive solidarity that almost any community, large or small, presents in the first instance to the representatives of external authority. In the hands of men whose loyalties, interests and values committed them to the centre against the periphery, to law against custom, to kingdom against community, to lord against kin,

[55] See especially Abulafia, *Christians and Jews*. The argument of this paragraph is stated more fully in Moore, *First European Revolution*, pp. 146–59, and the relationship between intellectual and religious revival, the redefinition of the Christian community and identity and the exclusion of heretics, Jews and Muslims magisterially expounded by Dominique Iogna Prat, *Order and Exclusion*.

it was a formidable and infinitely flexible instrument. If any single aspect of the twelfth-century revolution in government may be seen as decisive, it is surely the capacity developed by both secular and ecclesiastical powers to penetrate communities of every kind vigorously and ruthlessly, overriding the restraints of custom, and enlisting, or destroying, men of local standing and influence in the name of order, of orthodoxy or of reform. This is the foundation upon which the reshaping of European society and culture in the high middle ages was built; and this is the force which prevented the vigour of the nascent European state from running into the sands of tribal or dynastic loyalties and unchallenged local hegemony, as its counterparts under the Mamluks, the Ottomans and the Mughals, even under the infinitely more ancient and sophisticated bureaucratic traditions of the Song and the Ming, were destined to do.[56]

All this says nothing about the conscious motives or intentions of those whose thoughts and actions these pages have traced. It would be foolish to suppose that they foresaw, designed or intended the consequences which we have ascribed to their work. Even when we can read their writings we have no window into their conscience. Some were undoubtedly inspired by the highest ideals and the noblest aspirations; most doubtless supposed on most occasions that they were acting for the best. To guess to what extent, or for what reasons, they may have deceived themselves, or failed to scrutinise the influence of their interests on their judgements, is neither necessary nor useful to this discussion. Nothing would be achieved by replacing one simplistic explanation of the appearance of persecution in medieval Europe – that it was an inevitable, or at least a natural, response to the growth of real and perceived dangers – by another – that it was a device to secure power in the hands of an emerging and corrupt clerical class. That would presume, with a complacency that the most superficial reflection could not defend, that evil consequences arise only from evil actions, and evil actions only from evil intentions. It would also imply, equally indefensibly, that the depiction of the

[56] Moore, 'The Eleventh Century in Eurasian History'. For comparative discussion of the impermeability of local power structures as a fundamental obstacle to institutional and economic development, in the footsteps of Weber and Gellner, see Hall, *Powers and Liberties*, pp. 27–144; for a vivid account of the inability of Ming bureaucracy to penetrate to these levels, Huang, *1587*, pp. 130–55.

intellectual and institutional developments of the eleventh and twelfth centuries in the preceding pages, and of the men who brought them about, is complete. On the contrary, the contribution of the ideas, actions and institutions mentioned here to the formation of what we have called the persecuting society was only one aspect, and one which was not always accepted without challenge or hesitation, of some of the most profound and spectacular innovations which made this period a turning point in European history, the period when, for better and for worse, the continuous history of modern European society and achievement begins.

It was perhaps the most general and indispensable characteristic of the innumerable changes which made up that transformation that they involved a very much deeper and more pervasive penetration of society by the culture and institutions of the literate minority. That fact is implicit in all the labels for the period with which our text-books abound. Whether we choose to emphasize its idealistic aspects by writing of 'the reordering of Christian life' or 'the renaissance of the twelfth century', or prefer to stress the assertion and definition of social hierarchy and the expansion of governmental power in 'the age of chivalry', 'the revival of monarchy' and 'the twelfth-century revolution in government' is largely a matter of taste, though like all expressions of taste it reveals our values. It is the argument of this book that however that tremendous extension of the power and influ-ence of the literate is described, the development of persecution in all its forms was part of it, and therefore inseparable from the great and positive achievements with which it is associated. Whether they might have taken place without it is quite another question, and one which, perhaps thankfully, historians are not called upon to answer.

BIBLIOGRAPHICAL EXCURSUS: DEBATING THE PERSECUTING SOCIETY[1]

The recording of intellectual debts is a prime duty of the academic calling, but not always an easy one to discharge. The influence of Michel Foucault on this book is obvious and regularly pointed out, but in 1987 I was hardly aware of it. I was then acquainted with – it would be an exaggeration to say, 'had read' – only two of Foucault's books, *The Birth of the Prison* (*Surveiller et punir*) and *Madness and Civilization* (*Histoire de la folie*). I had consulted the latter in search of comparative material for this book, to be struck chiefly by Foucault's readiness to accept for the leper houses of medieval Europe the positivist account of their history and functions that he had rejected for the lunatic asylums which took their place.[2] My thinking about religion and society had been mainly shaped by the British anthropologists, especially Edward Evans-Pritchard and Mary Douglas. The immediate source of the insight into the nature of social classification on which the argument of this book was founded was Edmund Leach's *Culture and Communication*. The passage quoted from it at the end of Chapter 2 (above, p. 93) had struck me with the force of revelation, but if I knew that Leach was heavily influenced by Claude Lévi-Strauss, who influenced Foucault, I had given the matter little thought. My own questions about the possible social construction of popular heresy, and later of leprosy,

[1]   To minimise distraction most citations in this section are in the briefest form necessary to locate the full reference in the Bibliography.
[2]   Above, p. 56 n. 96.

had initially been stimulated from a quite different direction, by the then Professor of Psychiatry at Sheffield University, Alec Jenner, and *The Myth of Mental Illness*, by the American psychiatrist Thomas Szasz, which he recommended to me.

This may seem an unnecessarily pretentious way of making the obvious point that intellectual pedigrees are of limited usefulness in tracing the evolution and influence of ideas. Often we seek out ideas in their pristine, written state only after we have seized them from the air around us, as it were, because they seem to answer our needs. Conversely, they sometimes become current not so much because they are cogently argued or supported by great erudition – though certainly those qualities may contribute to the character and durability of their subsequent influence – as because their time has come. Indeed, it sometimes happens that new thinking catches attention in simplified, even vulgarized, form rather than at its subtlest or most scholarly best – a phenomenon of which some may consider *The Formation of a Persecuting Society* an example. However that may be, it is very much a product of its time, the 1970s and early 1980s, when the almost exclusive preoccupation of academic history with traditional structures of political, social and cultural power and their beneficiaries was being questioned with growing scepticism, but still effectively predominant. When I complained, in 1975 (Moore 1975: v), that heretics and their followers 'ought to occupy a larger place in the view of the early Middle Ages which we teach', I was unaware of Gavin Langmuir's scathing account of the exclusion of Jews from the history and historiography of medieval Europe, which had been published in 1966 – after rejection by the *American Historical Review* had proved its point (Langmuir 1990: 21–41).

My attempt to establish how far the analogy with lepers so commonly applied to heretics in the twelfth-century sources corresponded to reality quickly showed me how largely that reality had loomed, and how little it had been investigated (Moore 1976). The publication of John Boswell's *Christianity, Social Tolerance and Homosexuality* in 1980 stands in retrospect as a landmark, now celebrated and reassessed in a fine collection of papers under the editorship of Matthew Kuefler (2006). It was not only a pioneering work of great learning and originality in its field, but in discussing in some detail the climate of growing intolerance towards Jews and heretics as well as gay men in the later twelfth and thirteenth centuries was one of the first to point to the need for a common explanation of their predicament.

Medievalists in the early 1980s had barely begun to discuss in print other aspects of the history of sexuality (except in the context of canon law, magisterially surveyed by James A. Brundage in 1987), and still less to grapple with the implications of the social construction of gender, whose pertinence to the argument of *The Formation of a Persecuting Society* was pointed out, as far as I know, by only one reviewer.[3]

Growing interest in these 'minority', 'marginal' or 'subaltern' topics, as they were variously called, goes far to account for the cordiality with which *The Formation of a Persecuting Society* was welcomed, especially in North America. Since 1987 all of them have been received, as it were, into the mainstream of historical discussion – so far as the idea of a mainstream itself still has currency – and all have been enriched by a great deal of new research and writing of high quality, much of it (of course) highly controversial. It would be quite impractical, even if it were within my powers, to summarise that work here. This essay does not, and cannot, attempt comprehensive bibliographical or critical treatment of any topic in its own right. Its aims are first, to point to a number of developments that have had a particular bearing on the argument and conclusions advanced in *The Formation of a Persecuting Society*, and second, to respond to what have seemed to me some particularly telling or stimulating observations and criticisms. To the many whose comments are not taken up here I can only apologise: the omission does not mean that I am either ungrateful for their attention or indifferent to their views, but only that though scholarship is long, books are short.

Heresy

Understanding of popular heresy and of responses to it, the subject in which I have been chiefly interested throughout my professional life and the starting point of this argument, has been greatly enriched in recent years, though the nature of new approaches had been visible, just as the debates from which they emerged had been in progress, for much longer. The absence of any objective, hard and

---

[3] Miri Rubin, *Speculum* 65 (1990): 1025–7. Anyone who finds it hard to credit that serious professional attention to these subjects can be so recent a phenomenon need only consult the bibliography of Karras (2005).

fast distinction between orthodoxy and heresy in the popular religious movements of the high middle ages was put beyond serious question by Herbert Grundmann as long ago as 1935, though his work did not become widely known outside Germany until after the second edition of 1961. By then specialists were beginning to grasp the extent to which generations of scholars had accepted uncritically as reliable records of historical reality the accounts which inquisitors and other Catholic observers had pieced together from fragments of information often distorted or exaggerated, collected over long periods of time, from widely scattered places and in very different circumstances.

These sinister and largely imaginary descriptions of secret theologically coherent and hierarchically organised heretical sects were taken more or less at face value to provide the subject matter of almost all accounts of medieval popular heresy until late in the twentieth century, and in airport-bookstall history and historical fiction are still recycled as unquestioned and extremely lucrative fact. Robert E. Lerner's elegant dissection of how preconception, fantasy and credulity had created 'the heresy of the Free Spirit' in the later middle ages appeared in 1972, and my own assessment of how they had shaped perceptions of popular heresy before the inquisition in 1977. Critical reading of the sources and the traditional historiography founded on them has advanced enormously since 1987.[4] To mention only a handful of examples, the team of scholars led by Monique Zerner (1998, 2001) has shown how many of the key sources for the heresies of the eleventh and twelfth centuries were created, or improved, long after the event, and in the process of laying the groundwork for the preaching of the Albigensian crusade and the wider campaigns against heresy of the thirteenth century. Their work also provides a context for the bitterly resisted but ultimately irresistible critique, most powerfully marshalled by Mark Pegg (2001), of the idea that 'Catharism' ever constituted a unified or coherent alternative to Catholicism, let alone an organised counter-church. Carol Lansing's richly documented and wonderfully humane account of the pursuit of 'Cathars' in thirteenth-century Orvieto (1988) brings out the variety of purposes which the intellectual categories implicit in the notion of heresy might serve – explored at the level of political conflict by Scharft (1996) – and their irrelevance to

---

[4]   For overviews Lambert (2002); Fichtenan (1998). I have reviewed modern work on eleventh- and twelfth-century heresy at length in Frassetto (2006).

the passions and anxieties of ordinary people. That 'Waldensianism' was an equally and similarly artificial construct is an increasingly accepted conclusion, firmly set forth by Grado Merlo, of another rapidly growing and fruitful body of scholarship.[5] The history of the 'spiritual Franciscans' is bedevilled by the same issues (Burr 2001).

The relevance of such work to the present argument is its constant tendency to confirm that we must seek to understand the persecution of heresy, with all its consequences, by looking not to the victims and their alleged errors and misdemeanours, but to the persecutors and the wider society of which they were part. 'The Inquisition' itself has been exposed as a myth, and its history as such superbly written by Edward Peters (1988). From 1231 popes appointed individuals and teams 'to make inquisition into heretical depravity', independently of the diocesan bishop, as and when circumstances seemed to warrant it. In and after the sixteenth century inquisitors and their powers were institutionalised as standing tribunals in many parts of the Catholic world, but there was no general or permanent office charged with this responsibility in the middle ages (Kieckhefer, 1995). The sinister, all-powerful institution of the modern imagination was constructed from scattered and miscellaneous elements of fact and fantasy by pamphleteers and polemicists, philosophers, historians, and novelists, mostly Protestant – by a process, in fact, ironically similar to that by which the inquisitors themselves had constructed the heresies of the Cathars and Waldensians, the Free Spirit, the Witch Cult and the rest. But if they had less institutional substance in the thirteenth century than used to be supposed, the Dominican inquisitors were no less earnestly dedicated to their task of eradicating heresy (Ames 2005). To that end they developed, with the same zealous professionalism that their clerical contemporaries brought to the tasks of secular and of ecclesiastical governance, the techniques of record keeping, interrogation, and punishment, and of the management of public relations and the historical record, which advanced their task and sustained them in it, to the point where, in the words of James Given, 'The inquisitors were not mere slaves of reality. Their investigative techniques allowed them to create their own, tailor-made truth. Through their interrogation procedures the inquisitors could make concrete the ideas, fears and fantasies that

[5]　Merlo, 1984, 1991; for recent surveys in English Audisio (1999), leaning towards the inquisitorial representation in respect of organisation and continuity, and Cameron (2000), who is more sceptical.

resided only in their own minds. In a sense they could make these phantasms objectively real' (1997: 231).[6] They made them real, certainly, in the sense of being widely shared, not only in that the existence of specific heretical sects and movements was widely believed in, but in that the figure of the heretic himself or herself, as treacherous, manipulative, powerful and omnipresent now entered the European imagination, and its imaginative literature, under many guises (Sullivan 2005).

[handwritten margin note: Reference to Inquisitors Development stereotype through Inquisitors]

Jews

Since the 1980s we have seen a considerable advance in the integration of the history and historiography of Jews and Christians in medieval Europe, previously conducted almost without reference to one another. The emerging new perspectives are well represented in the collection edited by Michael A. Signer and John van Engen (2001). On the whole, it shows the twelfth century as a period of prosperity and cultural florescence for Jews as well as Christians, though its basis was both fragile and vulnerable (see also Jordan 1989, ch. 1). Both points are spectacularly illustrated by Norman Golb's remarkable studies of the Jews of Normandy (1985, 1998). Jewish communities, like Christian ones, were becoming more self-conscious, more aware (or creative) of their identity and traditions, and more eager to sustain them.[7] Despite the horrors of 1096, which will always be passionately revisited (Haverkamp 1999, Stow 2001, Malkiel 2002, Nirenberg 2002, Cohen 2004), contacts between the two communities in the following generations, at the intellectual level among others, were generally peaceable, occasionally even cordial. While the formulation of anti-Jewish teachings can be traced with growing clarity from the beginning of the twelfth century (Cohen 1983, Tolan 1993), and of anti-semitic stereotypes from its middle decades (Langmuir 1990, Iogna Prat 2002), we do not sense general or widespread hostility, or see the beginning of sustained persecution at the hands of secular rulers, until towards its end (Chazan 1973, Jordan 1989).

[6]   For further sophisticated analysis of inquisitorial activity and the assessment of its evidence Arnold (2001), Pegg (2001), Bruschi and Biller (2004).
[7]   A point too general and many-sided to be explored here, but illustrated in many of its aspects by the much discussed conversion-narrative of Hermann Judaeus, magisterially expounded by Schmitt (2003).

In general terms this relatively optimistic account (which, of course, is not unanimously espoused: cf. Stow, 1992) confirms and indeed reinforces that offered in *Formation*, and more fully in Moore (1992), particularly with respect to the sharper chronology now presented in Chapter 5 above. Nevertheless, important issues remain for debate. My scepticism of popular generation of anti-semitic stereotypes is contested, most persuasively by Robert Chazan (1997: 78–85), who finds them widely reflected in the Hebrew sources as coming from Christians of all social classes. He is supported by the extent to which hostility to Jews and Judaism was embedded in the structure of early medieval Christianity, even in the absence of Jews themselves. In Anglo-Saxon England, Andrew P. Scheil (2004: 3) maintains, 'the Jews were present as imaginative, textual constructs, manifest only in the distorted shadow cast by the Christian tradition'. In the most famous and important example, the allegation of ritual murder, the role of Thomas of Monmouth's account of the murder of William of Norwich is reduced by John M. McCulloh's evidence (1997) that the story that William had been murdered by Jews circulated in England and the Rhineland before Thomas wrote. In short, the people of Europe before 1150 were not wholly innocent of prejudice against Jews, and anti-Jewish myths and *topoi* did circulate among them. Such tales were not, or not always, simply inventions of the clerks, but were there for the clerks to draw on. Still, we should remember that the passing of stories and stereotypes up *to* the literate or down *from* them, socially speaking, were mutually reinforcing, not mutually exclusive processes: Scheil's textual constructs derived largely from Bede, and Ephraim of Bonn, one of Chazan's main sources, was writing quite late enough for the 'rich set of anti-Jewish imagery' which he perceived as current throughout Christian society in the second half of the twelfth century (Chazan 1997: 54–7) to have originated or been enhanced in the cloister or the court. Both the facts relating to the nature and currency of such materials and the sociology of their dissemination need further investigation. In short, I agree with Anna Abulafia (1995: 139) that the interaction between scholarly responses to Jews and Judaism and popular attitudes is a subject which demands a book in its own right; it might well show that I drew too sharp an antithesis between popular and clerical perceptions.

Nevertheless, the critical importance of the acceptance of hostile stereotypes and attitudes into literate culture, and their elaboration, propagation, and if necessary invention, by the literate, has been abundantly confirmed. A comprehensive and penetrating account of how it took place in probably the most influential individual case, that of Peter the Venerable, is provided by Dominique Iogna Prat (2002: 275–322). In the thirteenth century relations between Jews and Christians in England and France were undermined, above all, by royal policy (Stacey 1988, 1992; Mundill 1998; Jordan 1989). Royal greed, however, does not seem a sufficient explanation for that development: in the hundred years or so following the accession of Philip Augustus to the French throne in 1180 persecution was ratio- nalised and sustained by a growing determination among the rulers of Europe that the Jews were enemies of Christ, to be removed either by conversion or expulsion. That view was nourished in the universi- ties and popularised by the friars (Cohen 1982), but it was articu- lated and propagated with particular vigour and ruthlessness at the courts, ever more coherently and vigorously from c.1200 – and espe- cially, as Sarah Lipton (1999) has shown in her subtle and revealing exploration of the *bible moralisée* prepared for Philip Augustus c.1215, at the French court.[8] Robin R. Mundill (1998) has shown that thirteenth-century English Jewry was both wealthier and socially less uniformly ostracised than used to be thought, and attributes the expulsion of 1290 very largely to the personal hostility, based on religious zeal, of Edward I, encouraged by a coterie of ecclesiastical advisers.

The argument that the basis of growing hostility towards Jews on the part of the literate elite of Latin Christendom, in all its manifesta- tions, lay in undeclared competition for cultural prestige and hege- mony rather than directly for office, as I had suggested in the first edition of this book, has been set out in Chapter 5. For some Chris- tians it did not have to be so. Robert E. Lerner (2001) has shown how Joachim of Flora's vision of a third age, in which 'Jews and gentiles would be gathered in the flock of love', was maintained, in the face of persecution, by some of his followers and intellectual descendants until the middle of the fifteenth century. It is another reminder that, as Robert C. Stacey comments, there is still to be written 'a series of parallel histories of Jewish experience in a variety of political com- munities scattered unevenly across the landscape of twelfth-century

---

[8] For the creation and use of visual stereotypes see also Camille (1998), Strickland (2003).

northern Europe' (2001: 351). Such histories will cast much light on the formation of the persecuting society. They are unlikely to suggest that it was uniform, inevitable, or independent of contingency.

Lepers

The account of leprosy offered in *The Formation of a Persecuting Society* is susceptible to more substantive revision in consequence of recent work than that of any other topic, but it is not clear how the key question is affected, or that it is resolved, in consequence. The inclusion of lepers among the persecuted has been one of the most disputed aspects of the case, on the grounds that segregation is (allegedly) a medically sound – and therefore, by implication, essentially rational – response to the disease, practised in many cultures. This, however, is not the issue. It was not segregation in itself that brought lepers into this argument, but the special odium which was attached to their position, expressed not only in the rhetoric but also in the curtailment of legal rights and powers which assimilated them to heretics and other outcasts, and hence to the general model of exclusion.[9] Nevertheless, I should have pointed out, as Christopher Brooke (2000: 399–402) has done in a thoughtful discussion, that responses to lepers and leprosy in the thirteenth century were by no means simple: they evoked a range of religious and cultural responses which makes them and their condition a point of access to the spiritual climate of the period, as well as an essential context for their position in the present discussion.

It would not be too much to say that the advances since the late 1980s have brought medieval leprosy within the purview of modern historiography – and shown that the standard image of 'the medieval leper' then received, and described in *Formation* (not entirely without scepticism), was very largely a construct of late nineteenth-century medical doctors, shaped by their anxiety to demonstrate the efficacy and urgency of segregation as a means of dealing with an epidemic. Some of its more lurid aspects should be abandoned. It seems, for example, that the so-called 'leper mass' (above, p. 55) was celebrated rarely, if ever, and the English writ *de leproso amovendo* was used seldom, late and in exceptional circumstances. The best account of this work is now Rawcliffe (2006), from whom I take both of those

[9]   Above, pp. 152–3.

examples. Her account is focused on England but fully in touch with the broader context, for which see also Bériac (1988) – a useful popular survey, already somewhat dated – and Touati (1996 and 1998). It is probably fair to say that current thinking on the epidemic in continental Europe is most represented, if not dominated, by F.-O. Touati's views, founded on his monumental research on the leprosaria of the archdiocese of Sens, which unfortunately is not widely available outside specialist libraries. The pattern of foundation in this crucial region, comprising seven dioceses and the greater part of the twelfth-century Capetian kingdom, was similar to that already described above for England and Flanders: a trickle of foundations in the early twelfth century – a bare handful sooner – broadening into a flood which reached its height in the middle of the thirteenth.[10] To this Touati adds some important observations. The earliest leper hospitals were also, by and large, the most important, sited in the main cities, all of which had one by 1130, large, amply funded and permanent. The later foundations, often offshoots from them, were in secondary centres of population, and the latest in the least populous and most remote areas, and correspondingly themselves smaller, poorer, and often transient. This is also true of England. The selection especially of the earliest sites does not suggest that isolation was a desideratum: on the contrary, they were conveniently located both to benefit from and to enhance developing networks of communication. This is the starting point of a powerful and to my mind wholly convincing argument that the movement should be seen not primarily as a response to an epidemic, but as part of the great social expansion of the high middle ages, and specifically of the interlinked growth of rural settlement, towns and urban populations, and of religious institutions, which included both general hospitals and those specifically provided for lepers – by no means a hard and fast distinction. Finally, Touati does not see foundations tailing off in the early fourteenth century: new ones continued in large numbers until the sixteenth, as Borradori (1992) also found for the Pays de Vaux. The phenomenon goes beyond the scope of this essay, but calls into the question the view that new cases of leprosy fell off after the Black Death.

[10]   Touati's figures for foundations in the archdiocese of Sens, which may be compared with those in Table 1 above: a. 1100: 3; 1101–50: 33; 1151–1200: 55; 1201–50: 96; 1251–1300: 80; 1301–70: 128 (Touati, 1996: 65, where the figures are subdivided by diocese).

Touati rightly distinguishes between the foundation, conduct and social functions of the leper hospitals, which is the subject of his very fine research, and the actual course of the medieval epidemic of Hansen's disease, reactions to it and the treatment of those affected by it. The distinction is particularly relevant to his insistence (also developed in Bériou and Touati 1991) that the inmates of leper houses were regarded as members of a religious order, and that their confinement and deprivations should be considered in that light, rather than as an aspect of the persecution. This may well be true, but it says nothing about those who were unable to secure admission to a hospital, which (as I had observed, above p. 51) was a privilege rather than a punishment. As to the epidemic itself, we continue to be dogged by the lack of decisive archaeological evidence in the form of skeletons bearing the distinctive marks of lepromatous leprosy, though some have been found in excavations at Chichester (Magilton, 1989) and Putot-en-Bessin (Touati, 2004: 79) to add to those at Naestved (above, p. 71). Our ignorance of the course and trajectory of the epidemic is underlined by Touati's own argument that it reached its peak in the tenth century and was already in decline by the twelfth (1996: 81–5). This somewhat perverse proposition, based chiefly on the assertion that the superior climate and nutritional standards of the twelfth century would have been unfavourable to the dissemination of the bacillus, seems designed to bolster his case against seeing twelfth-century foundations as expressing the fear of contagion; it requires no such artificial support.

Nor does the history of *leprosaria* tell us anything about the treatment of those who were unable to secure admission to them despite being diagnosed or regarded as lepers, or who were expelled from them on disciplinary grounds, for which the hospital statutes invariably provide. Rawcliffe not only shows how distorted is the nineteenth-century account which established the modern stereotype of the leper as degraded outcast (affording interesting analogies with Peters on that of the inquisition[11]), but makes a strong case for doubting the extent and cruelty of segregation in England. Both regional and chronological differentiation are particularly to be desired on this issue, not least because it should offer the opportunity to compare the responses of the literate elite (including its interpretation of popular responses) with those of the population at large. The central

[11]   Cf. Rawcliffe (2006), ch. 1 with Peters (1988), chs. 7 and 8.

questions, for the present purpose, are whether social attitudes hardened towards those who were regarded as lepers, but who were not inmates of hospitals; whether a stereotype of 'the leper' which attributed anti-social as well as merely physiological characteristics to the sufferers was formed by thirteenth-century medical opinion; if so, whether and to what extent such stereotypes contributed to diagnosis, and to exclusion from the community; and how and by whom such diagnoses and decisions were made.

While it has become apparent that the answers to these questions will be neither as simple nor as universal as they seemed in 1987, it is by no means clear that they can be answered negatively, or that they are not worth asking. They underline the inadequacy to date of the archaeological evidence, potentially both precise and conclusive, and suggest that there is still room for systematic consideration of the fragmentary and miscellaneous literary sources, especially in saints' lives and miracle collections as well as in vernacular literature. For example, though I share Marcus Bull's impression (1999: 13) that leprosy appears surprisingly rarely in the records of miraculous cures – one reason for doubting Touati's view that the disease was at its height before the twelfth century – analysis of those that can be found should be rewarding.[12] Such materials, of course, present the problem of distinguishing between reflections of social perceptions and responses and reports of 'objective' reality – which is precisely why they might be capable of taking us, in some respects, beyond the places that the institutional record can reach.

Persecution and Society

The variety of developments, especially in twelfth-century history, in which scholars have observed the persecuting process at work, in whole or in part, more or less as it is described in this book, is so great that even if I had been able to keep abreast of all of them detailed comment on each would become repetitive without being illuminating. It might even be argued – as Alexander Patchovsky has said (2003: 32) – that persecution was ubiquitous, and therefore in

---

[12]   I do not see why segregation should account for this paucity, as Bull surmises, even if had been practised everywhere and throughout the period. Bériac (1988: 117–18) reports a clutch of lepers cured among the early miracles of Becket.

itself of no great significance, because 'societies normally, and European societies always, have been ruled by dynamic forces and could be defined as conflicting entities'. It will be evident that I could acquiesce in neither so general a definition of persecution nor so undifferentiated an account of its prevalence at any time. For the twelfth century, as we have seen, for all the limitations of the surviving evidence, we need not settle for such blandness. Persecution, or persecuting tendencies, were present widely, but not everywhere; in forms similar but not identical; from causes often, but not always, the same. The differences suggest that the functions of persecution, and therefore the reasons for its widespread adoption, were more various and complex than my account of 1987 described, though not that it was mistaken in seeking to embrace them in a common explanation.

The activity at the core of persecution is classification, in accordance with what Leach (1976: 36) called the freedom of human beings 'to carve up the external world into named categories, and then arrange the categories to suit our social convenience'. In the twelfth century the arrangement, or rearrangement of such categories – that is, of the perception of the external world, and the establishment of a common perception of it – was peculiarly necessary, because the world was changing, for Europeans, in almost every conceivable dimension (above, pp. 95–100). If it was to make sense old boundaries had to be redrawn more precisely and many new ones, social, cultural and intellectual as well as topographical, invented. The points at which, and the ways in which that process takes place offer a sensitive and vivid register of social change, and a discriminating account of the particular forms that it assumes in different times and places, and the tensions and forces which lie beneath them. 'It is not far-fetched', says Teofilo Ruiz, 'to link village communities' concerns with the boundaries delineating their landholdings and the ongoing shift in spiritual values' (2004: 152). It is not far-fetched, he has demonstrated, to link the profound changes in social relations and economic conditions which those concerns reflected with transformations in aristocratic family structures, and in the foundations and exercise of royal power – including among their consequences in late twelfth- and thirteenth-century Castile 'increasingly more virulent pejorative representations of Muslims and Jews' (35–6). The changes that Ruiz traces and places in context were quite specific, some even unique, to the region, but their combined effect was that 'Castile joined the rest of the West in the broad social and cultural transformation that slowly but inexorably propelled medieval men and women from heaven to earth and ushered their world into modernity' (154).

Boundaries have to be defined, and if they are to be useful, policed – sometimes over-zealously, to be sure, but the activity itself is indispensable to ordered society. Wherever they were in question, or were being newly established, we find some or all of the processes associated with persecution, including especially stereotyping and the construction of rationales for suppression or oppression. Religious and cultural, as well as geographical boundaries helped Latin Christendom to define its identity in relation to its Orthodox and Muslim neighbours (Tolan 2002, Iogna Prat 2002);[13] accounts of ethnic and cultural superiority justified the exclusion, and the conquest, of less organised peoples around its peripheries (Gillingham 1992, Bartlett 1993). In Latin Christendom the place of non-Christians – not only Jews, but Muslims (Powell 1990, Tolan 2002) – must be worked out, and non-Roman forms of Christianity 'reformed' or condemned as heretical. Within Christian society thus defined, the pursuit of heretics as well as of criminals provided occasions for policing the social frontier between the privileged and the unprivileged – or, as contemporaries said, the free and the unfree – which was a far starker and more universal division after the adoption, throughout lowland Europe, of large-scale cereal agriculture as the main source of sustenance and wealth. The reordering of the privileged into the legendary three orders, necessary to secure and control that wealth (Duby 1981) entailed, among other things, a radical revision of gender roles, excluding women, for instance, from the custody of memory (Geary 1994), as well as confining them within the bounds of matrimonial chastity or its religious counterpart (Duby 1983, Gold 1985, Venarde 1997), by idealising the desired patterns of behaviour and demonising alternative ones. Every aspect of the 'Gregorian Reform' meant redefinition and reordering of the clergy as well as the boundary between clergy and laity (Tellenbach 1948, and innumerable subsequent studies, recently surveyed by Cushing 2005). In the monastic world ever more precise specification of the routines of daily life and

[13] References in the discussion which follows are by way of example only, and heavily biased towards works which refer to *The Formation of a Persecuting Society*.

worship, promulgated and enforced by the ubiquitous processes of 'reform', defined boundaries within and between communities of bewildering variety (Constable 1996; and for a striking example of bureaucratisation in the treatment of religious, Conklin 1999). Separation of the clergy from the laity demanded the end of clerical marriage (Moore 1980, Elliott 1998). The invention of sodomy (Jordan 1997) facilitated the reform of monastic and cathedral clergy (Leyser 1995), and sodomy accusations also 'began to feature in attempts to discipline masculine subjects by patrolling and controlling gender barriers' among the laity by defining appropri-ately masculine behaviour and demeanour, especially for knights (Burgwinkle 2004: 200).

This list is very far from complete, and most of its elements will reward further research. It is not suggested that every form of conflict or control mentioned constituted 'persecution' in the full sense of the term. Still less is the existence or multiplication of such conflicts to be explained by the emergence or ubiquity of a 'persecuting mentality'. Insofar as any such thing can be identified it was the result, not the cause, of the frictions and tensions produced by profound social change, and can be understood only in that context. To this extent Patchovsky was right: social change generates conflict, and conflict tends to generate persecution. Analogies to most, quite possibly all, of the examples mentioned in the preceding paragraph could be found quite easily in 'societies with persecution', though it would not be easy to suggest one where so many of them were present at the same time, or where society and culture were so thoroughly permeated by their combined effects.

To remember the distinction between societies with persecution and the persecuting society, however, is to be reminded that the question central to this discussion is not only how persecution or persecuting behaviour originated in eleventh- or twelfth-century Europe, but how and why it persisted, to become not incidental, but part of the fabric of society. That, as Chapter 5 argued, takes us back to the clerks. The most obviously controversial assertion of this book was that the impetus to persecution was 'top-down' rather than 'bottom-up'. It raised questions not only about the extent to which popular sentiment or action contributed to persecution, but also about the constitution, nature and motivations of the 'top' to which I attributed the formation of the persecuting society – that is, the literate, and especially the functionaries and advisers of kings and other lords, secular and ecclesiastical. It is already clear from the

preceding discussion that these questions are not quite so easily sepa-
rable as I thought in 1987, or in practice as they are in logic. As far
as heretics and Jews are concerned, it has become more apparent
than ever that persecution itself, the ideologies that rationalised it
and the mechanisms that realised it, indeed came from the top, even
if, in respect of the Jews, there were also currents of communal
tension and popular prejudice to work on. The case of leprosy is
much less clear, but it may be said at least that while indications of
popular animosity in the twelfth century are lacking, the creation
and uses of the distinctively European stereotype, widely diffused in
the thirteenth, remain to be explained, albeit in the context of
complex spiritual and cultural responses to the disease and its victims.
In several though not all of the other instances mentioned above
'bottom-up' pressures may have played a part, to be identified (where
possible) and assessed in each particular case and place. It seems
reasonable to guess, for instance, though it is a guess, that whereas
the stereotype of the sodomite was almost entirely a clerical construct, that of the prostitute or immoral woman, which was dramatically clarified and energetically disseminated in the twelfth century,
drew on and tapped into traditional customs and attitudes in most
places and at all social levels (cf. Karras 2005: 96–108). Some of
these examples also illustrate Scribner's point (1996: 41) that 'the
dynamics of classification and stigmatization may have created
popular demands to which agents of the state may only have
responded', though it is fair to wonder how often the 'only' should
be assumed. Agents of the state have been known occasionally to
exaggerate the extent to which they acted under compulsion, or to
claim to do so in the name of a 'people' whose approval of their
actions is in fact less than clear, as in the case of the persecution of
Quakers in seventeenth-century New England cited in Chapter 3
above (p. 101n.). Nevertheless, Scribner was right that my theoretical
antithesis between a Durkheimian and a Weberian model may in
practice very often be a false one – or rather, that it may become so
after stereotypes have been created and placed in circulation, as I
had remarked at pp. 101–2 above.

Nevertheless, in every instance the stereotypes which were actually propagated, the mechanisms of persecution which actually operated in the new Europe were devised by the literate, moulded by their
concerns, interests and ideals, and at least on a very large proportion
of occasions deployed at their initiative. If interest in persecution and

its victims has been stimulated by a recent turn of historians' attention towards minorities, even to a focus 'not only on the marginal but on the grotesque' (Freedman and Spiegel 1998: 699), its explanation takes us straight back to one of the oldest preoccupations of traditional historiography, the construction and exercise of institutional power. Even in the fact that our focus is not on the lords, secular or ecclesiastical, so much as on their servants, there is nothing new. The most notable addition to the groundbreaking work of Murray (1978), Clanchy (1979) and Stock (1983) on which I drew in 1987 is the last work of R. W. Southern (1995, 2001); its greatest lesson, fundamental to the present argument, that in the twelfth century the growth of government and the growth of education were inextricably interwoven. The men who moved so easily between the one and the other created in doing so a unified and distinctively European culture deeply rooted, dynamic and pervasive because it found its home and employment for its votaries not only at the courts of princes, but in every centre of power and action.

Unity did not mean uniformity. The account of the French and Anglo-French courts staffed by the products of the Paris schools and the cult of chivalry which underlies my exposition, in its essentials long familiar, provides a serviceable model for this analysis, but it is not to be mistaken for a universal one. The influence of an alternative and rival tradition, with its roots in the Ottonian world, has been traced through our period, in diverse aspects, by C. Stephen Jaeger (1985, 1994, 1999). Another has been brought to light by Maureen C. Miller's stunning reconstruction of the bishops' palaces of northern Italy, whose political traditions and civic values stand in contrast to those both of the imperial courts and of the communes (Miller, 2000a and b). In short, the court cultures of twelfth-century Europe display the same intoxicating variety as its cloisters, its schools, its market places and town halls. The diversity of their origins and the intricacies of their tensions and combinations defy reduction to simple formulations: they were not just variations on a theme.[14] The common elements which are the focus of our present concern, the

[14]   It should be noted that the trial at Angoulême in 1028 cited above (p. 134) as an example of how sorcery accusations were particularly liable to arise out of the highly personalised politics of early eleventh-century courts has now been fully and revealingly analysed by Richard Landes (1995: 178–93).

courtiers' mastery of new forms of power and their reliance on the favour of the masters in whose service they deployed it, were precisely that, and no more – two common elements among many differences. But these two repeatedly combined in confronting routine, everyday issues as well as real or imagined crises, to create the flexible, persistent, imaginative deployment of power that brought the concerns and responsibilities of government ever more intimately into the lives of communities, equally in the guises of reform and its other face, persecution.

CONCLUSION: EUROPE AND THE MIDDLE AGES

It was no part of the object of *The Formation of a Persecuting Society* to propose a characterisation of 'the middle ages' in Europe, or of 'medieval society'. Regrettably, that has not prevented its title from supplying one. That for many who are unfamiliar with the contents of the book its title may have served to reinforce the infantile stereotype of a millennium of unrelieved savagery is a source of understandable irritation to medievalists, myself included. Irritation may lead to distortion, though happily not to persecution. Quite recently, for example, Alexander Patchovsky, a far more distinguished scholar of heresy than I (and one more than capable of thinking for himself), has been taken to task for being 'in thrall to Moorean perspective' – ironically enough, in the essay with which I have taken issue above (pp. 184–5) – to such an extent that he has 'failed to take cognizance of a growing body of recent countervailing literature' – as, no doubt, the present excursus has also done. Patchovsky's principal offence was to comment that 'The history of the high and late middle ages could effortlessly be written as a process of increasing consolidation in religious and legal theory and armed praxis in regard to Christian "Catholic" views on the eradication of the world they saw as deviant.' 'Of course,' adds the reviewer, 'Moore already wrote such a history. And, of course, Moore's history is a painfully overdrawn caricature. It boggles the imagination that Patchovsky does not appear to know any better.'[15]

[15] Cary J. Nederman, reviewing Bruschi and Biller (2004): *Speculum* 2003/4, 1047–8.

If it had been presented as a complete or balanced description of European society at any period *The Formation of a Persecuting Society*, to which this observation apparently refers, would indeed be a painfully overdrawn caricature, but neither it nor any other of my books purports or pretends to be a history of the high and late middle ages. I had hoped to avoid creating any impression of making such a claim with the statements that (on the first page) 'this book neither pretends nor attempts to offer in any sense a complete or even a fair account of European society and institutions in one of the most vigorous and creative periods of their history', and (in the closing paragraph) that it would be 'indefensible' 'to imply that the depiction of the intellectual and institutional developments of the eleventh and twelfth centuries in the preceding pages, and of the men who brought them about, is complete'. I can only regret my inability to make this point clear to Patchovsky's reviewer. He was not alone among my critics in failing to grasp it. Those reservations remain,[16] and are intended to be taken seriously.

Formation made, and makes, no claim about medieval Europe, or medieval society, as such. My assertion was that in the twelfth and thirteenth centuries – well into the second half of the middle ages as they are commonly defined – Europe *became* a persecuting society, *and that it has remained one*. Interestingly, nobody, to the best of my knowledge, has objected to the second part of that statement.[17] It is hard to avoid the inference that for at least some of those who have referred to my thesis as though it related to the whole middle ages, and to the middle ages alone, the reperiodization implied by my chronology is objectionable in itself. That the thesis impugns the traditional unity of 'the medieval centuries' and associates some of them directly, even organically, with one of the more repellent aspects of modernity, is to some readers, it seems, itself a source of resentment, an offence to the romantic medievalism for which escape from modernity is a prime, if usually unacknowledged, motivation.

If that is the case I make no apology, for romantic medievalism is a menace to the study of Europe in its formative centuries, and indeed to the rational study of history itself. My argument, however, is directed against the equal and opposite folly of assuming that nothing recognisably associated with modernity (which in this mindset is

[16]   Above, pp. xi, 171; in the first edition, pp. vii, 152.
[17]   Scribner (1996: 43) came closest: see above, p. 152.

more or less equated with virtue) had its origin earlier than the sixteenth century. These twin commonplaces agree in effect that nothing
that happened between 500 and 1500 had much to do with anything
that has happened since. Both, like the idea of the middle ages itself,
are the offspring – perhaps the bastard offspring – of the master
narrative of European history which presented the Renaissance and
the Enlightenment as, on the one hand, the heirs of classical antiquity, and, on the other, supplying the rational foundations of the
modern world – and hence the basis, and more or less explicitly the
justification, for the hegemony in the nineteenth and twentieth centuries of European and neo-European industrial power. (Resuscita-
tion has recently, and brilliantly, been attempted by Landes (1998).)
In its first formulation, current from the age of Petrarch (1304–74)
to that of Gibbon (1737–96), by consigning a thousand years to
'barbarism and religion' the master narrative performed the essential
function of enabling the men (as they were) of the Renaissance and
Enlightenment to assume with the maximum of continuity the role
which they claimed for themselves as heirs of the ancients. In a
revised version, as the nineteenth-century idea of progress which was
finally articulated in contrasting forms by Karl Marx and Max
Weber, the millennium of assumed stagnation served to underline
the dynamic quality of 'modernity', and provided an 'other' against
which it could be defined, reinforcing the Enlightenment caricature
of the 'feudal' and 'superstitious' middle ages.

How to respond to the exclusion of their field from the master
narrative has been a constant dilemma for scholars of the middle
ages. Romantic medievalism, an eighteenth-century invention, self-
consciously repudiated the narrative by valorising an alternative,
non-classical and even anti-classical character of its own, which
reached a peak of acceptance, perhaps, in the Gothic revival and its
aftermath. It continued, and continues, to be fuelled by a variety of
anti-modernist cultural and political movements. Around the beginning of the twentieth century, in reaction, those who championed
history as a scientific discipline in its own right began, rather
than challenging the master narrative, to claim a place in it for the
middle ages, by pushing the search for the origins of 'modernity'
back beyond the sixteenth century. In the account which had won
widespread acceptance by the 1950s the twelfth and thirteenth centuries occupied a crucial position as the period when the distinctive
institutions of Church and State took shape, and when the recovered

learning of classical antiquity was united with the grand synthesis of Catholic theology and piety to lay the foundations of the European civilization which in the nineteenth and for most of twentieth centuries reigned unchallenged as the acme of human achievement, and as recently as 1992 could still be hailed as 'the end of History'.[18]

Growing scepticism of the master narrative itself since the 1960s, tending towards its abandonment, has renewed the medievalists' dilemma. The gathering interest of the 1980s in topics and communities perceived as having been marginalized by the dominant discourse, which contributed greatly to the welcome accorded to *Formation* when it appeared in 1987, is one example of their response. From one point of view it may appear as an assertion of 'total history', rejecting the valuation of phenomena in the past according to their supposed contribution to some long-term development rather than to their interest in their own right. From another, it can also be described as, or as part of, a historiographical 'turn to the grotesque', and (with particular reference to medieval studies in North America) as a 'rediscovery of alterity' (Freedman and Spiegel 1998). One reason for the success of this turn, it is suggested, is that the 'otherness' of the world with which they deal 'in part has given medievalists their sense of professional legitimacy, since the very strangeness and difference signified by the distant past suggests a special virtue required for its study' (p. 679). That, in a nutshell, is the lure of sentimental medievalism. It is, of course, entirely bogus. Historians of every period derive part of their sense of professional legitimacy from the strangeness and difference of the past. One of the daily frustrations of medievalists is the facile presumption on the part of others that strangeness and difference are proportionate to distance in time. The corresponding advantage is that it may be a little bit easier for them than for their modernist colleagues to persuade an audience that the people of whom they speak and write were not 'just like us'. But it is an advantage that comes nowhere near compensating for the harm that is done by the patronising mirage of several centuries of static and immutable quaintness that is conveyed and nourished by the very word 'medieval'.

The unsatisfactoriness of 'the middle ages' as a historical periodisation is well brought out by an interesting collection of papers which

[18] Fukuyama (1992). It seems that Mr Fukuyama, ever optimistic, now thinks that History may continue after all.

contests the general presumption of modern political scientists that the theory of religious toleration is simply a product of the Enlightenment (Laursen and Nederman 1998). It explores aspects of the thought of a selection of figures from Abelard to Bayle which, without expressly advocating toleration, might seem in various ways to be conducive to it. Yet, while rightly rebuking over-simple periodization on the part of modernists, and rightly insisting on the variety and diversity of religious culture and practice in Europe before the Protestant Reformation, the collection fails to assess the extent to which acceptance of that diversity changed during the period with which it deals. The assertion that 'if medieval Christendom was not entirely an open society neither was it the closed and monolithic "persecuting society" that it has been portrayed' (23; *sic*) is quite correct – leaving aside the authenticity of the alleged portrayal – but it begs (that is, assumes an answer to) the crucial question whether this was equally the case at all times in 'the middle ages'. What is meant by 'medieval Christendom'? In the centuries before 1100 or so religious diversity was not the result simply of inability to coerce: as I had pointed out (above pp. 65–7), there were several factors at work, notably the autonomy of the bishops in their dioceses, to permit diversity, though certainly those factors did not include a positive approval of it, let alone recognition of any right to dissent on the part of individual believers or non-believers. That is why 'the tolerant middle ages' is not an appropriate designation of the period before 1000. Nor was the vigour of debate in and around the early twelfth-century schools an expression of toleration in any modern sense. As Constant Mews puts it, 'modern notions of toleration should not be read back into the *Dialogus* [*of a Philosopher with a Christian and a Jew*]. Abelard is never explicitly concerned in his writings with the right of alternative groups in society to hold dissenting views' (in Laursen and Nederman 1998: 39). Abelard's pupil John of Salisbury agreed with him in holding that heretics should be coerced by reason and not by power. Even so, Nederman argues, John's recognition of the ability of wise men properly to differ, rooted in Ciceronian scepticism, was both principled and potentially of wide application (Laursen and Nedermen 1998: 53–70). But vividly as both essays illustrate the creativity and sophistication of their subjects, giants in any age, the question remains what wider conclusions we are entitled to draw not only about their world, but about the direction in which it was changing.

The debate over whether the twelfth and thirteenth centuries saw a turn from an open and creative to a more closed and repressive society, a proposition classically formulated by Friedrich Heer (1961) in what remains one of the most attractive introductions to the period, can be conducted without reducing either position to a caricature. Of course, the complexities and contradictions of human life and thought in any society cannot be reduced to simple formulae without distortion: another, and wide-ranging collection of papers (Copland 1996) shows institutional frameworks under challenge and open to dissent in a variety of fields and contexts in the high and later middle ages. To return to the question of toleration, Christopher Brooke is unquestionably right, in a searching though brief discussion (2000: 400–2) that in a Europe 'in which Christians of different obediences and Christians and non-Christians freely mingled some measure of tolerance – of live and let live – must have been a very familiar phenomenon'. But, he continues, it is not until the early thirteenth century that we find, in the work of the poet Wolfram von Essenbach, a clearly articulated plea for the valuation even of heathen life as the work of God. Layman though he was, Wolfram was inspired in this by the stress on divine love which was an important element of twelfth-century theology. And it was no accident that this conscious concern for tolerance, or something very like it, appears just at the critical moment, in my chronology, of the formation of a persecuting society, any more than it was a coincidence that human rights and dignity were asserted with a fresh clarity and eloquence in the middle decades of the twentieth century.

Wolfram's eloquence is no less moving, and in itself no less important, because it did not prevail. But historians cannot choose between Ranke's injunction to recover the past *wie es eigentlich gewesen* and Marc Bloch's insistence that history is the science of change over time. We must try to satisfy both – but, like Heisenberg's physicist who cannot accurately measure the position and the velocity of a particle at the same time, we cannot achieve both at once. Most historical writing attempts to combine the two, but we need to remember with which we are engaged at each point. An argument such as Heer's necessarily understates what did not contribute to the changes that it is concerned to identify; a true description which weights everything just as it appeared to contemporaries must eschew the hindsight that alone can recognise consequences. *Formation* is addressed very directly and almost exclusively to change over time.

Historiographically it might be regarded as, among other things, a contribution to the elucidation of the reasons why the turn that Heer described, in itself very widely acknowledged, took place, and took place at the time it did.

Again, however, chronology is critical. Certainly the thought of Abelard and John of Salisbury offers a salutary corrective 'to those' (whoever they may be!) 'who maintain an ingrained prejudice against the possibility of intellectual and religious diversity during the middle ages' (Laursen and Nederman 1998: 55) – especially if 'during' means 'at any time in'. If, on the other hand, it suggests 'at every time in', the incurably prejudiced might be tempted to retort that if John of Salisbury had uttered his famous dismissal of belief in night flights and child sacrifices as the delusions of 'a few poor women and ignorant men with no real faith in God' (*Polycraticus* ii. 17) in the middle of the fourteenth, or even the thirteenth century, rather than the twelfth, he might have found himself in some difficulty. In the sixteenth century it would have been foolhardy in the extreme (cf. Stephens 2002). The history of the acceptance of witch beliefs by the literate, which can be traced from around the middle of the thirteenth century (Russell, 1972), and of its terrible consequences, was not discussed in *Formation* precisely because it was not a phenomenon of the early or central middle ages, and therefore not part of the process which I have described. It was, however, one of its early results, and one of the most obvious reasons for insisting both that the persecuting society was formed during the middle ages, and that for most of the middle ages persecution was relatively mild by later standards. My reply to the distinguished historian of early modern Europe who asks whether the sixteenth century saw 'the zenith of Moore's persecuting society' (Monter 1996: 32) is that he underrates in this respect not the thirteenth or the fourteenth century, but the twentieth.

The sketch so crudely formed in 1987 can now be painted with a far finer brush and an infinitely more nuanced palette. That is how understanding advances. I am immensely grateful to all the scholars – many more than could be mentioned in this brief survey – whose labour and acuteness has corrected my blunders and improved my perspectives. I do not think that the contours have been greatly altered. There is always a danger, in offering a broad and general hypothesis for debate, of seeming to make larger claims than one intends, and to do so more dogmatically. The danger grows as, in the struggle for clarity, one strives to avoid repeating the obvious warnings, reservations and qualifications that might have covered one's back. *The Formation of a Persecuting Society* is at least as guilty of these failings as can be excused in a short book on a big topic, and if it misled by over-simplification nobody but its author is to blame. Twenty years on I am tolerably satisfied that, qualified, rounded, given subtlety and variation by the ordinary processes of scholarly debate, its conclusions contain a useful truth about the course of European history. It is not the whole truth, and should not be mistaken for it.

BIBLIOGRAPHY

The following abbreviations are used:

Bouquet *Receuil des historiens de Gaule et de la France*, ed. Dom Martin
Bouquet et al. (24 vols, Paris, 1737–86, 1806–1904; vols. I–XIX,
repr. Paris, 1869–80)

Mansi *Sacrorum conciliorum nova et amplissima collectio*, ed. = J. D.
Mansi (Venice, 1776, repr. Paris and Leipzig, 1903)

PL *Patrologiæ cursus completus, seu bibliotheca universalis
omnium ss. patrum, doctorum, scriptorumque ecclesiastico-
rum*. Series latina, ed. Jacques Paul Migne (Paris, 1844–55)

RS Rolls Series, London

TRHS Transactions of the Royal Historical Society

Note: Versions of medieval texts are listed under the name of their author
or title, not that of the modern editor or translator.

Abelard, Peter, *A Dialogue of a Philosopher with a Jew and a Christian*
[Collationes] trans. P. J. Payer (Toronto, 1979).

Abelard, Peter, Collationes, ed. John Marenbon and Giovanni Orlandi
(Oxford, 2001).

Abulafia, Anna Sapir, *Christians and Jews in the Twelfth Century Renaissance* (London, 1995).

Acton, Lord, *Lectures on Modern History* (London, 1906).

Ames, Christine Caldwell, 'Does Inquisition Belong to Religious History?',
American Historical Review 110.1 (2005): 11–37.

Andersen, J. G., *Studies in the Medieval Diagnosis of Leprosy in Denmark*, *Danish Medical Bulletin*, 16 (1969), suppl.

Angold, Michael, *Church and Society in Byzantium under the Comneni*, *1081–261* (Cambridge, 1995).

Arendt, Hannah, *The Origins of Totalitarianism* (New York, 1976). (Originally published 1951.)

Arnold, John H., *Inquisition and Power: Catharism and the Confessing Subject in Medieval Languedoc* (Philadelphia, 2001).

Audisio, Gabriel, *The Waldensian Dissent. Persecution and Survival*, *c.1170–c.1570* (Cambridge, 1999).

Bachrach, B. S., *Early Medieval Jewish Policy in Western Europe* (Minneapolis, 1977).

Baer, Y., *A History of the Jews in Christian Spain*, vol. 1 (2 vols, Philadelphia, 1971).

Baldwin, John W., *Masters, Princes and Merchants* (2 vols, Princeton, 1970).

Baldwin, John W., *The Language of Sex. Five Voices from Northern France around 1200* (Chicago, 1994).

Barber, Malcolm, *The Trial of the Templars* (Cambridge, 1978).

Barlow, Frank, *The English Church, 1000–1066* (London, 1963).

Barlow, Frank, *Thomas Becket* (London, 1986).

Baron, S. W., *A Social and Religious History of the Jews* (2nd ed., 13 vols, New York, 1952–67), vol. IV.

⚹ Bartlett, Robert, *Trial by Fire and Water: The Medieval Judicial Ordeal* (Oxford, 1986).

Bartlett, Robert, *The Making of Europe: Conquest, Colonization and Cultural Change, 950–1350* (London, 1993).

Bautier, R. H., 'L'hérésie d'Orléans et le mouvement intellectuel au début du XIe siècle', *Actes du 95e. Congrès national des sociétés savantes* (Reims, 1970), Section Philologique et historique (Paris, 1975), 63–88.

Bautier, R. H., ed., *La France de Philippe Auguste: le temps des mutations* (Paris, 1982).

Bautier, R. H., 'La personnalité de Philippe Auguste', in Bautier, ed., *La France de Philippe Auguste*, 33–57.

Bautier, R. H. and G. Labory, eds., *Helgaud, Vie de Robert le Pieux* (Paris, 1965).

Bendix, Reinhard, *Max Weber: An Intellectual Portrait* (London, 1959).

Bériac, Françoise, *Histoire des lépreux aux moyen âge: une société des exclus* (Paris, 1988).

Bériou, Nicole and Touati, F-O., '*Voluntate dei leprosus*: les lépreux entre conversion et exclusion aux xiie et xiii siècles', *Testi, studi, strumenti 4* (Spoleto, 1991).

Bernard of Clairvaux, *Letters*, trans. Bruno Scott James (London, 1953).

Bienvenu, J-M., 'Pauvreté, misère et charité en Anjou aux xie et xiie siècles', *Le Moyen Âge* (1966–7), 72–3.

Blumenkranz, B., *Le juif médiéval au miroir de l'art Chrétien* (Paris, 1964).

Blumenkranz, B., 'Juifs et judaisme dans l'art chrétien du haut moyen âge', *Gli ebrei nell'alto medioevo*, 987–1012.

Borradori, Piera, *Mourir au monde: les lépreux dans le Pays de Vaud (xiiie.–xvii siècles)*, Cahiers lausannois d'histoire médiévale, 7 (1992).

Bossy, John, 'The Mass as a Social Institution', *Past & Present* 100 (1983), 29–61.

Boswell, J., *Christianity, Social Tolerance and Homosexuality. Gay People in Western Europe from the Beginning of the Christian Era to the Fourteenth Century* (Chicago, 1980).

Bourgeois, A., *Lépreux et Maladeries du Pas-de-Calais (x–xviii siècles)*, Mémoires de la Commission Départmentale des Monuments Historiques du Pas-de-Calais, xiv 2 (Arras, 1972).

Bournazel, E. and Poly, J-P., in Bautier, ed., *La France de Philippe Auguste*, 217–34.

Brody, S. N., *Disease of the Soul: Leprosy in Medieval Literature* (Ithaca, 1974).

Brooke, Christopher, *Europe in the Central Middle Ages, 962–1154* (3rd ed., London, 2000).

Brooke, Z. N., *Europe 911–1198* (London, 1938).

Brown, Peter, 'Sorcery, Demons and the Rise of Christianity: From Late Antiquity into the Middle Ages', in Brown, *Religion and Society in the Age of St. Augustine* (London, 1972).

Brown, Peter, 'Society and the Supernatural: A Medieval Change', in Brown, *Society and the Holy in Late Antiquity* (London, 1982), 302–32.

Browning, Robert, 'Enlightenment and Repression in Byzantium in the Eleventh and Twelfth Centuries', *Past & Present* 69 (1975), 3–23.

Brundage, James A, *Law, Sex and Christian Society in Medieval Europe* (Chicago, 1987).

Brunn, Uwe, 'L'hérésie dans l'archevêché de Cologne, 1100–1233', *Heresis* 38 (2003), 183–90.

Bruschi, Caterina and Peter Biller (eds), *Texts and the Repression of Medieval Heresy* (York, 2003).

Bull, Marcus, *The Miracles of Our Lady of Rocamadour* (Woodbridge, 1999).

Bullough, Donald A. 'Burial, Community and Belief in the Early Medieval West', in Patrick Wormald et al., eds., *Ideal and Reality in Frankish and Anglo-Saxon Society: Studies presented to J. M. Wallace-Hadrill* (Oxford, 1983), 177–201.

Burgwinkle, William, *Sodomy, Masculinity and Law in Medieval Litera-ture: France and England, 1050–1230* (Cambridge, 2004).

Burr, David, *The Spiritual Franciscans. From Protest to Persecution in the Century of the St. Francis* (University Park, 2001).

Bury, J. B., *The Later Roman Empire* (2 vols., London, 1923; New York, 1958 ed.).

Cameron, Averil, 'Byzantines and Jews: Some Recent Work on Early Byzan-tium', *Byzantine and Modern Greek Studies*, 20 (1996), 249–74.

Cameron, Euan, *Waldenses: Rejections of Holy Church in Medieval Europe* (Oxford, 2000).

Camille, Michael, *The Gothic Idol: Ideology and Image-Making in Medi-eval Art* (Cambridge, 1998).

Chadwick, Henry, *The Early Church* (Harmondsworth, 1967).

Chazan, Robert, *Medieval Jewry in Northern France* (Baltimore and London, 1973).

Chazan, Robert, *Medieval Stereotypes and Modern Antisemitism* (Berkeley and Los Angeles, 1997).

Chazan, Robert *Fashioning Jewish Identity in Medieval Western Christen-dom* (Cambridge, 2004).

Christina of Markyate, The Life of, ed. C. H. Talbot (Oxford, 1959).

Chronica regia Coloniensis, ed. G. Waitz, *Monumenta Germaniae His-torica, Scriptores in usum scholarum* 18.

Clanchy, M. T., 'Moderni in Education and Government in England', *Speculum* 50 (1975), 671–88.

Clanchy, M. T., *From Memory to Written Record: England 1066–1307* (London, 1979).

Clay, R. M. *The Mediaeval Hospitals of England* (London, 1909).

Cochrane, H. G. and Davey, T. F. (eds), *Leprosy in Theory and Practice* (2nd ed. Bristol, 1964).

Cohen, Jeremy, *The Friars and the Jews* (Ithaca, 1982).

Cohen, Jeremy, 'The Jews as the Killers of Christ in the Latin Tradition, from Augustine to the Friars', *Traditio* 39 (1983), 1–27.

Cohen, Jeremy, *Living Letters of the Law: Ideas of the Jew in Medieval Christianity* (Berkeley, 1999).

Cohen, Jeremy, *Sanctifying the Name of God: Jewish Martyrs and Jewish Memories of the First Crusade* (Philadelphia, 2004).

Cohen, Mark R., *Under Crescent and Cross. The Jews in the Middle Ages* (Princeton, 1994).

Cohn, Norman, *Warrant for Genocide* (London, 1967).

Cohn, Norman, *Europe's Inner Demons* (London, 1975).

Collins, Roger, *Early Medieval Spain* (London, 1983).

Conklin, George, 'Law, Reform, and the Origins of Persecution: Stephen of Tournai and the Order of Grandmont', *Mediaeval Studies* 61 (1999), 107–36.

Constable, Giles, *The Reformation of the Twelfth Century* (Cambridge, 1996).

Copland, Rita, *Criticism and Dissent in the Middle Ages* (Cambridge, 1996).

Cowdrey, H. E. J., 'Archbishop Aribert of Milan', *History* 51 (1966): 1–15.

Cowdrey, H. E. J., 'The Papacy, the Patarenes and the Church of Milan', *TRHS* 5/18 (1968), 25–48.

Cushing, Kathleen G., *Reform and the Papacy in the Eleventh Century: Spirituality and Social Change* (Manchester, 2005).

Denholm-Young, N., *Richard of Cornwall* (Oxford, 1947).

Dobson, R. B., *The Jews of Medieval York and the Massacre of March 1190* (Borthwick Papers no. 45, York, 1974).

Dols, Michael W., 'The Leper in Medieval Islamic Society', *Speculum* 58 (1983), 891–916.

Douglas, David and G. W. Greenaway, *English Historical Documents* II, 1042–1189 (London, 1953).

Douglas, Mary, *The Lele of the Kasai* (Oxford, 1963).

Douglas, Mary, *Purity and Danger* (London, 1966).

Douglas, Mary, *Natural Symbols* (London, 1970).

Duby, Georges *La société aux XIè et XIIè siècles dans la région maconnaise* (Paris, 1953).

Duby, G., *The Three Orders: Feudal Society Imagined* (Chicago, London, 1981).

Duby, G., *The Knight, the Lady and the Priest* (Harmondsworth, 1983).

Dupré Thesider, E., 'Le catharisme languedocien et l'Italie', *Cahiers de Fanjeaux* 3, *Cathares en Languedoc* (Toulouse, 1968), 299–316.

Eadmer's Life of St. Anselm, ed. R. W. Southern (London, 1963).

Eadmer, *Historia Novorum*, ed. M. Rule (Rolls Series, London, 1884, trans R. W. Bosanquet as *Eadmer's History of Recent Events in England* (London, 1964).

Eckbert of Schönau, *Sermones XIII contra Catharos*, PL 195, col. 11–192.

Elliott, Dyan, *Fallen Bodies: Pollution, Sexuality, and Demonology in the Middle Ages* (Philadelphia, 1998).

Erikson, Kai, *Wayward Puritans* (New York, 1966).

Etienne d'Obazine, La vie de St., ed. M. Aubrun, Publications de l'Institut d'Etudes du Massif-Central 6 (Clermont-Ferrand, 1970).

Fanning, Steven C., 'Lombard Arianism Reconsidered', *Speculum* 56 (1981), 241–58.

Fichtenan, Heinrich, *Heretics and Scholars in the High Middle Ages*, 1000–1200 (University Park, 1998).

Finley, M. I., *Economy and Society in Ancient Greece*, ed. Brent D. Shaw and Richard Saller (London, 1981).

Finucane, Ronald, *Miracles and Pilgrims* (London, 1977).

Foreville, R., ed., *Les mutations socio-culturelles au tournant des XIIè–XIIIè s. Spicilegium Beccense 11: Actes du Colloques internationales des CNRS Etudes Anselmiennes*, IVè session (Paris, 1984).

Fossier, R., *Enfance de l'Europe* (2 vols, Paris, 1982).

✳ Foucault, Michel, *Madness and Civilization: A History of Insanity in the Age of Reason* (London, 1967).

Foucault, Michel, *Discipline and Punish. The Birth of the Prison* (London, 1975).

Frassetto, Michael, ed., *Heresy and the Persecuting Society in the Middle Ages. Essays on the Work of R. I. Moore* (Leiden, 2006).

Freedman, Paul and Gabrielle Spiegel, 'Medievalisms Old and New: The Rediscovery of Alterity in North American Medieval Studies', *American Historical Review* (1998), 677–704.

Fukuyama, Francis, *The End of History and the Last Man* (New York, 1992).

Fulbert of Chartres, *Letters and Poems*, ed. F. B. Behrends (Oxford, 1976).

Gaudamet, Jean, 'Les ordalies au moyen âge', *Receuils de la société Jean Bodin* 17 (1965).

Geary, Patrick, *Phantoms of Remembrance* (Princeton, 1994).

Gellner, Ernest, *Nations and Nationalism* (Oxford, 1981).

Gernet, Jacques, *A History of Chinese Civilization* (Cambridge, 1982).

Gesta pontificum Cenomannensium: Bouquet, XII, 54–5.

Gillingham, John, 'The Beginnings of English Imperialism', *Journal of Historical Sociology* 5/4 (1992), 392–409.

Given, James, *Inquisition and Medieval Society: Power, Discipline and Resistance in Languedoc* (Ithaca, 1997).

Glanvill, *Treatise on the Laws of England*, ed. G. D. G. Hall (London, 1965).

Gli ebrei nell'alto medioevo, Settimani di studio del centro Italiano di studi sull'alto medioevo xxvi (1978), (Spoleto, 1980).

Gluckman, M., *Politics, Law and Ritual in Tribal Society* (Oxford, 1965).

Goglin, J-L., *Les misérables de l'occident médiévale* (Paris, 1976).

Golb, Norman, *Les juifs de Rouen au moyen âge. Portrait d'une culture oubliée* (Rouen, 1985).

Golb, Norman, 'Les juifs de Normandie à l'époque d'Anselme', in Foreville, ed., *Les mutations socio-culturelles*, 149–57.

Golb, Norman, *The Jews in Medieval Normandy: A Social and Intellectual History* (Cambridge, 1998).

Gold, Penny Schine, *The Lady and the Virgin: Image, Attitude and Experience in Twelfth-Century France* (Chicago, 1985).

Goodich, Michael, *The Unmentionable Vice* (Oxford, 1979).

Grabois, A., 'Ecoles et structures sociales des communautés juives dans l' occident aux IXe–XIIe siècles', in *Gli ebrei nell'alto medioevo*, 937–62.

Gratian, *Decretum*, ed. Emil Friedberg, *Corpus iuris canonici* I (Leipzig, 1879).

Grell, Ole Peter and Scribner, Bob, eds., *Tolerance and Intolerance in the European Reformation* (Cambridge, 1996).

Grundmann, Herbert, *Religiöse Bewegungen im Mittelalter* (Berlin, 1935, 2nd ed. Darmstadt, 1961), trans. Steven Rowan as *Religious Movements in the Middle Ages* (Notre Dame, 1995).

Guibert of Nogent, *Autobiographie: Texte et Traduction*, ed. E. R. Labande (Paris, 1981).

Guibert of Nogent, *Self and Society in Twelfth-Century France: The Memoirs of Abbot Guibert of Nogent*, trans. John F. Benton (New York, 1970).

Hall, John A., *Powers and Liberties* (Oxford, 1985).

✳ Hamilton, Bernard, *The Medieval Inquisition* (London, 1981).

Hamonis (of Savigny), *Vita B.*, ed. E-P. Sauvage, *Analecta Bollandiana* xiv (Brussels, 1883).

Haverkamp, Alfred, ed., *Juden und Christen zur Zeit der Kreuzuüge*, Vorträge und Forschungen 47 (Sigmaringen, 1999).

Heer, Friedric, *Mittelalter* (Zurich, 1961), trans. Janet Sondheimer, *The Medieval World* (London, 1962).

Helgaud (of Fleury), *Vie de Robert le Pieux*, ed. R-H. Bautier and G. Labory (Paris, 1965).

Hill, J. W. F., *Medieval Lincoln* (Cambridge, 1948).

Hopkins, Keith, *Conquerors and Slaves* (Cambridge, 1978).

Huang, Ray, *1587: A Year of No Significance* (New Haven and London, 1981).

Hugh of Lincoln, Magna Vita *of*, ed. Decima L. Douie and Hugh Farmer (2 vols, London, 1962).

✳ Hyams, P. R., 'Trial by Ordeal: The Key to Proof in the Early Common Law', in M. S. Arnold et al., eds., *On the Laws and Customs of England: Essays in Honor of Samuel E. Thorne* (Chapel Hill, 1981), 90–126.

Iogna Prat, Dominique, *Order and Exclusion: Cluny and Christendom face Heresy, Judaism and Islam, 1000–1050* (Ithaca, 2002).

Jaeger, C. Stephen, *The Origins of Courtliness: Civilizing Trends and the Formation of Courtly Ideals, 930–1210* (Philadelphia, 1985).

Jaeger, C. Stephen, *The Envy of Angels: Cathedral Schools and Social Ideals in Medieval Europe, 950–1200* (Philadelphia, 1994).

Jaeger, C. Stephen, *Ennobling Love: In Search of a Lost Sensibility* (Philadelphia, 1999).

James, Edward, *The Origins of France* (London, 1982).

Jocelin of Brakelond, The Chronicle of, ed. H. E. Butler (Edinburgh, 1949).

John of Salisbury, *Polycraticus*, trans. J. Dickinson as *The Statesman's Book of John of Salisbury* (New York, 1927).

Jones, A. H. M., *The Later Roman Empire, 284–602* (Oxford, 1964, 1973).

Jordan, Mark D., *The Invention of Sodomy in Christian Theology* (Chicago, 1997).

Jordan, William C., *The French Monarchy and the Jews, from Philip Augustus to the last Capetians* (Philadelphia, 1989).

Karras, Ruth Mazo, *Sexuality in Medieval Europe* (New York, 2005).

Katz, Jacob, *Exclusiveness and Tolerance* (Oxford, 1961).

Katz, Solomon, *The Jews in the Visigothic and Frankish Kingdoms of Spain and Gaul* (Cambridge, MA, 1937).

Kealey, Edward J., *Medieval Medicus: A Social History of Anglo-Norman Medicine* (Baltimore, 1984).

✳ Kieckhefer, Richard, *European Witch Trials: Their Foundations in Popular and Learned Culture, 1300–1500* (London, 1976).

✳ Kieckhefer, Richard, 'The Office of Inquisition and Medieval Heresy: The Transition from Personal to Institutional Jurisdiction', *Journal of Ecclesiastical History* 46 (1995), 36–61.

Knowles, David, *The Christian Centuries* (London, 1969).

Knowles, David and Hadcock, R. N. *Medieval Religious Houses: England and Wales* (London, 1971).

Kuefler, Matthew, *The Boswell Thesis. Essays on Christianity, Social Tolerance and Homosexuality* (Chicago, 2006).

Kuhn, Philip A., *Soulstealers. The Chinese Sorcery Scare of 1768* (Cambridge, MA, 1990).

Ladurie, E. Le Roy, trans. Barbara Bray, *Montaillou. Cathars and Catholics in a French Village, 1294–1324* (London, 1979).

✳ Lambert, Malcolm, *Medieval Heresy: Popular Movements from Bogomil to Hus* (London, 1977); 3rd ed.: . . . *from the Gregorian Reform to the Reformation* (Oxford, 2002).

Landes, David, *Revolution in Time* (Cambridge, MA, 1983).

Landes, David, *The Wealth and Poverty of Nations. Why Some Are So Rich and Some So Poor* (New York, 1998).

Landes, Richard, *Relics, Apocalypse and the Deceits of History: Ademar of Chabannes, 989–1034* (Cambridge, MA, 1995).

Langmuir, Gavin I., 'From Ambrose of Milan to Emicho of Leiningen', in *Gli ebrei nell'alto medioevo*, 313–68.

Langmuir, Gavin I., *Towards a Definition of Antisemitism* (Berkeley, 1990), includes

Langmuir, G. I., 'Majority History and Post-biblical Jews', *Journal of the History of Ideas* 27 (1966), 343–64 and

Langmuir, G. I., '*Judei nostri* and the Beginning of Capetian Legislation', *Traditio* 16 (1960) and

Langmuir, G. I., 'Thomas of Monmouth: Detector of Ritual Murder', *Speculum* 59 (1984), 820–46.

Lansing, Carol, *Power and Purity. Cathar Heresy in Medieval Italy* (New York, 1988).

Larner, Christina, *Enemies of God: The Witch Hunt in Scotland* (London, 1981).

Larner, Christina, *Witchcraft and Religion: The Politics of Popular Belief* (Oxford, 1984).

Laursen, John D. and Nederman, Cary J., *Beyond the Persecuting Society. Religious Toleration before the Enlightenment* (Philadelphia, 1998).

Lea, Henry Charles, *The Inquisition of the Middle Ages*, with a historical introduction by Walter Ullmann (London, 1963).

Leach, E., *Culture and Communication* (Cambridge, 1976).

Lerner, Robert E., *The Heresy of the Free Spirit in the Later Middle Ages* (Berkeley and Los Angeles, 1972).

Lerner, Robert E., *The Feast of St. Abraham. Medieval Millenarians and the Jews* (Philadelphia, 2001).

Lewis, Bernard, 'The Significance of Heresy in Islam', *Studia Islamica* I (1955): 43–63, also in Lewis, *Islam in History* (London, 1973).

Lewis, Bernard, *The Jews of Islam* (Princeton, 1983).

Leyser, Conrad, 'Cities of the Plain: The Rhetoric of Sodomy in Peter Damian's *Book of Gomorrah*', *Romanic Review* 86:2 (1995), 191–211.

Leyser, Henrietta, *Hermits and the New Monasticism* (London, 1984).

Lipton, Sara, *Images of Intolerance: The Representation of Jews and Judaism in the* Bible moralisée (Berkeley, 1999).

Little, Lester K., *Religious Poverty and the Profit Economy in Medieval Europe* (London, 1978).

Lombard Laws, ed. Kathleen Fischer Drew (Philadelphia, 1973).

Luchaire, Achille, *Social France at the Time of Philip Augustus* (New York, 1912).

Lukes, Steven, *Durkheim: His Life and Work* (Harmondsworth, 1973).

Lukes, Steven and Scull, A., *Durkheim and the Law* (Oxford, 1984).

McCulloh, John M., 'Jewish Ritual Murder: William of Norwich, Thomas of Monmouth, and the Early Dissemination of the Myth', *Speculum* 72/3 (1997), 698–740.

McNeill, W. H., *Plagues and Peoples* (Oxford, 1977; Harmondsworth, 1979).

Magdalino, Paul, 'Enlightenment and Repression in Twelfth Century Byzantium: The Evidence of the Canonists', in N. Oikonomides, ed., *Byzantium in the Twelfth Century Canon Law, State and Society* (Athens, 1991), 357–73.

Magilton, J., 'The Leper Hospital of St James and St Mary Magdalen, Chichester', in C. A. Roberts, F. Lee and J. Bintoff, eds, *Burial Archaeology: Current Research, Methods and Developments* (BAR, British Series, ccxi, 1989), 249–65.

Mair, Lucy, *Primitive Government* (Harmondsworth, 1962).

Malkiel, D. 'The Underclass in the First Crusade: A Historiographical Trend', *Journal of Medieval History* 28 (2002), 169–197.

Manchester, Keith, 'A Leprous Skeleton of the Seventh Century', *Journal of the Archaeological Society* 8 (1981).

Manchester, Keith, *The Archaeology of Disease* (Bradford, 1982).

Map, Walter, *De nugis curialium [sic]*, ed. and trans. M. R. James, revised by C. N. L. Brooke and R. A. B. Mynors (Oxford, 1983).

Marenbon, John and Orlandi, Giovanni, *Peter Abelard Collationes* (Oxford, 2001).

Martines, Lauro, *Power and Imagination* (New York, 1979).

Merlo, Grado G., *Valdesi e valdismi medievali* (Turin, 1984).

Merlo, Grado G., *Identità valdesi nell storia e nella storiografia* (Turin, 1991).

Mesmin, S. C., 'The Leper Hospital of St. Gilles de Pont-Audemer', Ph.D. thesis, University of Reading, 1978.

Mesmin, S. C., 'Waleran, Count of Meulan and the Leper Hospital of St. Gilles de Pont-Audemer', *Annales de Normandie* 32 (1982), 3–19.

Mews, Constant J., 'On Dating the Works of Peter Abelard', *Archives d'histoire doctrinale et littéraire du moyen âge* 52 (1985), 73–134.

Miller, Edward, 'Medieval York', *The Victoria County History of Yorkshire: City of York* (London, 1961), 25–116.

Miller, Maureen C., (a) *The Bishop's Palace: Architecture and Authority in Medieval Italy* (Ithaca, 2000).

Miller, Maureen C. (b) 'Religion Makes a Difference: Clerical and Lay Cultures in the Courts of Northern Italy, 1000–1300', *American Historical Review* 105 (2000), 1095–130.

Mollat, Michel, *Les pauvres au moyen âge* (Paris, 1978).

Møller-Christiansen, V., *Bone Changes in Leprosy* (Copenhagen, 1961).

Møller-Christiansen, V., *Leprosy Changes of the Skull* (Odense, 1978).

Monter, William E., 'Heresy Executions in Reformation Europe, 1520–1565', in Grell and Scribner (1996), 48–64.

Moore, R. I., *The Birth of Popular Heresy* (London, 1975).

Moore, R. I., 'Heresy as Disease', in W. Lordaux and D. Verhelst, eds., *The Concept of Heresy in the Middle Ages, Medievalia Lovanensia* I/IV (Louvain, 1976), 1–11.

Moore, R. I., *The Origins of European Dissent* (London, 1977; Oxford, 1985).

Moore, R. I., 'Family, Community and Cult on the Eve of the Gregorian Reform', *TRHS* 5th series, 30 (1980), 49–69.

Moore, R. I., 'Duby's Eleventh Century', *History* 69 (1984), 36–49.

Moore, R. I., 'Popular Violence and Popular Heresy in Western Europe, *c.*1000–1179', in. W. J. Sheils, ed., *Persecution and Toleration*, 4–50.

Moore, R. I., 'New Sects and Secret Meetings: Association and Authority in the Eleventh and Twelfth Centuries', in W. J. Sheils, ed., *Studies in Church History* 23, *Voluntary Religious Associations* (1986), 47–68.

Moore, R. I., 'Antisemitism and the Birth of Europe', in Diana Woods, ed., *Studies in Church History* 29, *Christianity and Judaism* (1992), 33–57.

Moore, R. I., 'A la naissance d'une société persecutrice: les clercs, les cathares et la formation de l'Europe', *La persécution du Catharisme XIIe–XIVe siècles*, Actes de la 6e session d'Histoire Médiévale organisée par le Centre d'Etudes Cathares/René Nelli, 1–4 September 1993 (Toulouse, 1996), 11–37, 295–304.

Moore, R. I., *The First European Revolution* (Oxford, 2000).

Moore, R. I., 'The Eleventh Century in Eurasian History: A Comparative Approach to the Convergence and Divergence of the Medieval Civilizations', *Journal of Medieval and Early Modern Studies* 33.1 (2003), 1–21.

Moore, R. I., 'Les albigeois d'après les chroniques angevines', *La Croisade Albigeoise*, Actes du Colloque du Centre d'études cathares Carcassonne, October 2002 (Carcassonne, 2004), 8–90.

Moore, R. I., 'Afterthoughts on *The Origins of European Dissent*', in Frassetto, ed., *Heresy and Persecution in the Middle Ages*, 291–326.

Moore, R. I., 'The War against Heresy in Medieval Europe', *Historical Research*, forthcoming.

Morris, Colin, '*Judicium Dei*: The Social and Political Significance of the Judicial Ordeal in the Eleventh Century', in Derek Baker, ed., *Church, Society and Politics. Studies in Church History* 12, (1975), 95–112.

Mundill, Robin R., *England's Jewish Solution, 1262–1290* (Cambridge, 1998).

Mundy, J. H., *Liberty and Political Power in Toulouse, 1050–1230* (New York, 1954).

Mundy, J. H., *Europe in the High Middle Ages* (London, 1973).

Mundy, John H., *Society and Government at Toulouse in the Age of the Cathars* (Toronto, 1997).

Murray, A., *Reason and Society in the Middle Ages* (Oxford, 1978).

Nederman, Cary J. and Laursen, John Christian, eds., *Beyond the Persecuting Society: Religious Toleration before the Enlightenment* (Lanham, MD, 1996).

Nirenberg, David, *Communities of Violence: Persecution of Minorities in the Middle Ages* (Princeton, 1996).

Nirenberg, David, 'The Rhineland Massacres of Jews in the First Crusade: Memories Medieval and Modern', in Gerd Althoft et al. eds, *Medieval*

Concepts of the Past: Ritual, Memory, Historiography (Cambridge, 2002), pp. 279–310.

Nithard, *History of the Sons of Louis the Pious*, trans. B. W. Scholz, *Carolingian Chronicles* (Ann Arbor, 1972).

Obolensky, Dmitri, *The Bogomils* (Cambridge, 1948).

Orderic Vitalis, *Ecclesiastical History*, ed. Marjorie Chibnall (6 vols, Oxford, 1969–80).

Otis, Leah Lydia, (a) *Prostitution in Medieval Society: the History of an Urban Institution in the Languedoc* (Chicago, 1985).

Otis, Leah Lydia, (b) 'Prostitution and Repentance in Late Medieval Perpignan', in Julius Kirshner and Suzanne Wemple, eds., *Women of the Medieval World* (Oxford, 1985), 137–57.

Otto of Freising, *Deeds of Frederick Barbarossa*, trans. C. C. Mierow (New York, 1953).

Parkes, J. W., *The Jew in the Medieval Community: A Study of his Political and Economic Situation* (London, 1938).

Patchovsky, Alexander, 'Heresy and Society: On the Political Function of Heresy in the Medieval World', in Bruschi and Biller (2003), 23–41.

✳Pegg, Mark Gregory, *The Corruption of Angels* (Princeton, 2001).

Peter the Venerable, *Tractatus contra petrobrusianos* ed. James Fearns, *Corpus Christianorum, Continuatio mediaevalis X* (Turnhout, 1968).

✳Peters, Edward, *The Magician, the Witch and the Law* (Philadelphia, 1978).

✳ Peters, Edward, *Heresy and Authority in the Middle Ages* (London, 1980).

✳Peters, Edward, *Torture* (Oxford, 1985).

✳ Peters, Edward, *Inquisition* (New York, 1988).

Poliakov, L., *The History of Anti-Semitism: I, From Roman Times to the Court Jews; II, From Mohammed to the Maranos* (2 vols, London, 1974).

Pollock, A. F. and Maitland, F. W., *The History of English Law* (2 vols, Cambridge, 1895, ed. S. F. C. Milsom, 1968).

Poly, J-P., *La Provence et la société féodale* (Paris, 1976).

Poly, J-P, and E. Bournazel, 'Couronne et mouvance: institutions et représentations mentales', in Bautier, ed., *La France de Philippe Auguste*, 217–34.

Powell, James M. trans., *The* Liber Augustalis (Syracuse, 1971).

Powell, James M., ed., *Muslims under Latin Rule 1100–1300* (Princeton, 1990).

Rawcliffe, Carole, *Leprosy in Medieval England* (Woodbridge, forthcoming 2006).

The Chronicle of Richard of Devizes, ed. and trans. J. T. Appleby (London, 1963).

Richards, P., *The Medieval Leper and his Northern Heirs* (Cambridge, 1977).

Richardson, H. G., *The English Jewry under the Angevin Kings* (London, 1960).

Riley-Smith, J., 'The First Crusade and the Persecution of the Jews', in. Sheils, ed., *Persecution and Toleration*, 51–72.

Roberts, J. M., *The Mythology of the Secret Societies* (London, 1972).

Roberts, Simon, *Order and Dispute: An Introduction to Legal Anthropology* (Harmondsworth, 1979).

Robinson, I. R., 'The Friendship Network of Gregory VII', *History* 63 (1978), 1–22.

Roger of Hoveden, *Chronica*, ed. W. Stubbs (Rolls Series, London, 1869).

Rossiaud, Jacques, *La prostitution médiévale* (Paris, 1988).

Roth, C., *The History of the Jews of Italy* (Philadelphia, 1946).

Rubin, Miri, *Corpus Christi: The Eucharist in Late Medieval Culture* (Cambridge, 1991).

Ruiz, Teofilo F., *From Heaven to Earth. The Reordering of Castilian Society, 1150–1350* (Princeton, 2004).

Russell, Jeffrey Burton, *Witchcraft in the Middle Ages* (Ithaca, 1972).

Scharff, Thomas, *Häretiker verfolgung und Schriftlichkeit: Die Wirkung der Kekzergesetze auf die oberitalienischen Kommunalstatuten im 13 Jahrhunclert* (Frankfurt, 1996).

Scheil, Andrew P., *The Footsteps of Israel: Understanding Jews in Anglo-Saxon England* (Ann Arbor, 2004).

Schmitt, Jean Claude, *La conversion d'Hermann le juif: autobiographie, histoire et fiction* (Paris, 2003).

Scribner, Bob, 'Preconditions of Intolerance and Intolerance in Sixteenth-century Germany', in Grell and Scribner (1996), 32–47.

Shahar, Shulamith, 'Des lépreux pas comme les autres: l'ordre de Saint-Lazare dans le royaume latin de Jerusalem', *Revue Historique* 267 (1982).

Sharf, Andrew, *Byzantine Jewry from Justinian to the Fourth Crusade* (London, 1971).

Sheils, W. J., ed., *Persecution and Toleration. Studies in Church History*, 21 (Oxford, 1984).

Signer, Michael A. and John Van Engen, *Jews and Christians in Twelfth-Century Europe* (Notre Dame, 2001).

Simons, Walter, *Cities of Ladies: Béguine Communities in the Medieval Low Countries, 1200–1565* (Philadelphia, 2001).

Smalley, Beryl, *The Study of the Bible in the Middle Ages* (Oxford, 1941).

Somerville, Robert, *Pope Alexander III and the Council of Tours (1163)* (Berkeley and Los Angeles, 1977).

Sontag, Susan, *Illness as Metaphor* (New York, 1978).

Sournia, J-C. and Trevien, M., 'Essaie d'inventaire des léproseries en Bretagne', *Annales de Bretagne* 75 (1968): 317–43.

Southern, R. W., *The Making of the Middle Ages* (London, 1953).

Southern, R. W., *St. Anselm and his Biographer* (Cambridge, 1963).

Southern, R. W., (a) *Western Society and the Church* (Harmondsworth, 1970).

Southern, R. W., (b) 'Henry I', in Southern, *Medieval Humanism and Other Studies* (Oxford, 1970), 206–33.

Southern, R. W., *Scholastic Humanism and the Unification of Europe I: Foundations* (Oxford, 1995).

Southern, R. W., *Scholastic Humanism and the Unification of Europe II: The Heroic Age* (Oxford, 2001).

Stacey, Robert C., '1240–60: A Watershed in Anglo-Jewish Relations', *Historical Research* 61 (1988), 135–50.

Stacey, Robert C., 'The Conversion of Jews to Christianity in Thirteenth-Century England', *Speculum* 67 (1992), 263–83.

Stacey, Robert C., 'Jews and Christians in Twelfth-Century England: Some Dynamics of a Changing Relationship', in Signer and Van Engen (2001), 340–54.

Starr, Joshua, *The Jews in the Byzantine Empire, 641–1204 (Texte und Forschungen zur Byzantinisch-Neugrieschen Philologie*, Athens, 1939).

Stephens, Walter, *Demon Lovers. Witchcraft, Sex and the Crisis of Belief* (Chicago, 2002).

Stock, Brian, *The Implications of Literacy: Written Language and Models of Interpretation in the Eleventh and Twelfth Centuries* (Princeton, 1983).

Stow, Kenneth R, *Alienated Minority: the Jews of Medieval Latin Europe* (Cambridge MA, 1992).

Stow, Kenneth R., 'Conversion, apostasy, and apprehensiveness: Emicho of Flonheim and the fear of Jews in the twelfth century', *Speculum* 76 (2001), 911–33.

Strickland, Debra Higgs, *Saracens, Demons and Jews: Making Monsters in Medieval Art* (2003).

Stubbs, William *Select Charters* (9th ed. Oxford, 1913).

Sullivan, Karen, *Truth and the Heretic. Crises of Knowledge in Medieval French Literature* (Chicago, 2005).

Sumption, Jonathan, *Pilgrimage: an Image of Medieval Religion* (London, 1975).

Synan, E. A., *The Popes and the Jews in the Middle Ages* (New York, 1965).

Szasz, Thomas, *The Myth of Mental Illness* (New York, 1961; London, 1972).

Taviani, Huguette, 'Naissance d'une hérésie en Italie du nord au xie. siècle', *Annales ESC* 29 (1974): 1224–52.

Tellenbach, Gerd, *Church, State and Christian Society at the time of the Investiture Contest* (Oxford, 1948).

Thomas of Monmouth, *The Life and Miracles of St. William of Norwich*, ed. and trans. A. Jessop and M. R. James (Cambridge, 1896).

Tolan, John, *Petrus Alfonsi and his Medieval Readers* (Gainesville, etc., 1993).

Tolan, John, *Saracens. Islam in the Medieval European Imagination* (New York, 2002).

Touati, F-O., *Archives de la lèpre: atlas des léproseries entre Loire et Marne au Moyen Âge* (Paris, 1996).

Touati, F-O, *Maladie et société au Moyen Âge: la lèpre, les lépreux et les léproseries dans la province ecclésiastique de Sens jusqu'au milieu du XIVe siècle* (Paris, 1998).

Touati, F-O., ed., *Archéologie et architecture hospitalières de l'antiquité tardive à l'aube des temps modernes* (Paris, 2004).

Trachtenberg, J., *The Devil and the Jews* (New Haven, 1943).

Turley, David, *Slavery* (Oxford, 2000).

Van Engen, John, 'The future of medieval church history', *Church History* 71 (2002), 492–522.

Varoqueaux, C, 'Découverte de vestiges médiévaux à Rouen, Rue aux Juifs', in Foreville, ed., *Les mutations sociales*.

Venarde, Bruce L., *Women's Monasticism and Medieval Society. Nunneries in France and England, 890–1215* (Ithaca, 1997).

Vitalis (of Savigny), *Vita B.*, ed. E-P. Sauvage, *Analecta Bollandiana xiii* (Brussels, 1882).

Wakefield, W. L., *Heresy, Crusade and Inquisition in Southern France, 1100–1250* (London, 1974).

Wakefield, W. L. and Evans, A. P., *Heresies of the High Middle Ages* (New York, 1969).

Wallace-Hadrill, J. M., *The Long-Haired Kings* (London, 1962).

Wallace-Hadrill, J. M., *The Frankish Church* (Oxford, 1983).

Ward, B., *Miracles and the Medieval Mind* (London, 1982).

Warren, W. L., *Henry II* (London, 1991 edn).

Webb, Diana., 'The Possibility of Toleration: Marsiglio and the City States of Italy', in Sheils, *Persecution and Toleration*, 91–112.

Weber, Max, *The Religion of China*, trans. H. H. Girth (New York, 1951).

Whitelock, D., Brett, M. and Brooke, C. N. L. (eds.), *Councils and Synods* I (Oxford, 1981).

Wickham, Chris, *Early Medieval Italy* (London, 1981).

William of Malmesbury, *De gestis regum Anglorum*, ed. W. Stubbs (2 vols, Rolls Series, London, 1887–9); trans J. A. Giles, London, 1847.

William of Newburgh, *Historia rerum Anglicarum*, II, xiii, ed. R. Howlett, *Chronicles of the Reign of Stephen etc.* (Rolls Series, London, 1884–5).

Yves de Chartres, *Correspondence 1090–1098*, ed. J. Leclerq (Paris, 1949).

Zerner, Monique, ed., *Inventer l'hérésie? Discours polémiques et pouvoirs avant l'inquisition* (Nice, 1998).

Zerner, Monique, ed., *L'histoire du catharisme en discussion. Le 'concile' de Saint-Félix (1167)* (Nice, 2001).

Index

China, traditional, 44, 106, 148;
  sorcery scare in, 151
Christina of Markyate, 119
Church, Roman: and heresy, 16–25,
  64–8, 125–7; and Jews, 26–7, 30–
  6; and popular sentiment, 108–9;
  and trial by ordeal, 117–21; not
  the principal agent of persecution,
  viii, 103–6, 127–8, 146, 158, 161
civil rights, exclusion from, 1, 7, 9,
  11, 56, 62, 124–5, 149–50, 152
Clanchy, Michael, 129, 188
classification, 92–3, 184–5
Clay, Rotha Mary, 107
Clementius of Bucy, 20, 34, 60,
  114–15, 117–20, 122
clerks, see literati
Cohen, Jeremy, 177, 179
Cohen, Mark R., 150
Cohn, Norman, 33, 116, 137
Cologne, burnings at (1143), 21, 109,
  114, 121, 157; (1163), 36, 111, 157
Compiègne, lepers at, 53
Conklin, George, 185
Conrad of Marburg, 9
conspiracy, against Christendom,
  alleged: of heretics, 114–15; of
  Jews, 112, 343–5; of Jews and
  lepers, 60
Constable, Giles, 186
Constance of Arles, 15, 134
Constance of Brittany, 52
Constantine, Emperor, 11, 44, 58
conversion, forced, of Jews, 28, 76,
  149
Copland, Rita, 194
Corpus Christi, feast of, 36
courts, 135–6, 138–41, 166–8, 179,
  188–9
Crispin, Gilbert, 31–2
crusades, 28–30, 110–1, 177
Cushing, Kathleen F., 185

Devil, the persecuted as agents of,
  33, 60–1, 84–5, 116

dissent: turned into heresy, 66;
  popular attitudes to, 107–9
Dobson, R. B., 32, 80
doctors, Jewish, 78, 139–40
Dols, Michael, 58n, 152
Dominican inquisitors, 87, 176
Douglas, Mary, 94–5, 172
dress, distinguishing: for Jews, 7, 11,
  62; for heretics, 11; in Islam, 150
Duby, Georges, 97n, 135, 185
Durkheim, Emile, 100–3, 187

Eadmer, 50, 72, 121n
Eberwin of Steinfeld, 114, 160
Eckbert of Schönau, 71, 160
education: and government, 128–9,
  188; Jewish, 78, 141
Edward I of England, 42, 113, 179
Edward II of England, 88
Egypt, leprosy in, 44, 69
Eilhart von Oberge, Tristan, 60
Elliott, Dyan, 185
Emicho of Leiningen, 28, 111
Eon de l'étoile, 23, 159
Ephraim of Bonn, 9
ergotism, 51
Erikson, Kai, 101n
Etienne, clerk of Orléans, 15
Eugenius III, Pope, 23, 53
Evans-Pritchard, Edward, 172
Everard of Bucy, 34, 114, 117
Exeter, lepers in, 53

family, see kinship, structures of
Fichtenau, Heinrich, 175n
'Flora', see John, bishop of Orléans
Fossier, Robert, 29n, 136
Foucault, Michel, 56n, 172
Fournier, Jacques, 92
Frassetto, Michael, 175n
Frederick I (Barbarossa), Emperor, 3,
  38, 161
Frederick II, Emperor, 36, 38, 105,
  108, 128; Liber Augustalis, 9,
  105n

slave societies, 147–8
slaves, Jewish trade in, 27, 77
sodomy, 86–7, 138, 173, 186
Soissons, trial and burning at (1114),
    109, 114–15, 117–23, 157
Song of Roland, 27
sorcery, accusations of, 33, 116,
    133–4, 188–9
Southern, R. W., 3, 188
Spelleke, leper hospital at, 54
Spiegel, Gabrielle, 188, 192
Stacey, Robert C., 179
state formation: as explanation of
    social change, 166–7; and moral
    repression, 104, 127–8; as source
    of persecution, 195–6; and
    violence, 103–4
Stephen of England, 161
Stephen of Fougères, 89
Stephens, Walter, 195
stereotypes, construction of, 33–6,
    57–61, 83–98, 111–16, 131, 142–
    3, 161, 174–7, 178–9, 183, 186,
    187–8
Stock, Brian, 127, 188
Stow, Kenneth, 177, 178
Strickland, Debra Higgs, 179n
striking of Jews, 31, 110, 145n
Sullivan, Karen, 177
Szasz, Thomas, 172

Talmud, burning of (Paris, 1240),
    9
Tanchelm of Antwerp, 20, 23, 94
Taunton priory, 54
Tellenbach, Gerd, 186
Theobald, Count of Champagne,
    40–1
Theodoric of Cervia, 72–3
Theodoric the Ostrogoth, 76
Theodosian Code, 27
Theodosius I, Emperor, 11
Thierry, bishop of Orléans, 15,
    134
Thomas of Marle, 39, 89

Thomas of Monmouth, 111–13, 116,
    135, 178
Tolan, John, 178, 185
Toledo, Council of (589), 13; (649),
    37
tolerance, toleration, 193–4
Touati, F.-O., 181–2
Toulouse, 9, 22, 24–5, 30, 91, 123,
    137, 162–4, 169; County of, 9;
    Council of (1119), 23; Counts of,
    see Alphonse, Raymond
Tournai, bishop of, 106
Tours, Council of (1163), 25, 158–9,
    165
transubstantiation, 36
Troyes, leper hospital at, 73
tubercular infections, 69, 75

Urban II, Pope, indifferent to
    sodomy, 87
Usatges of Barcelona, 38
usury, 40, 79–80, 92

Valdès of Lyon, 22,
Van Engen, John, 146n, 177
Venarde, Bruce, 185
venereal diseases, 70–1, 100
Verona, expulsion of Jews from, 30
Vézelay, heretics at, 119
Vilgard of Ravenna, 13
vintners, Jewish, 81
Vitalis of Mortain, 89

Waldensians, Waldensianism, 22, 66,
    84, 142, 176
Waleran of Meulan, 53
Wallace-Hadrill, J. M., 103n, 142
Walter Map, 129, 167n
water, trial by, see ordeal, trial by
Wazo, bishop of Liège, 16, 23
Weber, Max, 103, 105–6, 124, 187,
    191
wells, poisoning of, 60
Westminster, Council of (1200), 56
Whitby, abbot of, 54